Jacob Schoenhof

A history of money and prices

being an inquiry into their relations from the thirteenth century to the present time

Jacob Schoenhof

A history of money and prices
being an inquiry into their relations from the thirteenth century to the present time

ISBN/EAN: 9783744739542

Printed in Europe, USA, Canada, Australia, Japan

Cover: Foto ©ninafisch / pixelio.de

More available books at **www.hansebooks.com**

A HISTORY OF
MONEY AND PRICES

BEING

AN INQUIRY INTO THEIR RELATIONS FROM
THE THIRTEENTH CENTURY TO THE PRESENT TIME

BY

J. SCHOENHOF

AUTHOR OF "THE ECONOMY OF HIGH WAGES," ETC.

Die Leute glauben deshalb an das Wahre so wenig, weil das Wahre so einfach ist.
(People are so little inclined to believe in the truth, because the truth is so simple.)
GOETHE.

SECOND EDITION.

G. P. PUTNAM'S SONS
NEW YORK   LONDON
27 WEST TWENTY-THIRD STREET   24 BEDFORD STREET, STRAND

The Knickerbocker Press
1897

PREFACE.

IN the years 1869 and 1870 I contributed a series of articles on *The Labor Question* to a German periodical, then published in New York, under the title, *Die Neue Zeit*. In these articles I held that prices were to be considered not as simple units, but as results of all the factors involved in the processes of production and distribution, including the action of government in the exercise of its political prerogative. I held, further, that the wage-earners' well-being, and that of all people with small incomes, depends on the extent in which the profit-charges on the several price-elements contribute towards swelling prices. Feudal prerogatives, privileges, monopolies of all sorts, protective duties, and taxes upon production, as well as all infringements of the exercise of the fullest measure of individual freedom, fell under this ban as a matter of course. I held that the preferences conveyed under these titles, either as inherited rights transmitted from a passing state of society, or as the acts of legislation for the furthering of special interests, raise values beyond the compensation received by the classes engaged in production and distribution, and thereby operate to depress the working classes; and that it must, therefore, be the aim of enlightened statesmanship to remove them, or reduce them to the smallest possible dimensions.

An analysis of prices necessarily involves, therefore, the examination of all the elements of price-making, and these include, practically, all the economic, political, social, and ethical forces of the age.

As subjects of my analysis I treated the conditions of agriculture, mining, and industry, whether free or saddled with hereditary burdens, and other charges contributing to price-making, under the headings of

Wages,
Profit-rates,
Expense of distribution,
Taxation and tariffs,
Interest and capital,
Transportation,
Monopolies, and
Currency.

The views on prices and the cost of production which I held then, and which I have briefly stated above, have been confirmed by the varied studies which I had exceptional opportunities to pursue in my business career and under a special appointment of the Secretary of State, Mr. Bayard.

In 1885 I gave expression to the same ideas in my book, *The Industrial Situation*. The question of "the appreciation of gold" and "the depreciation of silver" had then begun to be agitated. The decline of prices was by writers of international fame attributed to resulting monetary changes. I contradicted this theory, and gave expression to the views already stated. In my earlier opinions I was still under the influence of the theory that the money-quantities in circulation affect prices. From this theory I had emancipated myself by 1885. I stated that prices were of the composite nature illustrated, and that the quantities of gold and silver in circulation had little to do with this rise and fall.

As was to be expected, my position was severely criticized. It was so radically opposed to the tenets of orthodox political economy that it needed more than even the broadest and firmest foundation of general facts to prove its correctness and have it take the place of the old, time-honored belief.

The acute phase into which the question has since entered has caused me to examine the prices of the period anterior, to the discovery of the American silver mines, and to carry the comparison down to the present time, for the purpose of determining by this exact process whether prices have actually risen with the vast increase in the money stocks of the world.

A careful examination of German, French, and English records from the thirteenth century to the present day has brought to light an overwhelming array of facts in support of my views.

The data furnished by each country corroborating the data furnished by the others, all doubt of the correctness of the conclusions to be derived from them is removed, and I am enabled therefore to demonstrate in the present volume:

That prices of commodities move in obedience to natural and inherent causes, independent of circulating money quantities.

What these causes are, and how they operate on prices, is fully set forth in the third part of this treatise.

The demonstration that price increase brought about by the issue of depreciated currency, or other inflating causes, has always acted detrimentally to the interests of the working classes has an important bearing on the labor question. The rise in prices of grain in the three countries, dating from the middle of the sixteenth century, the causes of which are fully explained, brought no corresponding increase in wages. The deterioration of the condition of the poor is directly traceable to this indisputable fact. All commodities excepting grain have suffered most remarkable declines since the time of smallest money supply, from which my examination starts.

In Appendix A I have summarized the price history of grain for the three countries, and brought prices and wage rates in comparison, to illustrate the deterioration of the condition of the working classes by the quantity of grain purchasable by the day's wage of a carpenter or a mason from the middle of the fourteenth century to the year 1882.

The workingman's condition has been one of degradation from the time of the rise in grain prices mentioned above. It begins to improve only with the technical and scientific progress of our time, and it is proved that the well-being of the poorer classes is closely interwoven with cheapness of commodities.

In Appendix B the leading views are given, which I gathered in an inquiry into the economy of production and the state of technical education in Europe, undertaken under the auspices of the Department of State in 1887. The statement is the preface to a report to the Secretary of State, and was separately published under the title *Influences Bearing on Production*. As the data contained in its pages bear directly on the present inquiry, and are frequently referred to in the third part, devoted to the subject "of price-making causes," I have considered it advisable to reproduce the matter at the end of this volume.

NEW YORK, December, 1895.

CONTENTS.

FIRST PART.

A CRITICAL REVIEW OF PRICE THEORIES AND MONETARY CONDITIONS 3–68

CHAPTER I.

THE ERRONEOUS PREMISES UPON WHICH OUR PRICE THEORIES REST 3–18

The basis upon which the present agitation rests. Statistics and "Index Numbers." What makes them unreliable. Violently diverging price quotations footing up in equal totals. Falling and rising prices produce equal totals. Present price average equal to average of 1845–1850. Rise and fall traceable to natural causes. War periods and consequent high prices from 1853 to 1857, and from 1863 to 1875. Reaction and general trade depression 1875 and 1879 lower prices 3–16

Wages have risen materially only in gold-paying countries under constantly declining prices of the products of these countries. Price of cotton same in 1854 as in 1889. Great price reduction in finished product 16–18

CHAPTER II.

THE PREVAILING MONEY THEORIES. THE MONEY METALS. THE VARYING RELATIONS OF OUTPUT DOES NOT AFFECT VALUE RELATIONS 19–44

No trace found in modern history that sudden increase raised or sudden decrease lowered prices. Resumption of specie payment in America adds over 60 per cent. to circulation in 1879 to 1882. Increase does not stem tide of declining prices even 19–26

The output of gold and silver examined from 1492 to 1894. Average of quantity-relations: 45 silver to 1 gold up to 1850 maintains high value ratio of 15.50 to 1. The output of the 1851 to 1870 period violently changes relation. Does not affect value. Real cause of decline in price of silver not in the cost, or quantity of output, but in the use as a money metal. Great increase in gold production. Gold the money of advancing civilizations. Silver in the past almost exclusively the money. Cause of its high value in undeveloped periods. The extraordinary yields of the gold mines. New modes of gold mining. Application of capital and science 26–34

The Standards of Value of Different Epochs. The low commodity value of early moneys. Purchasing power due to limited coinage. Silver money now commodity money. Reasons. States rising to power always adopted gold standard. Signs of ripeness and trading expansion. The gold coins kept their purity and weight while debasing of silver brought silver money to a hundredth part of its original device in some of the coinages. Florentines, the bankers of Europe, the same as the "gold florin" the standard of payment. German cities in the fifteenth century make bills of exchange payable in gold . 35–44

CHAPTER III.

THE DEMONETIZATION OF SILVER A RESULT OF ECONOMIC DEVELOPMENT 45–68

The silver product of the world. Low cost of production for the last dozen years. Output increasing rapidly in spite of declining commercial value. The value of money metals determined by their usefulness in the currencies of the world . 45–55

Credit money. When taking the place of metal money. Why the Jews were early organizers of credit payments. Drafts and transferable due bills amongst the oldest institutions of civilized commerce. Why large money payments were impossible. The fairs. Methods of clearing accounts. Early practice at fairs. The frequent debasement of the coins made payment by weight a necessity. An established fact all through the Middle Ages. The money of account. The true standard of prices. The bank of Venice, created in 1171, organizes and pays in bank credits. Followed by Florence and by the commercial free towns of the Empire 56–68

CONTENTS.   ix

SECOND PART.

THE HISTORY OF PRICES FROM THE MIDDLE AGES
TO THE PRESENT TIME 71–212

CHAPTER IV.

THE ECONOMIC DEVELOPMENT OF THE MODERN STATES.
THE RISING PRICES AND EXPANDING TRADE IN GERMANY PRECEDING THE AMERICAN INFLUX OF SILVER   71–86

Rise of prices in Germany in the last quarter of the fifteenth and in the first quarter of the sixteenth centuries. The large trading companies. The strength of the money power. The enormous profits and capital accumulations. The wealth of the Nürnberg and Augsburg merchants. All happening prior to the discovery of the American silver mines of Potosi and Guanajuato. General breakdown of Germany's economic greatness about the time of American silver finds. Exaggeration of account of silver production in Germany and of American supply prior to the second half of sixteenth century. Small amount of money in circulation. Great amount stored away in silver plate. Scarcity of money did not prevent rise of prices. Rise in foreign produce due to altered route to India. Effect in Germany, monopolizing tendencies. Former conditions favored small traders 71–81

Rise of prices due to change from feudal agricultural to modern industrial conditions. Productive methods little changed. Same experience in Italian cities in thirteenth and fourteenth centuries. Complaint of German merchants of high cost of living in Venice. Italy early example of advanced mode of trading 81–86

CHAPTER V.

DISTINCTIONS TO BE OBSERVED IN MAKING COMPARISONS OF PRICES IN DIFFERENT PERIODS . . . 87–111

1. *The Economic Positions.* The earlier periods. Barter and payment in kind 88–90
2. *The Nature of the Money under which Price Quotations are Noted.* The early price quotations in present denominations. The variations and the gradual deterioration a source of revenue.

But marks also an economic progress and shows forward step to money economy. The pound of silver the actual basis. First steps of recovery from dishonest coins by commercial towns of the Rhine. Cologne, the mark silver, and its honest coinage the basis of its commercial ascendency. France, chaos as great as in Germany. Debasement by the Valois kings. The English coinage. Strength of the crown keeps coinage in hand and preserves full value. Debasement by Henry VIII. Effect on prices not great, because of payment by weight of silver. Sad effect, however, on condition of working classes. Elizabeth's reform of the coinage. Value of new coin 1 to 3 of full value of earlier coins 90–101

3. *The Different Relation of Commodities in Different Price Periods.* High prices of all commodities pertaining to manufacturing industries. A few price quotations from the eleventh and twelfth centuries in coins of the time and value of to-day. High prices of cloths, linen, iron, metals. Absence of intercommunication depresses prices of animals. Effect of union with England raising prices of Highland cattle. Low price of meat and high price of corn proof of backwardness of agriculture. Modern grazing countries offer same phenomena as Europe in Middle Ages. The hide, the tallow, the wool, the only commercial value in certain stages of development. Prices at present in grazing states much lower than in Germany in twelfth century 101–109

4. *The Changed Character of Commodities in Progressing Periods.* The character of commodities has improved considerably since early periods under discussion. The weight of animals. The improvement of breeds 109–111

CHAPTER VI.

ENGLISH PRICE HISTORY FROM 1261 A.D. TO 1580 . 112–133

Evidence that money dealings and price quotations are by weight and not by tale. Uniformity of prices under progressing deteriorations from 1261 to 1540 in average prices further proof. Extreme price variations between years of plenty and scarcity. Analogy in Russia of to day. Price period 1261 to 1400 and of 1401 to 1540 compared in the old prices and in the equivalents of the new coinage 112–119

CONTENTS.

1. Prices of wheat, barley, oats, rye, malt, beans, and peas. Showing no rise over first two periods expressed in equivalent money relations. Rather lower. 2. Price of live stock not changed in 300 years. On basis of weight of animals, difference between 1450 and 1850 but 1 to 2 119–123

3. Farm produce. High price of wool in earlier period. Lower at end of sixteenth century. Farm produce dearer, greater demand in towns. Lowering in prices of building materials, iron, and metals. Causes of decline. Wages high from time of plague to Henry VIII. Not risen in proportion with change of money. Workingmen never recovered old position before debasement of the coins. No change in methods in handicrafts nor improvement in agriculture make prices stationary in industrial, and with increasing population higher in agricultural, products. Higher prices of southern and eastern produce. Reasons 123–133

CHAPTER VII.

PRICE PERIOD 1582 TO 1702 CONSIDERED . . 134–147

The financial condition of England inferior in every way. Small amount of circulation. Slow increase during seventeenth century from time of Elizabeth. Imports and exports. Slow development of commerce. No possible cause of high prices in money quantity therefore. Comparing average prices of 140 years (1400 to 1540) period with prices of seventeenth century in equivalent money. Great rise in cereals beginning with the years 1592 to 1602, to end of seventeenth century prices two to three times as high as in 1580. Causes, bad seasons, increasing population, and backward state of agriculture. England importing grain. Authorities . . . 134–138

Prices of animals doubled over fifteenth century. Meat not much increased proves increasing weight of animals in seventeenth centuries. Wool same as in fifteenth and sixteenth centuries. Due to extended sheep farming over tillage. Explains high corn prices. Prices of building materials nearly the same as in fifteenth century. Iron and metals somewhat lower than in fifteenth and sixteenth centuries, and change very little all

xii   CONTENTS.

                                                                   PAGE
through seventeenth century. Rise in wages from time of Commonwealth is followed by proportionate rise in prices of some of the industrial products. Dismal position when wages of two epochs are compared with relative corn prices. Prices of textile fabrics. No rise but rather lowering tendency apparent. Little change yet in character of manufactures or in technical methods. High prices of foreign commodities still prevailing. But become lower towards end of century 138–147

CHAPTER VIII.

PRICES OF EIGHTEENTH CENTURY DOWN TO PRESENT TIME 148–173

Commerce of England in seventeenth century. Changing conditions under William III. Heavy growth of foreign trade, increasing revenues and increasing circulation. Banking facilities totally absent under preceding reigns. Now become part of trade. Plate comes out more from the strong boxes and forms part of money stocks. Increased output of gold and silver over seventeenth century throughout eighteenth. England's rising power. Commercial and financial. Declining prices in wheat follow. Same in France. England exports corn, while previously importing. Improvements in agriculture and good seasons, despite growing population, reduce prices. High prices during French war. Great suffering of working classes. Insufficient rise in wages to cover difference. Comparisons by periods. High prices in the first half of nineteenth century. Getting lower with increase of money supply from new gold discoveries. Enormous increase of money followed by decrease in prices. Recent prices 147–161

Prices of live stock, meat, and farm products. Do not rise in proportion with corn. Nor fall in proportion. Reasons. Comparing English prices of meat from 1593 to 1893. Rise not very marked to end of eighteenth century. Same showing for butter and cheese. Reasons. Steadiness of price of English wool up to end of eighteenth century. Rise of price beginning with 1845. Rise up to 1877. Decline since. Extraordinary expansion of wool supply. Prices of *Australian* decline from highest point in 1872 to 1875. But not lower in 1885 than in 1846 to 1855 161–167

CONTENTS. xiii

PAGE

Prices of English pig iron, finished iron, copper, and lead compared from 1693 to 1702 down to 1893 to 1894. Steadiness of price up to 1838, excepting war periods. Great decline in iron prices following that time. Great decline in manufactured articles. Cloth and linen prices of seventeenth century and present time. Extraordinary decline in sugar, spices, rice, etc. 168-173

CHAPTER IX.

THE PRICE HISTORY OF FRANCE FROM 1201 A.D. TO 1890 174-212

The chaotic state of French currencies. The various standards and varying values of the coins at different periods. Corroborations of facts adduced in preceding chapters of uniformity of price-level and that payments were made on basis of weight instead of tale in recent work of Mr. G. d'Avenel. The price of land and its returns from 1201 A.D. to present time not materially different for period 1226 to 1325 and 1526 to 1750. Revenue from land is lower on account of decline of interest charges. Present revenue from land not higher than in thirteenth century. Returns to cultivator much higher . . 174-181

Varying price of grains. Fairly uniform average up to 1550. Great rise. The low state of commercial and industrial development and political factional disorganization would prevent influx of money through trade. Mines not prolific then. Foreign commerce insignificant. The natural explanation of rise in grain prices in increasing population and great backwardness in agriculture. The soil and the population. Discouraging conditions. Dearth, famine, and plague. Some low price periods intervene. Comparison of yields pro rata 1600, 1700, and 1875 to 1890 in grains of all kinds. Insufficiency of products to give bread all the year round in seventeenth century in return for possible earnings of a family. State under Louis XIV. Years of war and scarcity general. The high taxes. Testimony of John Locke and Vauban's description. The onerous system of taxation grinding and making improvement and good tillage impossible. Improvement under succeeding reign. Low prices in period 1725 to 1750. Average level not higher in 1727 to 1736 than in period 1250 to 1450 and in 1526 to 1550 182-194

Bread prices not materially changed. Meals at inns do not change in price average from 1200 to 1800. The rate of wages in agricultural, mechanical, and domestic pursuits for the same long period. Singular uniformity. Shows no rise correspondingly with change in grain prices. High prices generally succeeded by great mortality 195–198

Prices of wool and iron do not change. Prices of manufactures of wool. Very high in early periods. Decline in time coincident with increase in money stocks. French price history shows same general facts as in England. Prices lower in every commodity, excepting grain, since the increasing supplies of money entered into the exchanges 199–202

German Prices. From 1350 to 1838. The prices of grain show same relations as in England and France. High from 1580 to 1720. Thirty Years' War and other disturbing influences. Same proportions of rise. About 2½ times old prices. Wages but 50 per cent. higher. Other products. Prices recede considerably in eighteenth century. Remarkable agreement in the price facts of the three countries absolutely disprove the prevailing money theories 203–212

THIRD PART.

THE TRUE PRICE-MAKING FACTORS . . . 215–309

CHAPTER X.

RELATION OF THE SHARE OF LABOR TO THE COST OF THE PRODUCT 215–253

Confounding wages and cost of labor. Rise in wages going with decline in labor cost in progressing countries. Fallacious "natural laws." Spinning fine numbers, Fall River, Bolton, and Alsace. Little difference in piece rates but great difference in time wages. Highest wages connected with lowest cost. The cost of spinning yarns from 1804 to present time. Reduced to less than one tenth of old cost. Improvements accruing to working classes expressed in pounds of flour. Contrasting Saxony and Lancashire wages from beginning of this century. The former not one fourth those of England 215–230

Groundlessness of fear of Asiatic competition. Competition only possible in low counts with little labor and high part in the material. Asiatic wages and depreciated currencies exist in European countries. Have not been sources of danger to high wage countries on gold basis. Wages in Bohemia cotton mills. Low wages in Ireland no incentive to English capital. Russia's rate of wages. Infinitesimally small earnings as compared to American and English rates. Peasant industries. Building trades. Russian cotton industry and wages. Paid in depreciated paper rouble. Not above Indian or Japanese rates. The output contrasted. Great development in iron industry. Extraordinary fall in prices without material reductions in time wages. Great progress in mining. A forty years' history of a copper mine. Wages higher by 25 per cent., but cost of labor per ton but one fifth the old cost. Similar reductions in the cost of mining and of reducing the precious metals . 230–253

CHAPTER XI.

OTHER CAUSES OF PRICE DECLINES 254–270

Price of iron. Rapid decline after about 1835. Scientific improvements. Fuel and ore saving. Labor saving. Some comparisons between costs of to-day and of five years ago in Southern furnace work. High explosives, machine drilling, etc., in mining. Results on price and cost. Bessemer rails. Difference between cost of pig iron and finished product. Reduced 90 per cent. by improving processes, within 25 years. Wages higher 254–264

The scientific exploitation of waste. The creation of by-products. Their great commercial value. Improvements in agriculture. Scientific farming as conducted in America on truck farms. The net results even more gratifying. Facts and conclusions. 265–270

CHAPTER XII.

REDUCTIONS IN COST OF OTHER PRICE-MAKING ELEMENTS 271–284

Cost of production can only be taken relatively in agricultural products. Expansion of wheat fields under declining prices. Position of working farmer not desperate. Mortgages on identical farms diminishing, not increasing. Why wheat, corn, and cotton are raised in respective zones, despite continuous decline in price. Point reached in March lowest in wheat for three hundred years. The new means and methods of transportation. Elimination of distance as a price factor. Low prices on farms in distant sections of the country in the past. Rising prices with the progress of railroad building. Diminishing difference in price between receiving point West and New York. The benefit to the consumer and the producer 271–281

First effect of progress in Government seen in improving roads and water-ways. The splendid system of road building of the Romans. Advantage to English transportation in Middle Ages. Left to run down in later centuries. Wretched roads in the latter part of the eighteenth century complained of by writers. Canals not begun building before that time. Waterways generally unimproved. High cost of carriage. Quotations of rates paid for carrying goods. Similar conditions and high charges in America before railroad building . . . 282–284

CHAPTER XIII.

OTHER CAUSES CONTRIBUTING TO HIGH PRICES IN THE PAST 285–309

The many burdens on trade and industry considered. The armed convoys required to conduct trading fleets. Money carried on men-of-war. The expense considered. The high rate of profit necessary to cover the risks. The Dutch as the principal carriers on the high seas during the seventeenth century. Their grasping and monopolizing tendencies. An object of jealousy and hate 285–291

Monopoly of trading companies crush individual competition. Early profits succeeded by heavy losses to stockholders. Wastefulness in the absence of individual responsibility. Extra length of voyage. Monopoly on land. Degeneracy of the guilds. Become a source of grinding taxation and exaction by government. Effect on cost of production. Limitations of right to exercise a craft. Granting the right to work a prerogative of the crown. In Germany legal limitations extend to within recent years. Preventing progress and spread of

CONTENTS. xvii

manufacture. Taxes and dues. Made purchasable offices. Trade regulations very onerous. Influence of the "Economists" on freeing trade and industry 291–299

Duties and taxes. Custom's taxes. At first for revenue. Later for protection. How they grew. Effect of gradual abolition on prices. Effect on prices in America of removing wool tariff. Examples from recent tariff history. Low prices the effect of the removal of burdens on trade, commerce, and transportation, and of giving full sway to the agencies set in motion by enlightenment and liberal laws 300–309

APPENDIX A 311–323

A Summary of the Price History of England, France, and Germany, giving in parallel columns grain-prices and wages, with their purchasing power in bushels of grain, notably wheat and barley, from A.D. 1351 to 1882.

APPENDIX B 324–344

Introductory letter to the author's report on Technical Education to the Secretary of State, separately published under the title "Influences Bearing on Production" by the Department of State.

INDEX 345–352

FIRST PART.

A CRITICAL REVIEW OF PRICE THEORIES AND MONETARY CONDITIONS.

CHAPTER I.

The Erroneous Premises upon which the Prevalent Price Theory Rests.

THE prices of commodities and the quantities of money in circulation have been so closely linked together in the thoughts of the people, through the teachings of a purely deductive political economy, that it has become almost an axiom, not to be touched by doubting inquiry, that a rise or a fall of prices is to be ascribed to an increasing or a decreasing supply of money, and that any sudden change in this supply must, necessarily, be followed by sympathetic changes in prices. Several instances of monetary changes bringing about changes, though nominal only, in prices, lend seeming support to this view.

It would be futile to deny that a rise of prices would follow sudden expansion of a certain kind in the currency of a country. The people of the United States have it only too vividly in their recollection, to need reminding of the fact, that the paper circulation of the war period brought on an era of price inflation, that values for a time were doubled and trebled by the mere fact of the change in the currency. But this fact proves rather that the purchasing power of the money had decreased, because the people doubted the ability of the government to exchange its own money at par into the money of the world, *i. e.*, full-valued coin, then gold and silver. The money supply was by no means excessive at the time when the government paper stood lowest compared to what it is at the present time, when the circulation is about two to one of the amount prior to the time of the resumption of specie payment by the government. The value of the money came to parity only when it became a certainty that the government would redeem its pledges. It may with justice be said that a government promise to pay is not money, no more than the promissory note of a commercial firm. But it is as good as money so long as the credit of the firm is undoubted. If it should come about that more bills come on the market than the character of the house would warrant, the bills would become discredited very soon. Governments have to submit to the same rules of commercial ethics as private firms. The world is even justified in exercising greater caution with government issues. An extra-legal position is created for the government by being the law-making power, and examples are not wanting of its availing itself of its opportunities. Indeed, history does so abound with examples of the abuse of this easy " new way of paying old debts," that it is hardly necessary to do more than make passing allusion to the most prominent instances and to the disastrous results. Our own Continental money * and the Confederacy's money furnish the necessary reminders for

---

* In the early part of 1776 an English general reported to his government : " The Congress paper is in the highest credit ; though before the year closed paper money in the northern section of the country was struck with a mortal blight."—Albert S. Bolles, *The Financial History of the United States*, vol. i., p. 119.

At the close of the same year it was that General Putnam, in command at Philadelphia, issued an order : " Should any of the inhabitants be so lost to public virtue and the welfare of the country to presume to refuse the currency of the American States in payment for any commodities they may

this side of the Atlantic Ocean of the possibly worst outcome of honest intentions and "safe beginnings." Neither of these issues was ever redeemed. The latter issue for the valid reason that the authorities which had issued the money went out of existence. The Continental government, however, though terminating the war successfully, never honored its promises, undoubtedly as sacred when made as the promises, under equal stress, at the time of our late war. These are even yet awaiting redemption. They do not share the fate of their forerunners, because no one doubts the ability of the government to finally redeem its pledges.

---

have for sale, the goods shall be forfeited, and the person or persons so refusing, committed to close confinement." (December 12, 1776.)

But in matters of trade sentiment plays a small part. The threats and proclamations of the authorities seem to have had little damaging effect on the traders. They converted their cash fast enough into merchandise. The poorer people, wage-earners and salaried men, suffered most from the rapid depreciation. Toward the close of 1777 the inclination to barter had become general, "and as general an aversion to dealing in paper money of any kind," as John Adams wrote to General Gerry. In 1779 twenty paper dollars were given for one silver dollar.

Depreciation of the currency was by this time everywhere acknowledged, except by Congress, which still refused to recognize the fact. During the year depreciation had increased to forty-one dollars and a half for one in silver. But the next year (March, 1780,) the bill was passed, the famous "forty for one" bill, which destroyed the cobwebs, declaring forty dollars in paper equivalent to one in specie. But even these repudiation dollars, scaled down to $2\frac{1}{2}$ cents in silver, suffered in that very year a decline to one half their face value, until finally they became entirely worthless.

Josiah Quincy, writing to Washington, November 27, 1780, said: "Our new paper money, issued by recommendation of Congress, no sooner began to circulate than two dollars of it were given for one hard one"; and added: "I am firmly of the opinion, and think it entirely defensible that there never was a paper pound, a paper dollar, or a paper promise of any kind, that ever yet obtained a general currency, but by force or fraud—generally by both."

The "money" with which Mr. Law's name is indissolubly associated has given him that kind of immortality which Herostratos aimed at. With the difference, however, that Mr. Law undoubtedly thought seriously of his ability to extricate the French finances by his scheme from the chaos in which Louis XIV. had bequeathed them to the Regent. The French assignats had the same history. Beginning on a seemingly safe basis, the value of the confiscated lands, they were yet, by the momentum of the forces set loose, soon swept from their moorings into the tossing sea of utter bankruptcy and disaster. No less than 45,578 millions of francs of these "moneys" were issued. The story is ever the same. Lured into issue after issue by the easy way of disposing of first issues, when credit is yet unimpaired, governments are soon compelled by the growing difficulties, which were to be remedied by these stratagems, to meet them by ever increasing supplies of paper promises. Draconian laws, imprisonment and the guillotine, were invoked to enforce acceptance at par value. "Patriotism," however, powerful as it may be to fire the heart in other directions, seems to lose its power when it is to make men give up their possessions for a scrip which has no other value behind it than the promise of a discredited or doubted issuer. Under the regime of this "money" prices did rise in a phenomenal manner. Although maximum prices were prescribed under threat of execution, one franc in silver became worth from 800 to 1000 in paper. The American Congress declared everybody, who refused to take its money at par with silver, an enemy of his country, and subject to the confiscation of his goods. But this did not prevent a silver dollar being worth $100 in paper in 1781. Finally these issues became worthless and were not taken at all. Before the final extinction of the assignats society had fallen back upon payment in kind, upon barter, the starting-point of civilization. The French Constitution of 1795 made the pay of a member of the Directory 50,000 myriogrammes of wheat.* In America it was easier to fall back upon this makeshift, as the country had hardly emerged from that state of civilization of which barter and payment in kind are the characteristic features.

The lesson was not lost upon students of history, and Daniel Webster's words, "Of all contrivances for cheating mankind none has been more effectual than that which deludes them with paper money," will readily find endorsement.

We leave these "moneys" out of consideration as we enter upon our inquiry into the influence of the quantities of money in circulation upon prices.

The question here first arising is, What is Money? The word is derived from "Moneta," a surname of Juno, in whose temple money was coined. The standard coins and measures were originally deposited in temples, as afterwards in the churches of the middle ages. They were under the protection of the celestial powers. The German word "Geld" is most direct in its meaning. It is derived from "gelten," to be valid, to be of full value.

In this sense alone must we take the word, when we discuss the influence of money-supply upon prices; this alone is meant when the question agitating the public mind for the last dozen years is taken up.

Broadly stated by the advocates of the theory the case is this: A decline of prices having taken place, incontest-

---

* See Wilhelm Roscher, *Handbook of Political Economy*, vol. iii., §§ 52, 54. (One myriogramme = 22 lbs. avoirdupois.)

ably, and dating from the time of the closing of the mints of the Latin Union and the resumption of specie payments by the United States, it is evident that this price decline is due to the appreciation of gold consequent upon the demonetization of the "sister-metal," silver. The moneys of the world cut in two could no longer perform the functions which they performed before the link was broken, it is averred, and the consequence is apparent in the prices. *Hinc illæ lacrimæ.*

The Question of Evidence.

Before going into an argument upon the soundness of the reasoning, we have to examine the evidence presented by bimetallists, the general decline of prices as proved by the "Index Numbers" of statistical societies, the London *Economist*, and other statistical authorities. But here it is plainly shown that what is commonly accepted as the most substantial support of economic deductions, the world's trade statistics, is, by the use made of them, placed on such a footing that it rather misleads than guides, and opens the door to much of the loose reasoning which so often lands us in a quagmire.

In these "Index Numbers," figures representing ever so many different species of merchandise are brought together in long columns footed up, and the results are made the basis of comparisons. They are treated in solid masses. They are not analyzed so that the parts may be given their proper representation in the totals, or that an article of minor utility may be reduced to its proper position in the expense budget of the individual or the nation. Nor is the fact borne in mind that the prices of 22 commodities, as in the *Economist* numbers, 28 of the Statistical Society, 40 of Mulhall, 60 or 100 of Mr. Sauerbeck and Mr. Soetbeer, never rise and fall at the same time, or even rise or fall in equal proportion. The fall of one would balance the rise of another. Wheat may rise 6 points, corn 4 points, and pork 4 points, in all 14 points. Pepper, sugar, indigo, and salt may aggregate a fall of an equal number of points, in which case the same average price ratio would appear. If the fall of the last named four articles indicated a greater number than 14 points, a general price reduction would appear from comparing the "index numbers" of the two years. But what a difference to the poor, (or to the rich in the effect upon their own fortunes, too, if these important commodities in the household of the laboring classes should be subjected to a rise,) compared to the advantage of a fall in commodities, important enough in a commercial sense, but most insignificant when held against the great staples which compose the food of the millions.

How the most unequal price notations and violent fluctuations still bring out equal index numbers, can be seen from a return taken from the *Economist*. To explain the construction of the table I will say in that paper's own words (*Economist*, February 18, 1888), that "the basis of 100 represents the average prices of the six years 1845–50, and all the subsequent figures are calculated from that datum line. Thus as regards coffee (col. 1), the price of 1st July, 1857 was equal to 151, or 50 per cent. above the average price of 1845–50. In order to ascertain the *percentage* rise or fall between one date and another—as, for example, *coffee*—comparing 1st of July, 1857, when the figure was 151, with 1st January, 1866, when the figure was 179, or a difference of 28, the rise per cent. has to be measured with the quantity 151, and gives, of course, a result of 19 per cent. as the real advance." Of course, the reader will understand this well enough, as also that if 100 represents the price of coffee at 44s. per cwt., 80s. per cwt. in 1878 stands in the index numbers for that year as 182.

I will now give the index numbers of years which approach closely the numbers for 1845–50, though widely separated in time:

VARIATION OF PRICES AND APPROXIMATING TOTALS OF INDEX NUMBERS.

	1845–50	1879	1884	1888
1. Coffee	100	143	106	166
2. Sugar	100	55	54	49
3. Tea	100	111	92	64
4. Tobacco	100	156	200	244
5. Wheat	100	75	73	58
6. Butcher's meat	100	127	123	108
7. Cotton	100	73	92	90
8. Raw silk	100	113	117	117
9. Flax and hemp	100	80	76	66
10. Sheep's wool	100	107	98	111
11. Indigo	100	164	151	129
12. Oils	100	104	110	74
13. Timber	100	115	100	80
14. Tallow	100	83	113	73
15. Leather	100	146	139	133
16. Copper	100	72	71	91
17. Iron	100	77	69	67
18. Lead	100	84	70	90
19. Tin	100	77	104	173
20. Cotton, Pernambuco	100	71	74	70
21. Cotton yarn	100	88	99	90
22. Cotton cloth	100	81	88	87
Totals of index numbers	2200	2202	2221	2230
Price of Silver per ounce	60¼d.	49⅝d.	51d.	44¼d.

The fallacy of general averages is plainly apparent when such violent price variations can be shown in the 22 commodities as against one another and each one of them by itself, in the comparative columns, while they foot up a nearly equal total with the normal average of 100 for 1845–50.

Still, upon such loose evidence is based the argument that the prices of a certain period have risen or fallen. Now it cannot be denied that during the last forty years we have lived through high-price periods and low-price periods. The high-price periods show a higher total in the index numbers than the low-price periods, though the variations are not less marked. It is evident that times of great activity make their imprint upon prices as well as times of depression, and it is equally evident that such greater activity should be apparent in the total of any set of index numbers. This being actually the case, the fact is made use of by the adherents of certain political or economic theories to bolster up the claims of their schools with utter disregard of the inherent causes that gave rise to the changed price facts of the years put in comparison.

A decline of prices has taken place dating from a stated period, and as the decline in the price of silver, as compared with gold, is shown to have had its beginning at about the same time, it has become the almost unanimous opinion among the advocates of bimetallism or silver-monometallism that the decline in the price of silver is the cause of the decline in the price of commodities.

The co-existence, or rather the consecution of facts is made to prove that one is cause and the other effect. To obtain clearness as to the truth or falsity of this claim is of paramount importance at this juncture.

To prove the falsity of this claim it is necessary, as a

first step, to show the erroneous methods which gave so much plausible support to the prevailing price theories.

The decline in prices has lent weight to the argument of the silver men. But even in this their position is not correct. Here the times chosen for comparison are all important. To prove their case, the decade of 1866 to 1875 for the period of parity of silver and of high prices, and the year 1885 for silver decline and low prices, stand well together. And here it is where so much error proceeds from otherwise willingly accepted data. The times for comparison conveniently chosen, almost anything can be proven from "Index Numbers," which in themselves are so full of error as has been shown. Here chance has done the work for silver which no amount of forethought could have improved on. In economic deduction, however, everything depends on the sifting of data and taking like and like for comparison. The importance is far-reaching. Property, wages, and the well-being of all classes depend on legislation on finance and taxation. The legislator depends solely on what he understands to be facts. If these facts are spurious, what else can be expected but ill-advised and dangerous legislation?

Now let us see what these comparisons of prices on which this silver agitation rests actually show. The prices which I introduce are, of course, English prices. Prices of American commodities are unsuitable. For 1866 to 1875 they have the double inflation of the gold premium and the war tariff. But even in England the two price-periods are by no means equivalents, a fact constantly ignored by bimetallists the world over. The inflation of all prices during the decade of 1866 to 1875 by extraneous causes was greater than even during the preceding ten years, which had the inflating influence of the Crimean

WAR PERIODS AND PRICES.

war and the American war to carry. The decade from which bimetallists draw their conclusions bore the effects, not only of inflation and speculation left over from the American war, but also from the Franco-German war of 1870, with the intense commercial and industrial activity following the destruction of property in France and the gift of the Pandora box of five milliards to Germany.*

The price of pig-iron in 1871 averaged 58s. 11d. according to the returns of the Board of Trade; in 1872 it averaged 101s. 10d.; in 1873, 117s. 3d.; in 1874, 87s. 6d.; in 1886, it was back again to the old price, of the year 1871, to wit: 58s. 6d. Bar iron, in 1871, £7, 12s, 6d, was £11 in 1872; in 1873, £12 10s. 0d.; in 1874, £10 5s. 0d., and in 1876 it had gone back to £7 5s. 0d. the price of 1871.

Now suppose you have noted down in the one ten-year period: Cotton 148s., tobacco 104, pig-iron 125, bar iron 235, coal 21, to name a few articles chiefly affected by the two causes of war and speculation, and put opposite for 1885: Cotton 58s., tobacco 64s., pig-iron 42s. (28s. for Cleveland iron), bar iron 89s., coal 9s., and you can well

---

* The extraordinary fluctuations of prices taken from the same totals of "Index Numbers" during this period of parity can be seen from the following abstract (given in round numbers up to 1870) along with the current price of silver given in pence per ounce:

	Index Numbers.	Price of Silver.
1845-50	2200	59¾d.
1857	3000	61⅜d.
1858	2600	61 1/16d.
1865	3600	61 1/16d.
1866	3580	61⅛d.
1867	3040	60⅝d.
1868	2680	60¾d.
1869	2650	60 7/8 d.
1870	2689	60⅝d.
1871	2590	60½d.
1872	2835	60 7/16 d.
1873	2947	59¼d.
1874	2891	58 1/16 d.
1875	2778	56¼d.

imagine how easy it is to prove the case of a decline in price of commodities "due to the depreciation in the price of silver."

The prices of other commodities were likewise affected, though in a more moderate degree. We can see how apt we are to draw wrong conclusions when we do not apply to statistical data the scrutiny which no business man would fail to employ in his own transactions, but which he may be sure to leave safely locked up in his office desk when he is perchance called upon to apply them to national or international affairs.

The comparing of the highly inflated years with the depressed year gives, by taking the two examples cited above, 632 for the five articles named for the former period and 262 for the latter. The addition of a great number of articles of smaller fluctuations, of course, reduces the final proportions in the aggregate of figures usually taken by the different authorities for their "index numbers," and from which they prove the increase or decrease of prices. Now, if we go back a generation and take the prices of the same five articles for the year 1854, we have cotton 54, tobacco 51, pig-iron 79, bar iron 200, coal 23, in all 407. These same articles show for 1860: Cotton 60, tobacco 58, pig-iron 53, bar iron 130, coal 9, in all 310. The methods of production were not very different in 1854 and 1860. But the price aggregate is much higher in 1854 than in 1860, on account of the war demand for iron and coal. Cotton and tobacco, on the contrary, were lower. This shows the different influences operating on prices of different articles collected in the same columns, added up, averaged, and demonstrated on.

On the whole, the year 1860 would give the most normal basis for comparison. It was a year of peace and tranquillity and general business activity. It shows us 310 in the price aggregate, against 262 for 1885. Not a great difference, it must be admitted, to build a labored theory on.

The difference between 1860 and 1885 is only 48, on a basis of 310. If we take the year 1890, with high iron prices, we get 290, a difference of 20 only. I have taken articles of great magnitude in international commerce and in home consumption. Two are agricultural and three industrial products.

A selection of 45 articles, food, textiles, minerals, and sundries (for which 1867-76 is taken, as 100) averages only 75 for 1851; but for 1854, on the contrary, 102; for 1873, they show 111; for 1881, they show 85, and for 1885, fall to 73. This is not much below the level of 1851, when silver was at a premium over gold, and few of the revolutionizing improvements in productive methods had been set in operation. Mr. A. Sauerbeck, whose computation from the *Statistical Society Journal* serves in this instance, gives the average price level (taking as a basis 100 for 1867-76) for 10-year periods for 45 articles as follows:

```
1843 to 1852........................................  82
1853 to 1862........................................  99
1866 to 1875........................................ 101
1876 to 1885........................................  85
```

Whatever we may say of the method of obtaining them, the "index numbers" of the different compilers show the present price level to be not very different from that prevailing before the Crimean war.

But what about that commodity which, according to all the schools is the chief price maker—labor?

Labor is the only commodity which has constantly been

rising. From 1850 to the present time the rise has been continuous, and has maintained itself all over the modern industrial world.

Labor and Wages.

Labor is higher to-day than in the sixties and seventies, with their level of high prices. It is certainly 50 per cent. over the low-priced period of 1850 in Germany, France, and England. It is 100 per cent. higher in the United States.

If the fall in silver were the cause of the fall in prices, the rate of wages would have been affected likewise. A general cause must have a general effect. What is of greatest significance is the fact that wages have risen in so high a ratio only in the gold-paying countries. In the countries adhering to the silver standard the rate of wages has been stagnant, or undergone but slight changes.* All this can be demonstrated to a certainty, from which I must abstain now from want of space. The matter, however, has been so fully proved that the reader will not require more detailed facts than what will be given in the progress of these pages for his orientation.

The rise in wages is the absolute proof that the fall in the price of commodities is due to invention and science, to the most forcible application of mind to production the world has ever seen. This has made labor so productive that it can demand and obtain higher pay, and at the same time produce at greatly reduced cost. To show this conclusively we must abandon "index numbers" and averages and follow the safe road of comparison by concrete cases.

---

* See chapter X.

To find a case calculated to cover all the elements in the discussion we have only to fall back upon cotton and cotton manufactures and show their price relations in the two periods mentioned;

	1854	1889		1854	1889
	s. d.	s. d.		cents.	cents.
Raw cotton..........per cwt.	53.7	53.0	per lb.	11.6	11.5
Cotton yarn.......... " "	112.0	103.0	" "	24.3	22.3
Cotton cloth, plain....100 yds.	25.0	19.0	" yard	6.1	4.6
" " printed.. " "	34.0	25.0	" "	8.3	6.1

The gold price of cotton is the same as before the war. The price of the goods made out of the cotton, *i. e.*, the cost of the labor expended on turning the cotton into goods, shows the remarkable fall indicated above. The greater the proportion of labor to the value of the material, the greater the decline in the price. The raw cotton is equal in price. In the yarn we note a fall of 8 per cent.; in the plain goods of 24 per cent; and in the printed, of 27 per cent. The cotton is subject to the competition of countries which stand on a silver basis. India has been the chief competitor. The decline in the value of the rupee has haunted to no small degree the imagination of the cotton planter in America. If the fall in the price of silver were the cause of the fall in prices, then certainly cotton ought to have fallen correspondingly. Silver was over 61*d.* an ounce in 1854; it was only 42*d.* in 1889. The price of cotton, however, had not varied. No one can deny that the decline which has happened since 1889 is due exclusively to the two phenomenal crops of 1890 and 1891, which left an unconsumed surplus on hand, after the low crop year of 1892, of nearly 3,500,000 bales. In the year 1892-93 when the crop was but an average crop, the price rose, at one time, to the high figure of 10½ cents, though silver had had a further drop. Nothing plainer but that the over-supply is the cause of the great falling away of price in cotton, as seen again in the price decline following the large crop of 1894.

But the labor and cost of turning the cotton into yarn, the yarn into cloth, the cloth into prints, is all added in gold-paying England, which regulates the price of manufactures for all other exporting countries. If the theories which have been at the root of all this agitation were sound, then a rise ought to be manifest in that part of the prices which is added by labor, earning daily rates varying from 50 to 100 per cent. higher than in the early years of the fifties.

No better proof need be given of the economic fallacies generated by blindly following statistical compilations than in this illustration of prices of cotton manufactures. This is further illustrated by holding the results of this examination of a concrete case against what I have shown as the usual statistical method, that of averaging prices of a large number of commodities entirely unrelated and discrepant in their importance as articles of consumption, and drawing comparisons from them without regard even to war and other extraordinary influences on prices.

If experience must be the basis for all reasoning, facts must be the basis for economic deductions. But what are facts? Mere statistical tabulations and the indiscriminate use made of them are not facts and certainly not very reliable guides for legislators to follow.

CHAPTER II.

The Prevailing Money Theories—The Money-Metals—The Varying Relations of Output between them—Does not Affect their Value Relations.

NAMES of the highest authority have given weight to the doctrine that the quantity of the precious metals in existence determines the prices of commodities. Montesquieu * formulated the theory that "prices are fixed in the ratio of the whole of the commodities to the whole of the signs" (gold and silver), "compounded with the ratio of the whole of the commodities in the channels of trade to the whole of the signs in these channels. The establishment of prices depends always, fundamentally, upon the ratio of the total of commodities to the total of signs."

This view is generally accepted. Montesquieu, however, is not the originator of the theory. As far back as 1588 Davanzati in *Lezione sulle Monete* † says: "All commodities which serve to satisfy the wants of man are by convention equal in value to all the gold, silver, and copper. The parts are subject to the same rule as the whole." Montanari, in *Della Moneta* sets forth the same views, but adds the limitation "spendibile in commercio" (to be expended in commerce). Locke goes even so far as to say, there being now ten times as much silver in the world than at the time of the discovery

---

* Montesquieu, *Esprit des Lois*.

† Quoted by Wilhelm Roscher, *Grundlagen der National Oekonomie*, vol. i., §. 123, 21st edition.

of America, the value of every unit of silver is only one tenth as much as then compared with merchandise remaining unchanged. He is of the opinion that with money the demand is always equally strong, always up to the supply, while with merchandise this is not the case.

Wilhelm Roscher says of Hume * that he knows well enough that only the money in circulation and the merchandise in circulation have a bearing upon prices, but

---

* Hume, the historian, contradicts the deductive essayist in a manner that I cannot refrain from quoting here his statements referring to price comparisons of his time and that of Elizabeth and James I.

"The price of corn during this reign (James I.), and that of the other necessaries of life, was no lower, or was rather higher, than at present. By a proclamation of James, establishing public magazines, whenever wheat fell below thirty-two shillings a quarter, rye below eighteen, barley below sixteen, the commissioners were empowered to purchase corn for the magazines. These prices, then, are to be regarded as low, though they would rather pass as high by our present estimates. The usual bread of the poor was at this time made of barley. The best wool during the greater part of James's reign, was at thirty-three shillings a tod. At present it is not above two thirds of that value ; though it is to be presumed that our exports in woollen goods are somewhat increased. The finer manufactures, too, by the progress of arts and industry, have rather diminished in price, notwithstanding the great increase of money. In Shakespeare, the hostess tells Falstaff that the shirts she bought him were Holland at eight shillings a yard ; a high price at this day, even supposing, what is not probable, that the best Holland at that time was equal in goodness to the best that can now be purchased. In like manner a yard of velvet about the middle of Elizabeth's reign was valued at two and twenty shillings."

Referring to 1776 he says in footnote : "Money, too, we may observe was in most particulars of the same value in both periods ; she (Elizabeth) paid eightpence a day to every foot soldier."

He makes the very wise deduction from the facts in explanation of the higher cost of living at his time :

"The chief difference in expense between that age and the present, consists in the imaginary wants of men, which have since extremely multiplied. These are the principal reasons why James's revenue would go farther than the same money in our time ; though the difference is not near so great as is usually imagined."—Hume, *History of England*, vol. iv., Appendix iii.

"he does not strike the idea yet that the rapidity of circulation has to be considered." That the theory of money here reviewed and still current is untenable appears from the mere consideration of the sums of money and quantities of merchandise in existence at any one time. So it is pointed out by Mr. Michel Chevalier that the money quantities of France in existence in 1851 were estimated at between $3\frac{1}{2}$ and 4 milliards of francs, while the value of real property alone amounted according to official valuation to 83 milliards of francs. The value of realty is, naturally, determined by the development of industrial production. But even the values of circulating merchandise, *i. e.* the annual product going into the channels of commerce, bears no positive relation to the quantities of money in circulation.

The money quantities in existence in the United States in 1880 are estimated at about $1,400,000,000. According to my calculation,* taking the salable value of the crops at the shipping ports and adding the additional value given to the raw material by the manufacturing industries of the country, plus the distributing expenses and the profits of capital, the commercial value of the annual product in the consumers' hands was then $7,680,000,000. †

Here the proportion of money to annually circulating merchandise is as one to five.

But we have here a very important fact to chronicle which at once sets at naught all the arguments of the adherents of the mechanical price theory.

---

* See J. Schoenhof, *The Industrial Situation*, ch. xii., p. 103.

† This is below the prevalent estimates. But my estimates are based on an elimination of repetitions in values, and differ in this from the usually inflated American official statistics, in which an absence of critical acumen is frequently too manifest.

The resumption of specie payments in 1878 had by 1880 added something like $600,000,000 to the paper forming the only currency, except the specie circulation on the Pacific Coast. The quality of the currency was improved by the resumption act, and notwithstanding the large increase in quantity of money, no changes in prices were perceptible, except in articles of merchandise in which the change can easily be traced to other causes still fresh in everybody's remembrance. I will show this by the prices of principal commodities in 1877 and 1880.*

Names of Commodities.	Prices.	
	1877. Dollars.	1880. Dollars.
Corn, bu..............................	0.587	0.543
Wheat ".............................	1.17	1.25
Wheat flour, bs.......................	6.49	5.88
Cotton, pd............................	0.118	0.115
Leather "............................	0.239	0.233
Bacon and hams, pd..................	0.108	0.067
Lard, pd.............................	0.109	0.074
Pork ".............................	0.09	0.061
Beef, salted, pd......................	0.075	0.064
Butter, pd............................	0.206	0.171
Cheese "............................	0.118	0.095
Eggs, doz............................	0.259	0.165
Starch, pd............................	0.052	0.043
Sugar, refined, pd....................	0.116	0.09
Leal tobacco, pd......................	0.102	0.077
Pig-iron, No. 1, Anthracite, Phila., ton.	18.88	28.50
Bar iron, ton.........................	45.55	60.38
Iron rails ".........................	35.25	49.25
Steel rails ".........................	45.50	67.50
Cut nails, 100 lbs....................	2.57	3.68
Anthracite coal, ton..................	2.59	4.53
Bituminous coal, "...................	3.15	3.75
Standard sheetings, yard..............	0.118	0.115
Standard drilling, yard...............	0.0846	0.0851
New York mills bleached shirting, yard..	0.1246	0.1274
Print cloths, 64 x 64, yard...........	0.0438	0.0451

* See *Statistical Abstract of the United States, 1891.*

If we were to foot up the twenty-six articles here named we should undoubtedly get a higher total for 1880 than for 1877. Those eager for proofs supporting the quantity theory would certainly find it in the "index numbers" based on the totals so obtained. But we see that the increase is solely derived from higher prices of iron, steel, and coal. These, as everybody knows, were suddenly raised in a phenomenal manner by the great boom in iron which in the fall of 1879 began its meteoric course, from the great depression following the panic of 1873. The boom, as will be remembered, led to the panic of 1884, following which came another four years of depression and a repetition of the same alternations in almost the same quadrennial or quinquennial periods.

Iron, it must be noted here, is more influenced in this erratic manner than other commodities, because during long-continued depression iron furnaces are blown out to reduce the output. The deterioration of the plant, the time for repair and putting in blast when demand revives, is great enough to create a scarcity for a considerable length of time, which makes it almost certain that high prices follow in the wake of a period of stagnation. All articles of which pig-iron is the basis naturally follow in the same run of price inflation until the collapse, always certain to succeed extraordinary expansion, sets in again. Now if we take iron and connected branches, like coal, out of the columns, we find the prices of most of the other commodities to be essentially unchanged, while meat products are even considerably lower than in the year of the smaller money supply.

If the theory were correct that an expansion of the money supply raises the prices of commodities, it would follow that the adoption of a paper currency driving the demonetized specie into neighboring countries would raise the ordinary standard of prices there. But investigation has been unable to show that this was the case in similarly affected periods, as evidenced by Tooke and other writers,* neither can we find any trace of such an occurrence as the consequence of the American acts, regulating the money circulation of the years 1861 to 1875.

The geometrical treatment of prices, equating a given bulk of money with a given bulk of merchandise is certainly an easy method of solving a great problem. It need not surprise us that experts went to work to adduce proof by algebraic test so as to give an apparently mathematical basis of certainty to an array of otherwise unauthenticated assumptions. Evidence to the contrary, however, has been brought forward by some of the most painstaking investigators, but the doctrine still holds full sway and certainly supplies a sort of "scientific" basis to the agitation for the "rehabilitation of silver" and co-relative demands.

Arthur Young in 1811 published his *Inquiry into the Progressive Value of Money in England*. In his introduction he speaks of the pains he took in the collection of his data. "I examined," he says, "a multitude of authorities from which I extracted a great variety of prices, carefully referring to every authority, quoting the volume and page, and combining them with all to be

---

* "That the markets of the world are not so easily put in perturbation by an increase of the circulating mediums is authenticated among other things by the facts how the enormous outflow of the French metal money in consequence of the paper emissions of 1716 to 1720 and again of 1790 met with declining prices on the surrounding corn markets. And yet the former has amounted to four hundred million francs and the latter at least to one thousand million francs."—Wilhelm Roscher, *Grundlagen der National Oekonomie*, vol. i., page 369.

found in the books cited by Sir George Shurkburgh, as well as with the details, more numerous than had before been published, given by Sir Frederic Eden in his *State of the Poor*. These prices I reduced with much labor to the standard of our present money. The investigation occupied myself, an amanuensis, and an accountant, with other occasional assistance, much the greater part of ten months and at no inconsiderable expense."

According to this minute and careful investigation the whole advance in prices was not more than in the proportion of 1 to 3 from the fifteenth century to the year 1810. If we were to reduce the prices of 1810, inflated by war influences, to those ruling in the preceding period, the difference would not be more than in the proportion of 1 to 2. The increase in the stock of the precious metals, employed as money, however, was as 1 to 11. Adam Smith shows in his table of prices of wheat that the prices were lower in the first half of the eighteenth century than at the end of the sixteenth and during the seventeenth century.

Tooke, in his examination as to the *History of Prices* covering the period from 1793 to 1839, comes to the conclusion "that the alterations of prices originated and mainly proceeded from alterations in circumstances distinctly affecting commodities, and not in the quantity of money."

An examination of the facts has always made the point clear enough. And it is not a very encouraging sign of the progress of economic thought that every generation has to fight the battle over again. We can combat these ever-recurring aberrations only by fixing the attention of the speculative mind upon the main facts, and this we can accomplish only by strictly pursuing the historic method of inquiry.

We shall therefore give a more exhaustive treatment to this part of our discourse later on, and examine first the claim that the fall in the price of silver is due to the change in the ratio of the outputs of gold and silver.

The Relative Output of Gold and Silver.

Much is made by the bimetallists of Europe and by the silver-men of America of the demonetization of silver by the commercial nations of the world. It is treated as an injury done to the common people. Reversely it is made to appear that, if remonetization could be accomplished, it would work a miracle in curing the evils the body politic is suffering from. Manchester expects a never-ending demand for its cottons at highly remunerative prices. The territorial lords of Germany promise their tenants and the agriculturists prosperous times, high prices, good wages and (possibly) good crops. Our own advocates of " Free Coinage " expect and promise no less.

But it seems that in the discussions concerning the alleged conspiracy of the "money power," against "the people," in which it is claimed that through the degradation of silver the people are discriminated against, the positions of the two money metals are not properly understood, or at least the inquiries neglect to exhaust the subject. The relative positions in different periods duly considered would demonstrate the correctness of what I have endeavored to show, namely: that the fall in the price of commodities is one thing and the fall in the price of silver quite another, and that the two stand in but very remote relation to each other.

It is maintained that the decreased output of gold since 1875, as compared with silver, has caused the depreciation of silver.

As in the question of the fall in prices so in the comparison of output of the two metals, the discussions barely touch a longer period than that covered by the last two decades. But in order to have a clear survey of the field, we have to go back to the position which the two metals held to each other up to 1850, and then consider what it has become since. We shall see then that the depreciation of silver is due to natural and very powerful economic agencies, though different from those usually assumed. We find that in the whole period preceding 1850, the production of silver had in value constantly and continuously been far in excess of that of gold. It is estimated by competent authority that in the early years of the present century there were thirty-three tons of silver in the world to one of gold. If the price of silver were determined by ratio or quantity, the price ratio would have been in the neighborhood of 33 to 1, instead of 15½ to 1, the then existing ratio.

As regards the production of the two metals, Alexander von Humboldt, who had good opportunities for gathering information on the spot, estimates the product of the American mines from their discovery down to the year 1803 at 51 times as much silver as gold. Including all the known mines of the world gives the ratio of 45 to 1. (See Humboldt, *Essai Politique sur le Royaume de la Nouvelle Espagne*.)

The quantities of gold to silver were from the time of the opening of the silver mines of Potosi, *i. e.*, 1545, in proportion of about 3 gold to 97 of silver as the average of the 300 years. In the periods named here below the proportions average as follows in quantitative output:

	Gold. Per cent.	Silver. Per cent.
1493–1600	2.9	97.1
1601–1700	2.4	97.6
1781–1820	2.1	97.9
1821–1840	3.2	98.6

28   MONEY AND PRICES.

As can be seen this gives a ratio varying from 30 to 45 to 1, if these great time divisions are taken into view. Within these wider divisions variations of far greater extent occurred.

At no time, however, did the quantity-relation determine the value. From 1492 to 1520 the output averaged 5800 kilos gold and 47,000 kilos silver, which is about 1 to 8. The commercial ratio then was about 1 to 11. From 1521 to 1544 the output was 7160 kilos gold to 90,200 silver, or a change to 1 to 12½, without changing the ratio of the commercial values of the two metals. The discovery of the mines of Potosi in 1545 and of Guanajuato in 1556, changed the quantity-relation to an extraordinary degree without at all affecting the value of silver for fifty years.

ANNUAL AVERAGE OF OUTPUT OF GOLD AND SILVER IN KILOS, THE RATIO OF PRODUCTION, AND THE COMMERCIAL RATIO.

Period.	Production of Gold. *Kilos.*	Production of Silver. *Kilos.*	— Proportion 1 Gold to — Silver.	Commercial Ratio.*
1492–1520	5,800	47,000	1 : 8	1 : 10.74
1521–1544	7,160	90,200	1 : 12½	1 : 11.25
1545–1560	8,510	311,600	1 : 36⅝	1 : 11.30
1561–1580	6,840	299,500	1 : 44	1 : 11.50
1581–1600	7,380	418,900	1 : 56⅝	1 : 11.80
1601–1620	8,520	422,900	1 : 48¾	1 : 12.25
1621–1640	8,300	393,600	1 : 47½	1 : 14.
1641–1660	8,770	366,300	1 : 41¾	1 : 14.50
1661–1680	9,260	337,000	1 : 36¼	1 : 15.00
1681–1700	10,765	341,900	1 : 31¾	1 : 15.00
1701–1720	12,820	355,600	1 : 28	1 : 15.20
1721–1760	21,850	482,000	1 : 22	1 : 15.00
1761–1780	20,705	652,740	1 : 31½	1 : 14.60
1781–1820	15,660	771,000	1 : 49	1 : 15.50
1821–1840	17,250	528,000	1 : 30⅝	1 : 15.75
1841–1850	54,759	780,415	1 : 14¼	1 : 15.83
1851–1860	200,500	895,000	1 : 4⅖	1 : 15.40
1861–1870	195,000	1,220,000	1 : 6¼	1 : 15.50
1871–1875	173,904	1,969,425	1 : 11⅓	1 : 15.97
1876–1880	172,414	2,450,252	1 : 14¼	1 : 17.81
1881–1885	149,137	2,861,700	1 : 19¼	1 : 18.63

* From Soetbeer's *Materialien.*

The annexed table shows more closely the variations in quantity-relations, and the steadiness of values during long periods.

A great revolution in relative output is ushered in with the discovery of the gold fields of America. The tables are suddenly reversed.

In the thirty years following 1850 as much gold was produced as in the 357 years beginning with 1492, and enough in addition to nearly double the gold finds of the two first centuries after the discovery of America.

The ratio by quantity for the decade 1851–60 was 1 gold to $4\frac{1}{2}$ silver; for 1861–70 it was 1 to $6\frac{1}{4}$; and for 1871–80, when gold production receded again, it still averaged 1 to $12\frac{3}{4}$, as against 1 to 33, and even 1 to 56 in the times previous to the large gold discoveries.

Still the price relations of the two metals did not change perceptibly.*

The ratio of value was nearly the same the beginning of the seventeenth century as at the end of the fifteenth, although the production of silver had risen from 8 (gold being 1) to 56. This ratio decreased gradually and reached 22 (to 1 of gold) in 1760. But the price of silver,

---

* The average London price of silver in pence per ounce and the ratio of silver stood as follows under all these violent changes:

	Price of Silver per ounce. Pence.	Ratio. Average.	Quantities.	
			Gold. Per cent.	Silver. Per cent.
1831 to 1840.....	$59\frac{7}{8}$	15.75	3.3	96.7
1841 to 1850.....	$59\frac{9}{16}$	15.83	6.6	93.4
1851 to 1860.....	$61\frac{3}{8}$	15.35	18.3	81.7
1861 to 1865.....	$61\frac{1}{4}$	15.40	14.4	85.6
1866 to 1870.....	$60\frac{5}{8}$	15.55	12.7	87.3
1871 to 1875.....	$59\frac{1}{16}$	15.97	8.1	91.9
1876 to 1880.....	$52\frac{1}{8}$	17.81	6.6	93.4
1881 to 1885.....	$50\frac{5}{8}$	18.63	5.	95.

which had commenced to decline in the beginning of the seventeenth century, was not raised by this decrease. Quite the reverse. In 1600 about twelve ounces of silver were required to buy an ounce of gold; in 1760 it took fifteen ounces. Neither does the rising ratio of production up to 1820 have much effect on the price. From 1780 to 1820 we have an annual average of 49 to 1 again. But the price does not change more than a fraction.

We can get perhaps a better conception of the indifference of the price of silver to the quantitative changes in the two metals, which took place during the three decades succeeding the discovery of the California gold fields, when we compare the output by values.

Up to 1840 the output had been:

In Gold.	In Silver.	Relation of Gold to Silver—.
£590,000,000	£1,361,000,000	1: 2.31

In 1880 the totals stood:

£1,454,000,000	£1,789,000,000	1: 1.23

There was but half as much silver in the world, in relation to gold, when the decline in the price of silver became a prominent feature in the financial history of the world, as in the first half of the century. Since then the output has been:

	In Gold. £	In Silver. £	Relation of Gold to Silver.
From 1881–1888	148,000,000	154,000,000	1:1.04
" 1889–1894	176,000,000	205,000,000	1:1.16
" 1881–1894	324,000,000	359,000,000	1:1.10
Adding, up to 1880	1,454,000,000	1,789,000,000	1:1.20
Gives a grand total of	1,778,000,000	2,148,000,000	
As against 1850 of	667,000,000	1,428,000,900	1:2.14
Consequently 1850 to 1894, added	1,111,000,000	720,000,000	1:0.65

In the last 45 years 166 per cent. has been added to the gold product of 357 years and only 50 per cent. to the silver product, which was then, at the time of its highest value, more than twice as great in proportion to gold as now, the time of its lowest value.

If the relative quantities of the two metals produced determined the value, then the price of silver ought now to be nearly double what it was worth in 1850. Being worth 60*d.* then, it ought to be worth 110*d.* now. But in fact, it had gone down to 38*d.* before the closing of the India mint, and had since this event further declined to a price less than 30*d.* the ounce.

The Real Cause of the Decline in the Price of Silver.

The question, Why has silver fallen so low in price? finds answer by bimetallists in what they call, the conspiracy to demonetize silver, begun and directed by England, and now followed by all the leading commercial nations. They say: If all nations would agree to the free coinage of silver at a certain ratio, then silver would command the full value it held before the decline. Mr. de Cernuschi has even supplied the vocabulary with the necessary "scientific" terms. "Centripoise" and "centrivale" are to express the two values—the value determined by the economic conditions and the value given by the government stamp upon coin. And our own bimetallists go so far even as to say that America can give this higher value to a depreciated commodity single-handed, by saying this or that piece of silver is a dollar, when its real value in the markets of the world is but 60, 50, or 45 cents, as has been the case a short time ago.

We may ask in return: Why do all other nations withdraw their support from silver?

If the extreme changes in the rate of production (comparing the time prior to the new gold finds, and the period of these great gold discoveries) did not change the value of ratio, it is safe to ask why should silver decline in price now when the proportionate production of silver is but even with that of gold, and the output of the latter exceeds in quantity everything the world has ever seen.

The answer is here. If we take the ratio of production to represent also the relative quantities in existence at the different periods named, then we have for 1850 for every dollar's worth of gold about two and one eighth dollars' worth of silver. Much of the silver produced up to then had become absorbed in the arts, sent to the East, or otherwise removed from use. But so had much of the gold. The amounts of gold and silver money actually in existence are estimated by competent authorities for 1800 as £120,000,000 gold and £260,000,000 silver; for 1848, as £150,000,000 of gold and £280,000,000 silver. But in 1880, £700,000,000 of gold and £490,000,000 of silver were in existence, according to the best authorities. Neuman-Spallart estimates the gold money for 1889 as about £800,000,000, and the silver money of about the same value. Since then little has changed in the relative positions of supply in the two metals. We have nearly two dollars of gold money in existence for every dollar of the two metals combined, circulating in 1848. In fact, silver was scarce as a money metal, relatively more so even than gold, because of the more general demand for it. It was the circulating medium. Upon the continent of Europe the idea of money was closely associated with silver, but not with gold. The French "argent" means silver and money. In German, "versilbern" is to the present day equivalent to "turning into cash." The language of the people is the storeroom of history. Silver was the circulating medium, and the standard. The poorer and the more backward the nations, the bulkier the substance of their circulating medium. Even copper coin was an important element with the people of Continental Europe in the earlier part of this century, but

Silver was the Money

used in business transactions. The Southern German states had no gold coins of their own before the formation of the new Empire. From 1831 to 1840 only £28,000,000 of gold was produced and £52,000,000 of silver. This is still nearly two to one of silver to gold.

But from 1850 to 1880 the very opposite current appeared in regard to production. The world produced more than two dollars' worth of gold for every dollar's worth of silver.

The increasing output of silver for a time, seemed to change the general relations. But now for several years again the output of gold is in value considerably above that of silver, if we take the commercial value. The new gold finds, the introduction of deep mining, and the application of capitalistic and, therefore, scientific methods, where formerly only crude, individualistic exploitation prevailed, seem to readily fill the demand. The world's output of 1894 in gold is estimated at $175,000,000, the highest average on record. The quinquennial period of 1851-1860 gives only an annual average of $140,000,000.

The "Witwatersrand" mines in South Africa have developed from 494,869 ounces in 1890, as follows:

1891	729,238 ounces.
1892	1,210,868 "
1893	1,478,473 "
1894	2,024,159 "

as reported by the *Economist* of January 12, 1895. The last year's figure is equal to two thirds of the American annual average for 1851–55. Gold production has added to the supplies of the world in the precious metals since 1850 the sum of £1,111,000,000. Silver production only £720,000,000 (silver taken at the coinage rate of 15½ to 1).

Silver, being relatively scarcer than gold, would easily maintain its former higher price, were its serviceability as great in the coinages of the world as in the past.

But it is not the relatively greater or smaller quantity of the white metal in existence which has cast it from its position, but the abundance of gold brought into use since 1848. In spite of all the endeavors to prove the contrary, there seems to be enough gold in existence to answer the purposes of exchange. True, there is always a very strenuous endeavor to obtain an increase in the stocks of gold. But gold seems never to be wanting, except in times of scare and waning confidence in the stability of financial conditions, such as produced the panic of 1893.

But here come other factors in view. The use of money is not as great as it has been in trade. Of the thousand million dollars of coined money (gold and silver), very little appears in trade in America. With the progress of civilization and its concomitants, industrial progress and international confidence and good-will, the importance of metallic money as a means of payment is becoming smaller and smaller. Metal money is gradually being superseded by less expensive substitutes. In the advanced countries silver has outrun its usefulness. The mere fact of its cumbersome nature would declare against it as the standard money of the commercial world.

The History of the Standards of Value.

The history of the development of commerce among nations, from the ancient to the present world, shows that the changes of standard of value mark the progress from a lower state of civilization to a higher one. For the Germanic nations as well as for the Romans, we have it recorded in the name that their earliest measure of value was cattle. "Fee," "feoh," "vieh," the same as "pecus," means "pecunia," money (it is used so in old German chronicles), as "peculia," means peculiar, individual property, as distinguished from landed property, which among all primitive nations is property of the community.*

This is true not alone among the Indo-Germanic races, but among nations of the most varied types. The holding and cultivation of land in common was found among the American Indians, among the Malays, among the archaic-races which occupied Italy before the Roman period, as well as among the Slavs, the Chinese, and Hindoos. †

---

* How deep the commonalty of land and its cultivation in common was rooted in the German people is proved by the fact that even in the towns the lands were so held by the burghers. The free towns, the great commercial emporiums of the middle ages, held large tracts of land, and a large part of their population, in many the larger part, obtained their living from the land. In Frankfort-on-the-Main the burghers had common rights not alone in the grazing lands and forests but also in the fields, which, as we read in an ordinance of the town council of the year 1504, had to lie fallow every third year. "But not alone concerning the common mark, but also concerning private holdings in many towns, the town councils ordered how to cultivate the land, how to plow and to till, how to cultivate the fallow, to plant trees, cut, tie, and trim the vines, prop them, and the like." See G. L. von Maurer, *Geschichte des Staedte Verfassung in Deutschland;* also Johannes Janssen, *Geschichte des deutschen Volkes bei dem Ausgang des Mittelalters,* vol. I.

† See, for full particulars, Émile de Laveleye's important work, *De la Propriété et des ses Formes Primitives.* Also the works of Sir Henry Maine, *Village Communities, Ancient Law,* etc.

The traces of this common property in land are found to the present day in Germany and in Switzerland, in the still existing "Gemeindeacker," "Gemeindeweide," and "Gemeindeforst" (the communal acre, the communal pasture, and the communal forest). In this the present writer remembers from his boyhood the burghers of his own town (Oppenheim on the Rhine) to have had their allotments. The existence of a peculium implies that a step forward has been made in civilization. It implies that trade of a certain kind is possible, that interchangeable values and commodities are created. Now it is quite evident that animals of the size and value even of the inferior kinds bred on the grazing lands and in the forests of ancient Germany or other undeveloped countries * are not a sort of money taken to fairs and markets to be exchanged for whatever could be had from the conflux of itinerant or post traders of the Roman settlements.† But from the records in the ancient laws we can easily see that this "pecunia" was used as a money of account to compute values by and effect settlements on.

When the migration of nations had merged into a settled state on the territories which the European nations now occupy, the conquerors adopted the garb of the

---

* We know that cattle were used in the same sense as money, or as standard of payment by the old Persians, by the Homeric Greeks, and the fact that the picture of an ox is found on the coins of pre-Solonic Athens is a sure indication that tradition still connected the idea of money with cattle. "Fe" (the same as "Vieh," the German for cattle) is still to-day in Iceland the expression equivalent with property or money.

† Commerce goes back to the very earliest periods. Traces of an active trade are found in places where no Roman settlements were ever made. Important contributions to our knowledge on this subject are made by Professor Dr. J. Schneider, from his own personal examinations, *Die alten Heer- und Handelswege der Germanen, Roemer und Franken im deutschen Reiche.*

civilization which they had overthrown, and, of course, the monetary system as part of it.

That the Salian Franks, who had conquered Gaul had in use the Roman monetary system is proved by the many gold coins in our collections, bearing the Merovingian stamp, which, in grain and fineness, as well as in general type, fully correspond with the contemporary imperial solidus. "As the Roman pound of gold weighed about 327 grammes, the metal contained in the solidus was $4\frac{1}{2}$ grammes."* The pound was 72 solidi of the exact weight of 4.55 grammes each, making the pound 327 grammes.

The German nations on the right bank of the Rhine, as evidenced by the Ripuarian, Bajuvarian, and other German Codici, and later on, the Capitularies of the Carlovingian kings, adopted the Frankish money standard at a period quite too undeveloped to allow us to suppose that an actual monetary traffic could have existed.

"The importance of the monetary system of that time does not lie in its employment as a means of payment and exchange, but in its application to the calculation of the values of marketable commodities."

"At least with the tribes of interior Germany, money was certainly for a long period only money of account, explained by the fact that commercial transactions, which require metal money, were of too rare an occurrence to call forth an active demand for coins. By this almost exclusive use of money as an accounting medium, the peculiar system of determining values which we find among the Germans becomes comprehensible." †

Trading was done in kind, as up to a comparatively recent period, taxes, rents, and feudal dues were paid in produce. Cattle formed the basis for computation. The "Wergeld," the compensation for murder, theft, or other injuries, is stipulated in heads of cattle in the codes of the

---

* See Inama-Sternegg, *Deutsche Wirthschaftsgeschichte bis zum Schluss der Karolingerzeit*, vol. i.

† Inama-Sternegg, *Ibid.*

more ancient times. Only after contact with the Frankish monarchies, the Roman money takes the place of cattle in legal computations. Till we come to a regular commercial trading system, in which money becomes the means of payment, a money economy, many a century has to elapse from the time we are speaking of here.

In the periods of transition from a system of barter and payment in kind to a money economy, the cheaper, more common metals, are used. Their use denotes a low state of commercial and industrial development. The iron money of Sparta, the copper as of Rome, the copper currencies of the middle-age period (this comprises very recent periods, so far as the smaller traffic and wage-payments go) of modern Europe, all denote a similar state of development, or rather undevelopment. The silver standard took the place of copper with the rise and extension of trade. Rome's copper currency seems to have held itself till the middle of the third century B.C., as long as Rome contented itself with extending its dominion over Italy. It put into its treasury from the triumph over the Samnites (293 B.C.) 2,000,000 pounds of copper; in silver, only 1330 pounds. In 194 B.C., shortly before the first Punic war, it adopted the silver standard. But with the beginning of the imperium under Cæsar and Pompey, the gold standard appears. With the great rise of power, practically extending over the civilized world, directing the world's economic and political pulsation, the more efficient gold standard had to take the place of the cumbersome white metal. The solidus replaces the denarius, just as the denarius replaced the as, all in their proper time and when their mission had been fulfilled. Good enough for a provincial or even an isolated national existence, silver was found insufficient for a world-empire.

And what is trade but man grasping the poles in his ambition!

Macedonia began coining gold as soon as its ambition reached beyond its own confines. And, in fact, we find this the case with all the ancient monarchies.

The wide circulation of gold coins makes it imperative to preserve not alone this standard, but also the effigy of the ruler whose name has gone farthest among the civilized and semi-civilized nations reached by commerce. The Persian Darius and the Macedonian Philip and Alexander pieces circulated centuries after the periods of these great rulers, and were found far beyond the limits of their empires, an advantage not shared by coins subject to frequent changes. Stability in fineness, weight, shape, and device is essential to a commodity which, as money, is to circulate without question among heterogeneous peoples. Egypt and the Saracen states in the middle ages, in the period of their greatest power, had the gold standard. The circulation of their coins seems to have extended pretty far over Europe, as is attested by the fact (see Falke, *Geschichte des deutschen Handels*) * that the Numismatic Cabinet at Stockholm contains 20,000 Arabic gold coins. And gold coins were not circulated so much as they were hoarded among the barbarous nations of Europe, even after trade and industry had developed. Copper and silver were with them the paying mediums, sufficient for their stage of civilization. It is no idle fancy that ascribed magic qualities to gold in the middle ages. The magic lay in the difficulty of realization, of possession. He who could make gold, possessed the elixir of life: the elixir of life of trade. It is therefore natural that what nations had found this elixir, took to a gold cur-

---

* See Roscher, *Grundlagen der National Oekonomie*, vol. iii., §. 47.

rency because none other possessed the quality of insuring a continuous flow of life to the trade extending over the countries of the world. You cannot carry silver from Bagdad to Paris or Lyons, or from Cordova to Hyderabad, or from Florence to Novgorod, or from Bruges to Constantinople, in quantities sufficient to make a trade worth the trouble, or to use it whenever you have to make money payment. The bulk is sufficient to forbid large transactions, especially in periods like the middle ages, with roads and means of travel alike defective and full of risk to life and property. Well adapted for provincial and interior trading, silver becomes an awkward medium to do service in the markets of the world. Wherever and whenever it was the standard of payment, it marks a period of "medio evo," a middle age, a period of unripeness, of exclusive provincialism and separateness. When the Italian cities had grown to independence and thrown off the yoke of feudalism, they quickly stepped in to take the reins of the world's trade from the fading Califate and decaying Byzantium, and followed their lead in adopting the gold standard. Venice, Genoa, Florence, coined gold and made their payments on the gold standard as far back as the thirteenth century. The gold florin, the coin of Florence, soon became the commercial money of Europe,* on account of its widely known

---

* Sismondi is authority for the statement that the gold florin of Florence, dating from the year 1252, never changed its coinage weight, while the silver lira underwent very great changes. It was coined at first especially for the Mohammedan countries, but soon became the standard money for international trading. The same can be said of the gold coins of other countries, which were hardly used at home, but circulated abroad, as the French gold coins up to 1748 in Switzerland, Germany, and Italy, and the Dutch ducats. No foreign coins could circulate unless they had acquired and maintained a high reputation for honesty and the veracity of the legend. Unchallenged circulation in foreign countries is the best test of the full value of coins.

high character; and the Florentine traders became the bankers of the world. Without a gold currency they would have remained the provincial traders which the descendants of the Medici, the Pazzi, the Aridi, became again after the spirit that built the cities on the Arno and the Po had taken its flight. Another reason of the great preference given to gold, beside its smaller bulk, *i. e.*, higher value, is, that the coins cannot so easily be tampered with. Without a staple currency trading communities cannot maintain their positions. As far back as the fourteenth century, the commercial cities of Germany made bills payable in gold, and in the seventeenth century the rule had wellnigh been universally adopted all over Europe.

The saying of the elder Mirabeau in *La Monarchie Prussienne*, "One can not gain, one can only steal, a profit from the coinage," is very appropriate when we regard the different games that were at different times played with the currencies of Europe. It is superfluous to explain in words why gold is less subject to the invidious attempts. It suffices to say that it has at all times been the safe basis upon which the world's commerce has rested, and therefore this brief historic sketch may not be without its useful application to the conditions now surrounding us.

It may also be of use to call attention to the fact that the high valuation of silver, as compared with gold, has been usual with countries in a backward state, and that, reversely, a lower valuation is the sign of a more advanced civilization. This, to a very large extent, is owing to the fact that, in undeveloped countries, silver is the chief currency, and therefore in constant demand, on account of the limited monetary transactions. It is the economic and industrial condition which governs the demand, and not the fiat of legislators and rulers.

Tacitus says that the German people had neither silver nor gold previous to their contact with Rome. Of those who had entered into relations with the Roman settlements he adds: "They aim more after silver than gold, not from preference, but because a number of silver pieces are more convenient in making a trade in promiscuous and inferior articles of merchandise." (Tacitus, *Germania*, ch., v.)

According to Roscher, in the time of Nadir Shah (1750), the Kurds gave weight for weight, silver for gold.

In India, at the time of Alexander's invasion, silver to gold was valued as 1 to 2. But in consequence of the widening of commerce, brought on by it, the ratio soon reached 1 to 5 or 6.* In Athens, when she was at the zenith of her glory and power, the ratio, according to Herodotus, was 13 to 1. The Rome of the undeveloped era, in 189 B.C., left it optional with the Æolians to pay their tribute in silver or gold, at the weight ratio of 10 to 1.

In the middle ages silver had a much higher value

---

* "When Vasco da Gama rounded the Cape, the new-comers first plundered the coasts; but finding that their brigandage aroused sufficient resistance to render it dangerous, they began to trade, at first by exchanging their stolen silver for gold at the Indian ratio of 6 to 8 for 1. In Bombay, in 1774, the legal ratio was nearly 15 to 1 ; in 1800 = 15 to 1.

"In Kordofan, between Darfoor and the Nile, thirty years ago, the trade in gold was monopolized by the Pasha, but gold was sold clandestinely at the rate of $8 in silver for 430 grains of fine gold. In Shoa, nine silver dollars were paid per ounce troy of fine gold." (The ounce of gold is worth nearly $20 in coinage value of silver.)—Alexander Del Mar, *A History of Money*. Quite in keeping with these facts may be quoted the statement from Ritter's *Erdkunde* that in Africa gold stands the lower, compared to silver, the farther the country is from contact with the civilized world.

compared with gold than in the later centuries. In the Carlovingian period, the Roman ratio of 12 to 1 still prevailed. But this soon gave way to a higher value of silver. Besides this, the ratio varied yearly from one country to another. In England, from 1104 to 1227 A.D., according to Th. Rogers, the ratio was 9 to 1; in 1257 I find it quoted at 9.10 to 1.* In 1292 it is quoted as 12.6 of silver to 1 of gold.† But it has to be remembered that this is the price paid for gold by the goldsmith. Gold had no circulation as money. Henry III., in 1257, struck the first English gold coins, the gold pennies. He could not get them into circulation despite his stringent ordinances that made them legal tenders. England's commerce was in too backward a state to require such costly currency. A hundred years later, in 1344, when England had become somewhat more progressive, Edward III. had no difficulty in getting gold coins, the rose nobles, into circulation.

In Florence the relation of silver to gold in the coinage was as $10\frac{1}{2}$ and 11 to 1, with some extreme variations interspersed, in the long period of 250 years, from 1252 to the end of the fifteenth century.

In Germany, in the limited transactions in which gold and silver came into play, from the middle of the eleventh to the middle of the thirteenth century, the ratio touched as low as 8 and ran as high as 11 and 12 to 1.‡ In the

---

* See W. A. Shaw, *The History of Currency*.

† In 1344 we find it again at 11.04; in 1346 at 11.50; in 1353 at 11.15; in 1412 at 10.33, and in 1464 at 11.15.

‡ Inama-Sternegg, *Deutsche Wirthschaftsgeschichte*, gives a number of payments made in gold and in silver as well as ordinances, making it compulsory to pay partly in gold and partly in silver. The transactions as well as the agreements are all based on weight, and, consequently, by stating the relative quantities we are informed how one metal was valued by another

beginning of the seventeenth century the ratio was 12.16 to 1. In Flanders, however, it was 13.22, and in England 13.5 to 1.

No common ratio existed, and with one country's hand on the throat of another, each imagining its salvation depending on the spoiling of the other, none could very well exist. A common ratio means mutual confidence and good-will, and this was not a distinguishing feature of the statecraft of the time. These differences gave cause to very grave disturbances in the monetary situation. The exportation of the undervalued metal was a natural consequence, endeavored to be prevented by summary laws. It availed little that the hangman occasionally exercised his office. The true remedy of an international agreement or of a single standard was not even within the comprehension of the times. The frequent alterations in the coins and declarations of their values were endeavors to find correctives for evils which were too patent not to be made the subject of remedial action. That these conditions resulted in curtailing the circulation still more than was occasioned by the general monetary situation of the times, is too evident to need more than passing mention.

---

in different times and places. Occasionally the ratio of 12 to 1 is met with, but generally the ratio of 10 to 1 is found in computations of the tenth, eleventh, and twelfth centuries, dealing with the two metals.

CHAPTER III.

The Demonetization of Silver a Result of Economic Development.—The Positions of the Two Metals: Past, Present, and Prospective.—The Real Standard of Payment not in Coins.—The Money of Account the Actual Measure of Payment.—Maintains itself Independently.

Gold and Silver. Production and its Cost.

WHATEVER the influence of the cost of production on the supply of a commodity in general, it cannot at all be said that it would be determining in regard to the production of silver and gold because of the generally overlooked quantity, the adventurous spirit in search after gain. The production of gold has, on the whole, hardly paid the average of wages ruling in Australia and in America. The fortunes made by the few are balanced by the disappointment of by far the greater number. The hope of good luck keeps up the search even in the face of loss of savings brought from other occupations into the mining camp. Gold mining, which receives the greatest yield from individual effort, keeps all the adventurous faculties keenly on the scent. It has been added to largely of late by deep mining. From these combined sources larger and larger yields are flowing, sufficient to keep the reserves increasingly supplied, without subjecting the value to very great changes.

The gold of the South African regions is mostly obtained from deep mining. These mines, only lately added to the fields of productiveness, yield now about one fourth of the annual output. Capital has largely come into play as a factor, superseding in a sense the adventuring gold-digger. Under capitalistic exploitation abandoned fields are recovered, and in places where layers are suspected, shafts are sunk and gold is obtained in large and paying quantities. Under these conditions America is also yielding considerably increased quantities. The quantity for 1894 is estimated at 42 million dollars, while in 1893 the yield was but 36 millions. The last six years show the gold product of the world to have been:

World's Product of Gold.

	Fine ounces.	
1889	5,973,780	$123,489,200
1890	5,749,320	120,465,300
1891	6,320,195	130,650,000
1892	7,077,165	146,297,600
1893	7,605,904	157,228,100
1894 *	8,420,000	174,000,000

The heaviest output of gold ever reached before this new era was during the five years 1856–60. Then the annual average was 6,486,262 ounces, $135,000,000. The present output overtops this average by about 30 per cent. The average for the five years ending with 1894, is larger by nearly 10 per cent. than that of the five years 1856–60.

It is impossible to say what the future of gold mining will be. One thing, however, is certain, that capital sunk in an enterprise cannot be withdrawn at will. A gold digger carries his capital on his back and his machinery on

---

* Estimated.

his shoulders. He can transfer these easily to any locality, and, if the new field does not yield more than the one he abandoned, he can bury his disappointment in a change of occupation. But shafts have to remain where they are sunk, and only lead to further investment until the last ton of quartz is extracted and the last dollar is expended and the shares are extinguished, whatever the promises of the prospectus. The expectant Midas is gulled over and over again. But whether he falls with the thousands buried on the road of expectation or wins a prize in the great lottery, the gold itself shows no trace of the emotions that its birth evokes. It takes its place in the money stocks of the world, whether the cost of production per ounce is £3 17s. 10d. (the mint price), £1, or £7. From what we know of the European gold finds, we can venture to say that rivers and valleys are by no means exhausted treasure stores.

The best authorities hold that,

> "By the disintegration and crumbling away of the rocks which contain the auriferous veins, the contents of these are swept down to lower levels, and the gold by its density always seeks the lowest places among the moving materials. The auriferous gravel deposits in alluvial formations, the golden sands of the rivers are thus produced, and have been gathering for long ages past, and forming deposits out of reach of such agencies."

This process of disintegration has certainly been going on some hundreds of thousands of years, and the river beds and valleys have been depositories of gold from time immemorial. But the search after gold dates but a few thousand years back. The gold hunters never went deeper than the surface.

As a fact, Germany and Austria, the oldest gold producing countries of Europe, furnish to-day not less than $3,000,000 of wash gold annually. This is not a very great sum compared with the present (1894) product of some $175,000,000. But it is an important figure when we consider that the annual average production from 1492 to 1520, according to Soetbeer, did not exceed the sum of $4,000,000. The average for the period beginning with 1521 and ending with the sixteenth century was but $5,000,000 a year. The greater part of this came from the New World. The auriferous rivers of Germany and Austria-Hungary produce therefore from three fourths to three fifths as much gold at present as was supplied by the whole world (annually) more than a century after the discovery of America.

More readily accessible and economically more productive means may be found in the newer development in the gold-mining industry, but the existence of gold in inexhaustible quantities is more than conjecture.

If man does not grow too wise to waste his energies on the finding of a symbol for wealth, and does not confine himself to providing the articles which diffuse comfort and well-being, settling accounts by means less wasteful than the present, the search for gold need not certainly be abandoned because of the exhaustion of the stores of mother earth.

The Silver Product.

Silver is not found in alluvial deposits. It can only be obtained by mining, and the investment of capital becomes therefore a necessity. The old process of separating the metal in the ore was by smelting. The Peruvians and Mexicans were acquainted with this method and employed portable furnaces. Scattered over a great surface on account of the difficulty in obtaining fuel, the fires blazing in Peru attracted the attention of the Spaniards and puzzled them. The discovery of the silver mines of Guanajuato and of Potosi would not have benefited the world much had it not been for the timely discovery by Medina in 1557 of the process of amalgamation. The difficulty of obtaining fuel at a convenient distance from the richer mines, mostly situated in high altitudes, would have made the employment of capital too hazardous. The easier supply of mercury at a reduced cost helped not a little in promoting the progressive yield of silver.*

The cost of obtaining the metal even by the method of amalgamation was very high. The working system was as crude as it possibly could be. The description which Alexander von Humboldt gives, leaves it in doubt whether any progress had been made in the two hundred and fifty years from the opening of the mines to the time of his visit.

An idea of the difference in cost of production, past and

---

* The Almaden mines, mortgaged to and controlled by the Fuggers from 1525 to 1645, were more fully exploited and produced in greater abundance. Under free competition with the quicksilver from the Istrian mines a much lower price could have been obtained. But under the Spanish government few of nature's gifts were permitted to become unalloyed blessings. The court of Madrid as late as the end of the last century reserved to itself the exclusive right of selling mercury, made its own price, and allowed only a certain quantity of foreign mercury to be imported. Possibly to secure to himself a part of the profits from so promising a monopoly, "the minister, Don Antonio Valdes, conceived the whimsical and audacious project of regulating from Madrid the distribution of mercury among the different mines of Mexico"†; and for the purpose of its execution he ordered the viceroy in 1789 to draw up statistical tables of all the mines of New Spain, and to send to Europe specimens of the veins which were worked. Of course the project failed because the viceroy found in the slow Spanish method a safe ally. "Not a single specimen was ever sent to Madrid." ‡

† Alexander von Humboldt, *Essai Politique sur le Royaume de la Nouvelle Espagne*.
‡ Ibid.

present, may be formed when we notice the process by which the bulk of the product was obtained in the richest silver mines of the world, as found in operation by Alexander von Humboldt, and in operation up to our time in all mines except those operated by new capital companies.

> "Subterranean geometry was entirely neglected and no plans were in existence of the works already executed. Two works in that labyrinth of cross galleries and interior shafts may happen to be very near one another, without its being possible to perceive it. Hence the impossibility of introducing, in the actual state of most of the mines of Mexico, wheeling by means of barrows or dogs, and an economic disposition of the places of assemblage. A miner brought up in the mines of Freiberg, and accustomed to see so many ingenious means of conveyance practised, can hardly conceive that in the Spanish colonies, where the poverty of the ores is united to a great abundance of them, all the metal which is taken from the vein should be carried on the backs of men. The Indian tenateros, who may be considered as the beasts of burden of the Mexican mines, remain loaded with a weight of from 225 to 350 pounds for a space of six hours. During this time they ascend and descend several thousand steps in pits of an inclination of 45°. In ascending the stairs they throw the body forward, supported on a staff, generally not more than three decimetres (about a foot) in length. They walk in a zigzag direction, because they have found from long experience (as they affirm) that their respiration is less impeded when they traverse obliquely the current of air which enters the pits from without."

Of no less crude a character was the system of draining the mines. Instead of employing proper pumping apparatus they drew up the water in bags made of two cow hides sewed together, by ropes operated by horse or mule whimseys. The expense of all this was enormous, especially as the bags, constantly rubbing against the shafts, had to be renewed every week. Speaking of the mine of the Count de Regla, Humboldt says that " the expense of these machines which drew up the water, not by means of pumps, but by bags suspended on ropes, then amounted to more than 750,000 francs per annum."

Equally wasteful was the system of extracting the silver from the ore. More than half the mercury was found by Humboldt to be wasted in the crude process of amalgamation employed.

It is easy to estimate the difference in the cost of production between such barbarous working methods and those of the present time. It is not necessary to describe the difference. The reader is sufficiently familiarized with the progress constantly made in mining engineering. Drawing his attention to the methods of former times will be sufficient to prepare his mind for the great revolution in the price of silver caused by the changed methods of production.

The Declining Cost of Production and Rising Output of Silver.

Silver is largely found in connection with other metals in the silver-bearing ores. The by-product is of considerable value and with the present low cost of reduction, frequently pays the expense of mining and leaves the silver a profit to the mine owner.

In his statement to the Royal Commission appointed to inquire into the recent changes in the value of the precious metals, Professor Roberts Austen, chemist to the Royal Mint, gave the available information from all the silver-mining countries. He classifies silver production by the nature of the ores and the processes for reducing the metals.

The latter are (1) From refining of native gold; (2) Desilverization of lead; (3) Desilverization of copper and cupriferous products; and (4) Treatment of silver ores proper.

The products and corresponding cost for the year 1883-4 (the full data ready at that time), were as follows:

Section	Fine silver in ounces.	Cost per ounce fine.
I.............	508,000	0s. 2½d.
II.............	30,726,000	2s. 0d.
III.............	7,200,000	1s. 11d.
IV.............	49,920,000	1s. 5d.
	88,354,000	Average 1s. 8d.

This includes the highest cost level of production under antiquated methods as well as also the lowest cost under the newest developments.

This latter level was even then known as remarkably low. The "Bonanza King" mine, situated near the highest peak of the Providence Mountains, 520 feet deep and the ore to be hauled a distance of two miles had a cost per ton of ore for mining, hauling, and milling of $25.70 which yielded silver to the value of $179. This, taking the average price at $1 per ounce is barely 15 cents cost for the 371 grains of fine silver (25.70 cost in 179. product = 1:7) which make the silver dollar.

It is further stated (from official reports) that the value of the silver ore treated in California, varies from $50 to $500 per ton, a great proportion yielding in the mill over $100 per ton. "As a considerable proportion was produced at a cost of only $6.50 per ton, it is not probable that the mean cost of extraction exceeded that at the 'Bonanza King,' say, $25 per ton."

But it is not America alone which broadened out her silver product. The Broken Hills Mines, in New South

Wales, produced silver at a cost, including mining charges, 1s. 1d. (26 cents.) per ounce of fine silver, " if the lead be considered of no value." The product in 1886 was 871,665 ounces of silver and 1,991 tons of lead. If the lead were counted at $50 a ton only, it would nearly have covered the cost of production and leave the silver output almost a profit. The 10,397 tons mined and reduced at a cost of £4 12s. 0½d., or $22.34 = $232,200, less lead $100,000, leaves $132,000 as the cost of the 871,665 ounces of silver, which is 15 cents per ounce. But it was expected that the cost of production would be considerably reduced, and undoubtedly has been so reduced judging from the developments. The product was increased so rapidly that it amounted to 9,000,000 ounces in 1890. In 1891 the Australian silver mines yielded 10,900,000 fine ounces ; in 1892 the product was 14,600,000 ounces and in 1893, 22,300,000 ounces.

The predictions advanced when public attention had first been drawn to the future of these mines, have become more than verified by these astounding yields. Mexico, too, brings constantly increasing quantities to the markets under the improved methods put into operation by capital and modern enterprise. In 1889 the product was 40,000,000 ounces; in 1893 it had grown to 48,000,000 ounces. The United States in 1889 produced 54,000,000 ounces ; in 1892 this had risen to 69,000,000 ounces, an increase of nearly 30 per cent. in four years and in 1893 the product was 65,000,000 ounces.

The annual average price per fine ounce according to the tables in the report of the Director of the Mint stands in the following relation to the world's output for the last ten years :

	Value per fine ounce. Dollars.	Product in fine ounces.
1885	1.0645	92,004,000
1886	.9946	93,276,000
1887	.97823	96,124,000
1888	.93897	108,827,000
1889	.93572	120,214,000
1890	1.04633	126,095,000
1891	.98786	137,171,000
1892	.87102	142,940,000
1893	.78031	161,776,000
1894	.637449	166,601,995

The steadily decreasing price rather stimulates than deters production and proves the correctness of the scientific estimates of the best informed authorities of ten and fifteen years ago. We can safely assume the profitableness of silver mining when in the face of adverse price-circumstances such results are produced.

If the closing of the mints of Europe, America, and India has not alone not checked production but supplies have increased in the ratio shown above, what would not be the result in output if an extra stimulus were given, by an artificial price set by an international agreement? A greater decline in price than any yet recorded would be the inevitable and not very remote consequence.

The expectations of gain were inducements powerful enough to make people go into so hazardous an undertaking as silver mining when the methods of production were as crude as we have seen and the results far more doubtful than under present methods. Adam Smith says that the profits of the undertakers of silver were never very great in Peru. From the authority of Frezier and Ulloa he quotes

THE INCENTIVE TO MINING.

"That when any person undertakes to work a new mine in Peru, he is universally looked upon as a man destined to bankruptcy and ruin, and is upon that account spurned and avoided by everybody. Mining, it seems, is considered there in the same light as here, as a lottery, in which the prizes do not compensate the blanks, though the greatness of some tempts many adventurers to throw away their fortunes in such unprosperous projects."

The tables have been turned; we have seen how the output has increased, stimulated undoubtedly by the great profits realized by the mine owners. Through causes sufficiently explained, silver has now become an industrial product, merchandise. The agencies engaged in promoting mining operations are of such a nature that it would be difficult to speculate upon the future status of silver in the market. Equally difficult would it be to speculate upon its future position as an industrial object. But its career as a money metal must be considered closed, since we know that any stimulus of demand by coinage and international agreement would even accelerate the increasing flow, which has marked its history in the last half dozen years.

The mere knowledge of the quantities easily procurable and waiting to be called to light, must work toward destroying its value as a money metal. The ratio of gold to silver depends on their use in currency, as Thorold Rogers observes. The functions which formerly the two metals exercised jointly, can be easily fulfilled by gold alone, because of the great quantities put into circulation, its smaller bulk making it a more convenient means of payment in countries with an expanding and expansive money economy, and because of the aid which other means of payment supply to the modern world.

Credits and Credit Money.

Credits and credit paper have even in former times played a considerable part in the balancing of accounts.

In England and in America they, with other modes of clearings, have superseded the use of money in commerce almost entirely. It is not even a new mode of payment, payment without money. We find it as far back as the days of the Babylonians. It is said that the Jews invented bills of exchange. They are credited with it at different places and at different times. They were transmitters of the civilized methods of antiquity to the modern nations of Europe, and while these nations were progressing from barbarism to civilization, the Jews were the only vehicles * through which international commerce and the complicated money and banking business of the world could be conducted. When the people had advanced sufficiently to take up the larger transactions of trade, the Jews were quickly enough driven away or shut up in ghettos. With everybody's hand upon them and upon their property, they had to keep this in a movable state so as to easily transfer equivalent value to any place that might offer them shelter in case of forcible ejection from the country of their birth. This naturally had a tendency to quicken their undoubted ability in conducting the larger operations of international finance. Having their co-religionists in every part of the inhabited world, they formed a sort of Hansa of their own, which needed no stringent articles of association to enforce strict compliance with their obligations and no

---

* The mediæval monks at a somewhat later period undertook a great part of commercial business, and transfers of payments were made through them.

law to give effect to their bills drawn upon each other. Reversely they could draw funds from different parts of the world and it is quite in keeping with this, as it is in evidence, that they became the bankers of the world. It is easy to understand why the Christian nations should ascribe to the Jews the invention of a system so mysterious to them as the writing of a sum on a piece of paper, addressed to an unknown person in a distant place, signed by the Jew in characters unknown to the Christian, and receiving that sum of money either himself or through a third or fourth person, at any time thereafter.

But did not Tobias, seven or eight hundred years before Christ, collect a sum of money from a man in a distant country on the presentation of a promise to pay? Gabael, living far away in Media, recognized his signature, though given some thirty years before in Nazareth in the ancient kingdom of Israel which had ceased to exist. The money was paid without hesitation. But it was not anything more than a common occurrence under the laws of the ancient monarchy.

Cicero when he returned from his pro-consulate in Cilicia, left the value of his spoils at Tarsus and took a draft on Rome to avoid by so doing the danger and risk of sea travel.* This transaction could not have been possible except as an incident and part of an organized system of banking.

The Jews were even then the chief conductors of the financial operations of the Roman world. Trading was not a gentleman's vocation. It is looked upon in all agricultural aristocracies with disdain. A Roman senator was led to execution for the great offence of being engaged

---

* At least this is the interpretation given by Wm. Roscher, *Grundlagen der National Oekonomie*, of the passage in Cicero, *Epist. ad Fam.*, ii., 17, 1.

in a manufacturing trade. Robbing the nations and spoiling the people were more in the line.

The Jews found, therefore, things well prepared at an early stage, when they took possession of a field which constantly widened in the centuries following the fall of the Roman Empire. Their knowledge of the trading methods of ancient civilizations reached back a thousand years when they came in contact with the nations that were forming out of the ruins of mighty Rome.

It is doubtful whether at any time of extensive mercantile activity, where trading with distant countries was a self-evident condition, credit payments and transfers from debtor to creditor did not exist in one form or another.

The burnt clay, the glass, leather, fur, iron, and copper money of ancient nations, issued in limited quantities undoubtedly, and stamped by the government may have sufficed for home trading.* Like the Chinese cash these money substitutes answered the purpose for which they were intended. But the squaring of foreign accounts between the Phœnician city republics or Carthage and their colonial dependencies or federated sister-republics, could not be undertaken with these money-signs.

The farther we go back the more difficult it would seem to have been to square accounts by means of money payments. The precious metals were not so abundant and transportation was not so safe in ancient and even quasi-modern times as to warrant the assumption that foreign trading was largely based on their agency.

It is therefore reasonable to assume that methods of payment existed not very dissimilar to our own credit

---

* In early stages trading is always in kind. The savage and barbarian are suspicious of being cheated by anything but what he can perceive to be of equivalent value to him.

payments, transfers, and promissory notes. For the later period of the middle ages we have decided proofs of the employment of such methods.

The Settlements at Fairs.

The fairs of Europe gave opportunities for the early introduction of a system of clearings. It is natural that the opportunities offered by a meeting of traders from distant parts at regular intervals of time, should be improved upon.

The large trade settlements were made quarterly or semi-annually. In Germany, within my own recollection, bills of exchange, and open accounts even, were made payable at the Leipsic or Frankfort fairs, held in the fall and in the spring of the year. At some of the fairs merchants assembled on fixed days for the settlement of accounts.

Very stringent laws governed the payment of acceptances, or of accounts made payable at the fairs. This was made necessary, undoubtedly, by the difficulty of keeping the debtor within the reach of the fair authorities. This is only a reminiscence of the system dating back many a century.

At Lyons the system of clearings was carried to such perfection that it finds no equal, even in our time. Merchants were compelled to present an account of their debits and credits in a sort of pass-book, called " bilan "— open debts as well as bills payable. They addressed themselves to one another in order to find whom they were indebted to, and to transfer accounts due them in liquidation of accounts payable by them.

When they had completed their arrangements, they assembled on the sixth day of the fair, when all these settlements were properly carried into legal form under proper ceremonies and under the superintendence of the "provost marchand," aided by six syndics, two of whom were French, two Italian, and two Swiss or German. The amount of indebtedness thus discharged yearly, at the four fairs, was estimated at from 50,000,000 to 100,000,000 of crowns by English writers at the close of the seventeenth century.* The whole amount of coin required to pay the balances, it is said, could not possibly have exceeded a quarter of a million.

Examples could be multiplied *ad infinitum*, were it necessary to more than touch upon the fact that many methods were in existence at early epochs by which commercial transactions on a large scale were made possible through credits and credit payments.

When nations have come to the state of maturity in which the civilizing ties of commerce are knit, they usually find methods by which they can conduct and settle their transactions. Money is of immense value in spreading and facilitating commerce. But it must not be forgotten that its employment is a means and not an end. Neither must it be overlooked that the introduction of money as a means of effecting payments does not change the nature of trade. It remains an exchange of commodities all the same, whether a woollen manufacturer sells his woollens to a wool merchant in exchange for his wool, or whether he sells his woollens to a third party, who pays over to him the amount in money, and he takes that money and pays it over to the wool merchant in payment for his wool.

The fairs were well calculated to bring about a system

---

* Doubtlessly a somewhat exaggerated statement, but it indicates the magnitude of the transactions covered by clearings.

of commercial usages by which money payments were easily dispensed with, and the most simple and effective methods of payments, by transfers of debits and credits, could be employed. It did not at all interfere with the price of merchandise that no money was needed in transactions covering many millions on one clearing day.

Indeed, it is doubtful whether these large transactions and clearings could have been effected with money.

Money payments, if they had been possible then, considering the limited quantity of circulating mediums, would have been a most difficult task, on account of the monetary situation. All the nations of Europe congregated at the fairs. Each had different coinage. The coins were often debased, clipped, sweated, or in other ways deprived of part of their original metal value or weight. To do the examining and figuring of the values of the moneys thus presented for settling an account going into the thousands would have consumed many hours of most valuable time.

Germany alone, with its many dozens of assorted states and moneys, not of the highest reputation at their best, would have offered insuperable difficulties.* We know

---

* From my own experience I can speak of the labor entailed by a remittance forty years ago in Germany. To send a money package of a few hundred florins from Carlsruhe or Baden-Baden (where the moneys were still more varied) to Saxony, for instance, required the conversion of florins, and of half a dozen of the subsidiary coins of the South German monetary system into thalers, the monetary standard of North Germany. Then came the Austrian florin, the German kleinthaler, the kronenthaler, the conventionsthaler, the Brabanter thaler, all different from the Prussian thaler. The franc and the five-franc piece had quite a circulation in that part of Germany, as well as the money of Switzerland. They were all included in the different statements that had to accompany the remittance. But these were only the larger silver coins. Many five- and ten-florin rolls had to be made up of three- and six-kreutzer pieces—two and four cents respectively. These

what the position of the English coins was toward the close of the seventeenth century, when the system described above was under its fullest development. The character of the moneys all through the six centuries, from the revival of the trading spirit, was never a very high one.

They were subject to the rapacity of all the thieves, crowned and uncrowned, who preyed upon commerce, and who knew of no better means of cancelling obligations than cutting down the value of the coins. To this question I shall return again. Here I allude to it only on account of the necessary mention of the remedy which trade at an early time called to its aid to save itself from the destructive consequences of the constant depreciations and variations of the coins.

---

had to be carefully counted, sorted, and packed. Many a spurious piece was apt to steal in if not carefully watched. The Coburger Ernst was mean enough to steal out of the six-kreutzer pieces enough silver to make it worth only one half the value expressed on its face. The dreibaetzner (12 kreutzers = 8 cents) and the sechsbaetzner (24 kreutzers = 16 cents), in rolls of ten and twenty florins, were not insignificant parts of these mail remittances. The gold coins had to be handled in the same way. There were the frederic d'or, the louis- or napoleon d'or, the ducat of Austria, the five- and ten-florin piece, and several other gold coins, which went all in to the general column, and had to come out in the final summary as so many thalers, if going to a thaler country, or as so many florins if to a florin country. It is easy to imagine that so kaleidoscopic a currency gave quite a good schooling to the commercial aspirant charged with the duty of reducing the heterogeneous elements to uniformity. But this was nothing compared to conditions existing before the establishment of the North-German and South-German coinage unions, which chaotic conditions will be dwelt upon in another place. That, under such conditions, the money-changer had a very prominent and lucrative position in the republic of commerce can well be understood. Many of the great banking houses of Frankfurt and other places of the present day were known in my time either actually or traditionally by that name.

The Money of Account.

But merchants did not reckon by these debased coins, but by the ideal money, *i. e.*, the full value standard money, the money of account. Payments were made by computation of weight into the money of account. The price quotations of the past can be understood only on this well supported theory.

This reduction of moneys to a common money of account, and settling of accounts by transfers was first practised in Europe by the Bank of Venice. Originated in 1171, it was soon one of the great instruments of commerce of the Republic and of the trading world. Instead of money the bank used a substitute for money, the bank credit. Instead of the varying coins it had the constant money of account—the zecchino d'oro.* This was the standard of Venice, just as in the succeeding period the Florentine gold coin was the standard of reckoning in all the money transactions of Europe. The fluctuations in the gold coins were slight,† but none at all can occur in the uncoined money of account. It can easily be imagined what great advantage the system of paying in bank credits, at first forced upon the bank by circumstances, offered to the trading world of that time.

The matter is of such importance at this juncture that I may be permitted to give a brief outline of the working

---

* The zecchino, as well as the florin, follows the bezant, which again is the successor of the aureus of Rome.

† Soetbeer, taking his information from a Florentine publication of 1765, gives the weight of the gold coin for 250 years as follows: 1252, 72 grains; 1296, 72 grains; 1324, 70$\frac{1}{2}$ grains; 1345, 70$\frac{1}{2}$ grains; 1375, 71$\frac{3}{8}$ grains; 1402, 68 grains; 1422, 71$\frac{3}{8}$ grains; 1460, 71$\frac{6}{7}$ grains; 1462, 71$\frac{6}{7}$ grains; 1464 to 1495, 72 grains (72 grains of Florence are equal to 53 grains English).

of this system of payment, from the pages of Mr. Stephen Colwell's volume, *The Ways and Means of Payment* (Philadelphia, 1860):

"It is worthy of remark that this very efficient mode of adjustment discovered and used largely at this early period in the history of commerce, was not dependent for its efficacy on the guarantee of the republic. The guarantee sprang out of the mode in which the bank originated: this convenient method of liquidation sprang from the use of this new substitute for money.

"The coin in circulation in Venice was, in many respects, a nuisance of the most vexatious kind. It consisted not only of the variety which the mints of Italy at all times afforded, but of that vastly increased variety which had accumulated from the coinage of more than a century. Besides this multiplicity of the new and old coins of Italy, was the coinage of many countries of the far East, with which Venice carried on a vast commerce. To make all the payments of the domestic and foreign trade of Venice in these coins, of different degrees of purity, and many of them much deteriorated by wear, required time, patience, and skill, which but few merchants could adequately command. The facilities offered by the government, through the bank, saved all this. The government took the coins one time for all, giving therefor a corresponding credit in the bank; and allowed the depositor or lender to transfer this credit claim upon the republic in payment of his debt, in place of transferring or paying over the coin in cash payment. Whatever men can employ in payment of debts, they will be willing to receive in payment, and this independent of any legal compulsion.

"Experience soon evinced the power and convenience of this mode of payment. The bank credits were divisible to every desirable degree, and they could be transferred with a readiness, speed, and safety, beyond all comparison, superior to any mode of paying in coin. The same sum or credit might be kept in such rapid circulation, as to effect an amount of payments, in a specific time, far beyond any possible movement in coin. This rapidity became a great economy, for a much less sum of credit was made to effect a given amount of payments with far greater speed than could have been attained with coin."

The same writer in another place gives the following account of the superior character of this ideal money of the Republic as compared with the circulating mediums of payment, which in no country of Europe were so carefully guarded against debasement and adulteration as in the Republic of Venice.

"In Venice, where the money of account was undisturbed for upwards of five hundred years, and was the medium in which the values stated in bills of exchange and bank credits were expressed, the chief payments during all that time were made in *bank credits*, bearing a premium of twenty per cent. over the precious metals. Any attempt by the Venetian government to debase the coin would have been futile and ineffectual, unless the bank had been at the same time destroyed, and the money of account broken up. Many changes were made in the coins of Venice, but their true value, in every instance, was at once marked by their value in the bank money." *

All the moneys, mutilated or sound, turned in by depositors were weighed and assayed and accounted for at their true value, and not as the tale read on the face. This carries the proof, if one were needed, that wherever money debasement was a characteristic, that money was credited by the intrinsic value of weight, and not by the extrinsic character of tale. By this means everybody dealing with Venice was made sure at all times that his account would be squared in the full value of the money of account. The Venetians knew that trade follows sound money. The only money sure to be always of full value was, in one sense, not money at all.

Hamburg adopted the same policy in creating the mark banco. The accounts were all made out and settled in this, the money of account, which was not coined. It was valued at about 25 per cent. more than the mark current—the coin in circulation.

The Bank of Hamburg found it necessary for self-preservation to adopt the expedient. To guard against the continuation of losses arising from a debased coinage, the system of reckoning all moneys, turned in, by this

---

* Article by Stephen Colwell in *Bankers' Magazine*, July, 1857.

5

newly adopted money of account was introduced. All moneys were assayed, weighed, and credited by this standard. The bank money thus established proved, of course, according to all authorities, the least variable of all Europe.

In England, up to the coinage act of 1816, the money of account was something different from the money in circulation. The unit of account was the pound sterling. This was not coined money, but it represented a certain value in gold, and this value of gold was put into the sovereign, which henceforth stood as the coin representing the pound sterling. It was, therefore, the full value of the money of account which created the full value coin—*i. e.*, as then determined: 5 pennyweights 3 171-623 grains of standard gold, and at the value of £3 17s. 10½d. the fine ounce.

From the reign of Charles II. until the year 1816, when the sovereign was coined, the pound sterling was not represented by any piece in the coinage. The guinea was intended to be of the value of a pound, but, not having been correctly adjusted, its greater value was at once shown by its greater price expressed in the money of account; and the price of gold fluctuating, it varied correspondingly in price until the year 1717, when it was fixed by Sir Isaac Newton at twenty-one shillings. The guinea as a coin has disappeared, but as a money of account it still holds sway. You ask the price of a commodity of a somewhat large value, and it is named as so many guineas and half-guineas. Donations, subscriptions, and bets are made in guineas, and not in pounds or sovereigns. Fees of doctors, lawyers, and of professional men in general are accounted in guineas, as well as the clothing made by the fashionable merchant-tailor.

Though the "livre" was superseded by the "franc" in the coinage of France a hundred years ago, to this very day the word "livre" is employed to express value. People speak of so many "livres de rente" in stating a man's income. No one would say "cinquante mille francs de rente."

The "pistole" was proscribed in France under Louis XIV., but the Norman peasants were found by Mr. d'Avenel at a country fair in 1892 to be still using the term "pistole" and "demi-pistole" in formulating the price of their cattle. I remember the "pistole" to have been frequently mentioned by visitors at Baden-Baden, but do not remember ever having seen one. The louis d'or is still the unit mentioned in sportsmen's wagers all over France.

Prices are made and people figure in moneys which have long since gone out of existence. The common people in Europe cling to the names of coins which have not been seen within the memory of the living generation.

In Carlsruhe I remember that eggs, butter, and certain minor agricultural products were sold by the "batzen." * No batzen existed. It had disappeared dozens of years before. But still everybody buying or selling farm produce would have been troubled, had he had to change his reckoning suddenly from the uncoined money of account to the coined money which was of entirely different denominations.

America figured in pounds and shillings when no such money was in existence. The Spanish shilling, the eighth part of a dollar, is still the money of account in small dealings in New York.

---

* The batzen was four kreutzers, equal to 2.66 cents American money.

Innumerable examples could be added from the financial history of all nations. We all have something entirely different in our mind when we trade or figure money values than the coin or money in circulation. We always think of a full value money of account, which the money in circulation seldom represents. Our silver dollar is certainly a debased coin. The silver certificate and other paper currency are taken at the full value because of the implied government promise that they will be redeemed at the full value of our money of account, represented by 23.22 grains of fine gold and called one dollar.

The idea of your money of account follows you into foreign countries. If you go to France you translate the francs, in England the shillings or pounds, in Germany the marks, into your dollars, your medium of payment—your own money of account—before you get the value of the commodity into your head.

We get certain things and ideas so firmly fixed in our minds that we do not inquire into their genesis and true relations. We are not given to inquiry into relations of things that grow up with us and form a part of us. Erroneous notions are often more apt to take hold of us than true ones, just because of our familiarity with the objects. Thus, if we speak of money, we are dealing in our minds with something quite different from what we see constantly before our eyes. Only we don't give the matter thought. We think the thing we see is the same as that we do not see, and do not analyze.

SECOND PART.

THE HISTORY OF PRICES

FROM THE MIDDLE AGES TO THE PRESENT TIME.

CHAPTER IV.

The Rising Prices and Expanding Trade in Germany Preceding the American Influx of Silver.

The Wealth of the Trading Houses.

FROM the middle of the fifteenth century down to the great upheaval of the Peasant War in 1525, we hear repeated complaints and admonitions of Reichstag, provincial diets, town councils, princes, and popular agitators against high living and lavish expenditure on finery. The dress regulations were published in endless repetition, without, seemingly, making any impression on those for whose guidance they were intended. That they were directed mainly against the working and the middle classes it is needless to say. Burgher and peasant enjoyed an amount of well-being which was not to be seen any more from the days of the Reformation and its barbarizing wars until a new era was to dawn in the second half of the nineteenth century.

With the destruction of the aspirations of the people centring in that social revolution, things soon began to change. Germany entered into that path of evil which led to the Thirty Years' War, a war that made a dreary waste of a country which for nearly a century had vied with the Italian city republics in leading Europe in civilization, developing art, industry, and commerce to a degree that gave it for a time the first rank in Europe. But in connection with this historical fact, it is important to mark that, within this period of German ascendancy in industry and commerce, prices rose and living became dear to a formerly unknown degree. The chief complaint was directed against the big trading houses and the large trading companies which the former established. These concerns were forestallers in the worst sense. They bought up not alone the spices of India and the silk of Italy, cotton and sugar of Egypt, but, and this gave rise to deep resentment, the crops before they were harvested, the produce before it came to market. An Austrian ordinance says: "No company shall be permitted hereafter to buy up Hungarian or Austrian cattle in droves on pain of confiscation of the animals; all buying up and driving away into other countries is prohibited." A company started to monopolize the trade in soap was by law enjoined from going into operation. It seems the "trusts" of our days had their prototypes some four hundred years ago in Germany, and met with the same popular indignation. The Jews had been driven out of Germany, but the Gentile soon found that his own flesh and blood was the worse leech. Geiler von Keysersberg, one of the foremost preachers of the time, says that they were "greater and far worse deceivers and oppressors of the people than the Jews have ever been; they not alone gather into their monopolies the plunder of foreign merchandise, easily dispensed with, but also the commonest necessaries of life, as corn, meat, wine, and the like, and screw up prices to satisfy their greed and avarice, and fatten on the toil of the poor."

The Reichstag sitting at Cologne in 1512 saw itself compelled to take steps against the usurious, forestalling, capitalistic companies. A very stringent anti-trust act was passed, in which it was ordained "that henceforth it shall be prohibited to carry on such injurious practices, whereby the Holy Empire and all the Estates have suffered considerable loss and damage." It was ordered that "if these merchant companies should dare to produce an unseemly dearth, then all authorities shall with diligence and severity abolish such dearth and order honest and tolerable trading, and if they neglect this duty then the imperial fisc shall proceed and act as determined in the law." "Thou shalt not" has at all times been an easy expedient of the law-maker. The fathers, however, were not more successful with the execution of the law than the children are to-day.

The money power had become stronger than the executive power. Many members of the town councils were members of the great stock companies, the emperor's councillors were "in with the merchants with their money, but in secret only" ("Doch nur im Gehaim"), as an old Augsburger, Lucas Rem, says in his diary.

Of Ambrose Höchstetter, of Augsburg, a contemporary relates,[*] that he bought up whole lines of goods, and paid higher prices than their market value, to drive out other merchants, who could not afford it. "He then made a rise in the goods in all countries, and sold them just as he wished. No merchant with 50,000 florins or 100,000 florins could stand against him, because he made profits as he chose. He bought up the quicksilver in all the kingdoms and countries dearer than the common price, and paid 8 florins the cwt.," so that he could press the other merchants by his foxiness. When he had brought all the quicksilver

---

[*] Clemens Sender's, an Augsburger citizen's statement quoted by Johannes Janssen, *Geschichte des deutschen Volkes*, vol. i.

into his hands, he sold it again for 14 florins the cwt. Pepper rose in the six years from 1512 to 1519 to three and four times its former price; sugar, in 1516 at 11 florins, stood in 1518 at 20 florins the cwt.; almonds rose from 8 florins to 12; nutmegs to seven times their old price within the same period.*

Now, whatever the guilt of the merchant companies and the great trading houses in bringing about this rise of prices by forestalling, whatever help the speculators and great capitalists, the Fuggers,† the Welsers, the Höchstetters, and their kind may have derived in creating their great monopolies from the altered route of the trade of the East by the discovery of the passage to India around the Cape of Good Hope, it will not be contradicted that these high prices could not have been obtained, and certainly not maintained, had consumptive demand not become general, for what had been considered luxuries of the very rich but a generation previously. Of pepper alone some 30,000 cwts. were imported, annually, an article considered so precious at a former period that it was used as money in trade.

The profits must have been enormous. Lucas Rem relates in his diary (on Augsburg's commercial history, 1491 to 1546) that Bartholomew Rem put 500 florins into the business of Ambrose Höchstetter on profit share. Money was put on deposit with Höchstetter by rich and poor, princes, counts, and knights, as well as peasants, servants, and laborers. He held as much as a million florins from

---

* See Wm. Zimmermann, *Allgemeine Geschichte des grossen Bauernkriegs*.

† The memory of the people is a long one. To the present day these quinto-cento private tax-gatherers, by what the people considered unfair means, are pilloried in the people's language. "Fuggern" (to Fugger) is in southern Germany, in my own memory, synonymous with cheating or taking undue advantage in a trade.

these various contributors on profit sharing. Now, our friend Bartholomew Rem wanted an accounting, and his share of the profits on his investment of 500 florins for the six years from 1511 to 1517, and the court gave him 24,500 gold florins as his rightful due.

The accumulations of these merchant princes reached fabulous sums for the times, and would make quite a respectable showing even in our days of rapid fortune making. The fortune of the Fuggers is stated by our authority, Lucas Rem, at 64 million florins in 1546, when a division was made by the members of the family. The Fuggers had risen from simple linen weavers. But in those days little was left of the old simplicity of the master craftsmen in the patrician merchant adventurer. The Höchstetters especially are reported as leading lives of excessive prodigality. Our informant, Lucas Rem, tells us that "his (Höchstetter's) son Joachim, and his son-in-law, Franz Baumgartner, spent on one banquet 5000, and on another 10,000 florins, and gambled away 10,000, 20,000, and 30,000 florins in one sitting." But they came to a bad end. The house of Ambrosius Höchstetter failed, and the head of the house ended his days in the debtors' prison.

I give these facts at greater length, perhaps, than the narrow limits of this essay would otherwise warrant, because this all happened long before any additions were to be made by the American silver mines to the circulating mediums of Europe. The mines of Potosi and of Mexico were not to open up their treasures for two generations from the time of these price revolutions, and of great changes and improvements in the mode of living of the more modest classes, of extravagance and lavishness among the patricians and great merchants of the free cities of the tottering Holy Empire. The stories accepted by most writers of the vast treasures sent to Europe by the discoverers and their followers are found, on investigation, to have been great exaggerations. Roscher says, from official documents, that from 1522 to 1545 no more than 1,125,111 piasters in gold and silver were shipped by way of Vera Cruz to Spain. Soetbeer estimates the whole annual output of the precious metals for this period as 25,770,000 marks. L. von Ranke says that about the year 1525 not more than 2,000,000 franks a year were imported into Spain, and only after 1550 about four to six times this amount.

Alexander von Humboldt, who examined very carefully the annals and records in America and in Spain, is certainly the very best authority on the subject. After analyzing the reports of different authors of the time of the conquest, comparing them with one another and with the official records, he summarizes as follows for the period prior to the discovery of the mines of Potosi:

Period.	Average annual importation of gold and silver from America into Europe.	Remarks relative to the History of the Mines.
1492–1500	Piasters. 250,000	Discovery of the West India Islands; Gold-stream works of Cibas; expedition of Alonzo Nino to the coast of Paria; voyage of Cabral. The fleets did not arrive every year in Spain, and that of Ovando was considered immensely rich, though it was only laden with 2560 marcs of silver (about 20,000 ounces).
1500–1545	3,000,000	The Mexican Mines of Tasco, Tultepeque, and Pachuca wrought; Peruvian mines of Porco, Caraugas, Andacava, Oruro, Carabaya, and Chaquiapu (or la Paz); spoil at Tenochtitlan, and at Caxamarca, and Cuzco; conquest of Choco and Antioquia.

The piaster was changed at a period not well defined, and upon which Alexander von Humboldt was in doubt. The new piece is equal to our dollar; while about one dollar and seventy represents the value of the old piece. In the former case we have $250,000, and in the latter something over $400,000 for the period 1492–1500, and $3,000,000 or $5,000,000 for 1500 to 1545 as the annual average of specie shipments from the new world to Europe. True, the mines of Germany, under capitalistic exploitation, yielded greater sums than under the old system of mining by " Knappschaften." Much complaint is raised of the "Raubbau," the exhaustion of the lodes which had given bread and sustenance to generations of sturdy men, of whom the father of Martin Luther is a fitting type. The Fuggers, the Höchstetters, and others are mentioned in the same terms as our own great mine operators are spoken of to-day. Doubtless this added largely to the available money stocks, but considering the expansion trade had taken, the greater absorption in the arts in consequence of the general growth of wealth, the amounts mentioned by the more moderate chroniclers would have been easily absorbed.

The sums mentioned by most writers of the time, and eagerly fastened upon by more recent authorities, have, however, found considerable diminution, the same as the fabled quantities from the American discoverers, under the searching light turned on the archives and government records by competent investigators.

The sums stand frequently discredited by their impossible dimensions. But they are permitted nevertheless by modern writers to form part of their argument. So when it is stated that the mines of Schneeberg in the Erzgebirge yielded for the first thirty years after their opening 325,000 cwts. of silver. This is equal to 11,000 cwts. per annum, or nearly 500,000 kilos. For 1487, we are told in another place, the yield for three months was equal to two tons of gold, which is equal to 8000 kilos per annum.* Soetbeer's estimate of all the gold annually produced following the discovery of America, 1493 to 1520, is only 5800 kilos for the world; and of all the silver mines of the world, 47,000 kilos per annum. This is only one tenth the quantity said to have been the yield of one silver mine situated in the Duchy of Meissen, now part of the Kingdom of Saxony.

The Great Quantities of the Precious Metals— Taken as Hoards and Money Reserves.

The descriptions of the display of jewelry and of the quantities of plate in the possession of people of moderate means may seem to be somewhat exaggerated. The unanimity of writers on the economic condition of the Germany of that time does, however, admit of no question of the great quantities of the precious metals absorbed in plate, vessels, and ornaments, both sacred and secular. Aeneas Sylvio Piccolomini may have had an object in

---

* The recklessness with which historians of repute copy these exaggerations of older, uncritical writers may be seen from the statement which is taken from Johannes Janssen, *Geschichte des deutschen Volkes*, vol. i., p. 354 : "Das zu Schneeberg im Erzgebirge im Jahre 1471 entdeckte Silberbergwerk war eines der reichhaltigsten in Deutschland. In den ersten dreissig Jahren warf es beinahe 325,000 Centner Silber ab." Another statement of his is: "Im Jahre 1478 betrug eine vierteljahrige Ausbeute zwei Tonnen Goldes."

Janssen is copied by other writers, as he copies the writers of the eighteenth century, and they again the uncritical writers of the sixteenth. The above statements are from F. E. Fischer, *Geschichte des deutschen Handels, der Schifffahrt, Erfindungen, Kuenste und Gewerbe*. Hannover, 1785-1794.

writing up in glowing colors the condition of Germany, so as to give to his own countrymen the example of the thrift, progress, and general well-being of the German people, still in the enjoyment of their independence and liberty, at a time when the Italian republics of the Middle Ages were beginning to fall a prey to petty tyrants. But Froissart is not less emphatic in the praise of the conditions of the people of the empire. German writers of the time are unanimous in pointing to the wealth of the German burghers as illustrated by their rich possessions of gold and silver plate. Wimpheling, one of the best known writers of the time, mentions that "the merchants eat off dishes of pure silver and gold, and I have myself dined in Cologne at such a table with eleven other guests." And we are told further that "German merchants in foreign countries frequently have sent from home gold and silver ware weighing from thirty to fifty, and even one hundred and fifty pounds, and make considerable display with their plate and drinking vessels, especially when strangers are present."

When we take into account this general authentication of the extensive use of the precious metals for other purposes than circulation, then it will be conceded that the increase in production is an insufficient explanation of the changes in prices that we read of.

This greater absorption in plate and ornament, it must be remembered, marks periods where wealth loves display, and when the idea of wealth is associated with these visible signs of it. With the enjoyment of display, however, is also connected the advantage of having property in such shape that it is easily concealed and transformed into whatever condition is made most profitable by the exigencies of the times. Gold and silver plate unites in an admirable manner the requirements for all these purposes.

The great extent of its possession denotes a period of growing wealth, but is also significant of under-development and, as in this instance, of uncertainty as to the stability of the value of the coins. Private hoarding in this form is the natural consequence of such a state as existed in the Middle Ages and up to comparatively recent times. The period of law which subjects the State to the same code of ethics that governs the individual does away with it and finds a safer repository in banks and in transferable signs of real or personal property. The period we are dealing with was eminently not of this nature. The coins of the time, of which we shall presently hear more, were not of such character that a prudent merchant would care to lay in a very heavy stock. Plate, however, was sure not to be tampered with. It was money, or could be turned into money at its full weight value at all times. In England, up to very recently, it was given the government stamp, and frequently made use of in payments. The custom throughout the Middle Ages was to weigh to the smith the metal purchased or delivered from the treasure-box, and to pay for the work separately. Thorold Rogers in his researches has found this to have been the custom in England. And the same rule prevailed in Germany and other countries. Stephan Beissel, in his very valuable contribution, *Geldwerth und Arbeitslohn im Mittelalter*, gives a number of examples from the records of the Chapter of St. Victor at Xanten.

The holdings in plate by people of wealth were therefore, in times such as those we are treating of, something of which the present has little conception. Lord Burleigh, according to Hume, left at his death between 14,000 and 15,000 pounds weight in silver plate, and this was worth nearly as much as all his other possessions. For a man in his position this was considered very moderate. According to Giustiniani, Cardinal Woolsey possessed silver plate to the value of 150,000 ducats. Excessive as these amounts may appear, they are quite within credibility and mark a general condition in keeping with the theory advanced above. The treasure stores then, were as the banks, the bonds, and mortgages of the rich to-day; the trinkets and ornaments were the savings banks of the poor. But though never so easily turned into money in times of need, it is equally certain that as long as they were kept in their form and in their concealment, they were non-existent as circulation. It is, therefore, safe to assert that what silver had been added to the world's hoards up to the time of this expansion in trade and rise in prices in Germany, was only to a very limited extent turned into money, and that whatever additional money was coined, was so necessary, and complying so fully with an eager demand for it, that it could have had no possible influence on prices.

The True Cause of the Change in Prices at That Period.

Now in treating of prices we have here again to take exception to the rule of lumping different commodities and making a general price for them as indicating the price unit of a period. Even in the general awakening of the fifteenth and first part of the sixteenth century we do not find that all commodities were affected. The rise is chiefly observed in whatever goods came from far distant countries, principally from the East. This, as has been observed, was largely due to a greater demand, but, principally, to the altered trade-routes which made Lisbon for the time being the great emporium for the Indies. Venice and Genoa had been the chief markets for the Levantine and Eastern traffic before the discovery of the new route to India. They were easily accessible to the German trader. Venice lay at the very doors of the Empire, while the other Italian cities were still considered as members of it. Men of small means could engage in direct trade and keep up an active competition, and so keep prices within accustomed proportions. All this was changed when the chief port for the India trade was transferred beyond the Pillars of Hercules and the pack horse had to give way to the trading galleon that plied between Lisbon and Ghent and Antwerp. The Flemish and Rhenish towns, but chiefly the Nürnberg and Augsburg merchants, were not slow to take advantage of these altered conditions. In fact, the latter are entitled to part of the glory of the discoveries. Peuerbach and Regiomontanus* had so far extended and solidified the mathematical and astronomical knowledge of the time that the navigation of the oceans had become something more than a matter of prowess and of chance. Regiomontanus published a thirty-three years' calendar, the first of its kind published in Europe, and the *Ephemerides* were considered of priceless value by navigators. His improved astrolabe had a wide distribution in the East, and is said to have been bought by the Venetians for its weight in

---

* Regiomontanus was born in the year 1436 and died in 1476. His real name was Johannes Mueller. Born near Koenigsberg in Franconia his honest German name was, in the manner of his time, changed into the adopted latinization of his native place.

gold. The German mathematicians thus became the guides of the pathfinders to the new ocean routes.

The men of Nuremberg and Augsburg took foremost rank among the adventurers and helped intellectually, and what is here of importance to mention, financially, in the opening of the gates to commerce by hitherto unknown paths.

Nuremberg, an interior town of Germany, became the seat of manufacture of the best nautical instruments, compasses, maps, and mathematical tables. Regiomontanus made his lasting home at Nuremberg, because, as he wrote to a friend: "I find there readily the instruments indispensable for astronomical observations, and can with ease enter into communication with the men of science of all countries, as one may regard that city, on account of the travels of its merchants, as the central point of Europe." Martin Behaim, the traveller and cosmographer, disciple and friend of Regiomontanus, showed the way to East India on his globe six years before Vasco da Gama made his famous voyage.

The prominent position of the Nürnberger and Augsburger is shown in the fact that in 1504 the King gave all German merchants the right of separate jurisdiction. The Welsers obtained the privilege of sending their own trading vessels with the royal fleet that sailed to India. Two of the three German ships which accompanied the squadron in 1505, are said to have been the biggest ever fitted out. These vessels returned in 1506, and though the equipment had cost the sum of 66,000 ducats, yet the enterprising merchants made a clear profit of 175 per cent.

So it will be seen that the change that came over the trading world by reason of the discoveries, threw double treasures into the lap of Augsburg and Nuremberg, first, by giving them a monopoly of the East India trade and enabling them to charge whatsoever they saw fit in excess of the old ruling prices; and secondly, by giving them the wealth of Ormus and of Ind at first cost, without paying toll to the middlemen on the Adria and on the Ligurian Gulf.

Thus we can comprehend that the story of the great wealth mentioned above of the men whose names have become household words, even as that of the Rothschilds of to-day, was born of reality. They were the men to grasp the new spirit. Assisting in the scientific awakening of the Renaissance they also understood to reap the golden harvest, which commerce had in store for the venturesome trader.

That the expansion of trade in the fifteenth and sixteenth centuries, and the great revolutions in the commercial and economic world, which ushered in a new era, should have been possible without any greater additions to the moneys of the world than what has been stated above, from authentic sources, must put the current money theories to a very serious test. That price increases could occur of the nature described, makes the strain more severe yet, if, indeed, it leaves these theories anything to stand upon.

Corroborating Facts from the Italian City Republics.

Besides this direct evidence of a formidable rise in prices occurring without an increase in money, and due solely to the greater demand and to changed conditions of society and of trade, we have the corroborating evidence in the prices ruling in the Middle Ages in the trading republics of Italy. There the change from mediæval conditions of trade to the advanced mode of trading had taken place at a comparatively early period. Instead of being hoarded, money was put in rapid circulation, barter was replaced by money payments, and money economics, and the bank and the banker took charge of the circulation, keeping the moneys actively employed. The Lombards and the Florentines were the bankers of Europe. The wealth of the Medici of Florence,* the Pepoli of Bologna, whose income is stated by Sismondi † as amounting to one and one half millions of francs, and others, was analogous to that of the Welsers and Fuggers of the later period in Germany. The great losses which the Florentine bankers suffered by the bankruptcy of Edward III. are sufficient proof of their opulence.‡ The houses of the Bardi and the Peruzzi had to go under, as the profligate king owed them 1,365,000 goldflorins; according to Cibrario, 28,000,000 francs. The goldflorin of 1334–1394 was worth, according to the best authorities, ten reichsmark. In French money the goldflorin equals 12 francs, or about $2.40. The amount quoted by Cibrario would be, therefore, an overstatement and be equal to 16,380,000 francs only. Still quite a respectable sum for that time.

But the price of wheat in Italy is said to have been three times that ruling in Paris in the period of 1289 to 1379, while the general dearth in the fifteenth century is attested by the complaints of the foreign ambassadors at

---

* See Roscoe, *History of Lorenzo il Magnifico.*

† Sismondi, *Histoire des Républiques Italiennes du Moyèn Age.*

‡ In 1422 Florence had 72 banks; in 1472 only 33; as Roscher says, probably in consequence of the more oligarchic concentration of wealth. The Florentine banks were so widely distributed that they were called, "il quinto clemento." The Medici alone had 16 banking houses in different European cities.

the Papal court (Raumer's *Hist. Taschenbuch*). It is the opinion of an authority (Pagnini) that in Florence prices of commodities measured in silver rose but little, and not at all against gold from the fifteenth to the eighteenth century.

CHAPTER V.

Consideration of the Varying Factors in Connection with Prices. The Distinctions Necessary to be Observed.

THE difficulties which meet us in making price comparisons covering recent periods, of which I treated in the first two chapters of this essay, naturally increase the further back we trace our inquiry. Even if we eliminate the absurd combination of commodities to make up a price unit for comparison, it will be readily understood by students of economics that other almost insuperable obstacles meet us at every step. Unless we understand their nature and are prepared to give them thorough examination, we shall fall short of a proper estimate of the question: "The influence of the money-quantities in circulation upon prices."

I will class the different considerations we have to observe under a few general headings and give a brief explanatory statement concerning them:

1. The economic position of the period.
2. The nature of the money under which price quotations are given.
3. The character of commodities,
   - *a.* Differing as articles of commerce, or
   - *b.* Articles for home consumption or immediate use.
4. The changed relations of commodities in progressing periods.

1. The Economic Positions.

The remoter periods of the more advanced states of modern Europe had what is called in German "Naturalwirthschaft," "paying in kind." Taxes, rents, fines, moritariums, etc., were so paid, and trading was done on the basis of valuations according to a standard of account. At first this standard was the head of cattle; later on the pound of silver, with its divisions, took its place. But this by no means implies trading through the medium of money, "Geldwirthschaft." It would therefore be fallacious to make comparison with these early periods of developments, which, however, are by no means extinct, and are found wherever conditions exist akin to those in which Germany, England, and France found themselves prior to the thirteenth century. We find in the monastic records a multitude of price notations in *solidi* and *denarii*, going as far back as the sixth century and becoming quite frequent in the eighth and ninth centuries. This may partly be on account of the greater number of settlements made in the interval, secular and ecclesiastic benefices, etc., which formed the great territorial tenures, but is undoubtedly, to a very large extent, due to progress in economic development. The price records are of high value in another sense, which will be dealt with later on. For regular comparative use they would not be more valid than prices of horses or cattle on the pampas of Argentina twenty years ago and to-day. European travellers may have been astonished to meet beggars on horseback in the streets of Buenos-Ayres*; Americans know that in border settlements horseflesh is cheap enough for an impecunious man to own a horse. The

---

* Burmeister, *Reise durch die La Plata Staaten.*

means of a mere living are easily obtained. But without a horse a man would be a hermit or an outcast.

Trafficking in kind has been too long a marked condition in the United States, reaching down even to present times, to need any extended exposition to American readers.

The Beginnings of a Money Economy in Christian Europe.

The change in Europe's economic condition was prepared by a foreign civilization. The Caliphate and the Saracen kingdoms were, by unity of religion and language, well fitted to take up and spread the civilization of the classic world. The commerce of the world as well as the money of the world was attracted by them. When the power of the Caliphs had given way to effeminacy and was finally shattered by the Mongol invasion, the seeds sown in Spain had long been giving fruit, and Europe was beginning to turn to the Peninsula for light and guidance out of the darkness. The services of the Arab to mankind in preserving and extending the stores of knowledge in geography, medicine, algebra, and chemistry, and introducing the use of the mariner's compass, the pendulum, and the decimal system of numbers were in themselves enough to make the centuries following their dominion their lasting debtors. Without their work the era of European progress could not have opened as it did from the time following the Crusades. By this strange phenomenon the Christian nations were brought in contact with a higher civilization, and a new vision was opened out before them.

Soon the Adriatic and Ligurian cities became the heirs of the fading Moslem empires, although up to the fifteenth century Egypt still held high rank among the trading peoples of the Mediterranean.

The North gradually fell in line. From Italy through the medium of the empire up the Rhine to Flanders, and over the Alps along the Danube, civilizing and liberalizing tendencies became manifest. The free cities all along these trading routes soon became the centres of trade, poetry, and art, and the strongholds of freedom. In the same way, only somewhat earlier, the cities of Provence and up the Rhone had benefited from the Hispano-Arabic teachers, chiefly through the instrumentality of the Jews. Thus the great sleep was broken. Again commerce and trade could pave the way for industry and art to spread and create conditions analogous to those in which civilized communities in all ages have moved.

2. The Nature of the Money under which Price Quotations are Noted.

Henceforth money was not alone a measure of account, but became a means of payment. Gold and silver coins were first employed in real commerce, while home-trading still adhered to barter. Whatever the nature of the dealings, however, it is most important to know the kind of money in which these payments were effected, or by which the reckonings were made. Without such knowledge the history of prices is an unintelligible jumble of figures.

The early coins, as pointed out above, were the coins of imperial Rome. The Merovingian and Carlovingian kings naturally adopted the coinage and monetary divisions of the empire whose prefects they styled themselves, until Charlemagne put the imperial crown upon his head. As the kings of the Franks did not overthrow the empire, but did assume its prerogatives and powers, they continued to use the administrative machinery they found, having nothing to put in its place. Moneys, weights, and measures being necessary adjuncts of civilization, had, as a matter of course, to be borrowed from the conquered. With the decline of the Carlovingian house the moneys begin to fall in value. Charlemagne still held the coining of money as a prerogative of the crown. But with Louis the Debonnair the practice is introduced of giving the privilege over to certain bishoprics and towns, Pruem and Corvey being the first named and others following in quick succession.* But at first the right of coinage is given reluctantly and sparingly, with reservation of the royal power to regulate and supervise. But even this changed with the extinction of the dynasty. The separation of the kingdoms severed the coinage relations previously existing. In the Trans-Rhenan division the separate coining, gradually becoming the privilege of the towns, of the bishops, and of the rising dynastic houses, marks an economic progress, although we note a continuous diminution in the value of the coins. The increased demand for money denotes the change in the trade conditions noted above. This demand could not possibly have been met by the central power, even had its weak constitution permitted the exercise of a prerogative which, in the low development of society, would have taxed the mechanical and administrative skill of the time quite beyond its powers.

The pound of silver, the original unit of value, divided into 20 shillings (solidi), each of 12 pence (denarii), in the

---

* See Inama-Sternegg, *Deutsche Wirthschafts-Geschichte des 10ten bis 12ten Jahrhunderts.* Louis the German to Worms and Strassburg ; Arnulf to Hamburg ; Louis the Child to Eichstaedt, Osnabrueck, etc., etc.

course of time was made to yield two and three times as many pieces of the same denominations.

The gold solidus, or aureus, of the Roman Empire was the unity of account in the German part of the Frankish monarchy at this earlier period. This solidus contained 3.88 grams, which is about equal to $2.54 of our money. The denarius, the twelfth part of the solidus, was worth, therefore, in our gold value 21 cents. Some of the extant imperial denarii of that time show a gram weight of 3.23, which is equal to that price, if silver and gold are rated as 1 to 9, the relation of the time, according to the recorded transactions and agreements allowing substitution of one metal for another or of purchases at this ratio.

But the silver denarius in this comparison and part of the later silver money of account (240 of which make a £ sterling, a pound or livre of France and the Pfund Heller of Germany) in the best Carlovingian coinage was 1.7 grams of silver, and was worth about 12 cents gold value of our time.*

It was not long, however, before it was found that there was a source of gain in the privilege of coining money, and the spiritual and territorial magnates of the empire did not hesitate long to turn it to advantage. The best Carlovingian denarius is unalloyed—in the 12th century 8 per cent. of alloy is found in the money. But the chief depreciation is in the reduction in metal which gradually reduced the moneys to a fraction of their original weight,

---

* The gram = 15.12 grains, and at 1.7 grams this denarius weighed 25.7 grains of silver. Silver had a higher value and counting the ratio of 9 to 1 against 16 to 1, the American coinage value, makes the 25.7 grains equal to 45.68 grains in to-day's coinage. The dollar is 371.25 grains; 45.68 grains are therefore 12.33 cents. At the ratio of 15.50 to 1 the value is 12.72 cents.

so that the English penny of to-day is but an eighth part of the imperial denarius.

The cause of this reduction is, to a large extent, the eagerness of the bishops and members of the empire to take advantage of the seigniorage, the charge for coinage. They retained at first a certain proportionate number of pieces in payment of mint charges. This was soon extended into the right of making the weight of the coins lighter and increasing the number minted from a given weight of silver. The advantage derived from the exercise of the mint privilege was rapidly improved upon. The privilege was turned to account by the members of the empire, at their accession to their respective governments. Even this arrangement does not seem to have sufficed, and frequently recoinage was undertaken on the slightest pretext. With increasing multiplication of the coins, extension of trading, and the doubtful character of much of the money in circulation, it frequently became necessary to recoin the foreign pieces and give them the territorial stamp to make them more easily recognizable.*

---

* We must, however, not forget that the debasement of the coins was not entirely in the nature of a forced loan which is never returned, or the kind of robbery practised by the Valois Kings and the English Henry VIII. The lowering of the standard in Germany and in France, proceeding from the 12th and 13th centuries, was largely in obedience to popular demand. So was the multiplication of the coinages and the exercise of the minting privilege by the bishop towns, the territorial lords, and the commercial free towns.

The heavy coins of the original standard were entirely unsuitable as a circulating medium. They could not possibly have served in local trading and could only have been used in payment in other than ordinary daily transactions. Their very nature and high value prove the absence of a money economy, and that payment in kind was the well-nigh universal rule.

The smallest coin, the silverpenny, the denarius, often more than a day's wages, was of too inconveniently high a value to be used in ordinary dealings. We can imagine a state of society out West with dollars as the smallest de-

Up to a late period the imperial coins were of higher value than those of the states, bishops, dukes, counts, princes, lords, and towns of the empire, all of whom had gradually acquired the privilege of minting. The chaos became as great in the coinage as in the political condition of the Holy Roman Empire. The commercial towns, however, had begun to emancipate themselves from the domination of their feudal lords. Some of them discovered at quite an early period the important economic law that trade clings to and follows sound money. Chief and first among them were Cologne on the Rhine and Ratisbon on the Danube. Cologne, the queen city of the Rhine, stuck to good money, while even the episcopal cities of Metz, Treves, and Mayence reduced the denarius, still weighing in the tenth century about 1.45 grams, to 0.6 grams, as in the case of Metz, and 0.7 grams in the case of Treves and Mayence, at the beginning of the thirteenth century.

The money of Cologne, in consequence, became the standard of payment for centuries for the traders of the Rhenish states, just as the money of Florence, the gold-florin, for the trade extending beyond state and national borders.

---

nominations used in settling of accounts, when the daily dealings are not squared before a certain amount has accrued.

But when the social organism becomes more flexible, when the state of mediæval exclusion and territorial independence changes to a condition of commercial mobility and national and international communication, money economy gradually obtains the ascendency, and a demand for coins which will answer the daily requirements becomes more and more a necessity.

The lowering of the value of the coins in the Middle Ages is therefore a sign of the revival of the trading spirit and of a step forward in civilization.

The stability of the English coinage up to a very late period is sufficient proof, if no other existed (but of that there is abundance), of a much slower industrial and economic development.

With the progress of the centuries we find further deviations and variations in the coins. We find the stueber (stiver), the albus, the florin, the thaler, the grot, the obolus, the scutum, from which the *écu* is derived.

In the chaos which characterizes the monetary situation from the early Middle Ages to recent times, and which would make it impossible to read the history of prices in Europe, the weight and fineness of the coins gives us a helping hand. It is either by the coins themselves, found and collected, or by comparative statements of contemporary writers, that we can trace the value of moneys to a fixed standard.

The mark of Cologne furnishes us this standard for Germany up to the reform of the coinage in 1873. As early as the end of the tenth century we meet the mark.* It weighs 8 ounces, = ½ lb. of Cologne, equal to 234 grams, or 468 grams to the pound of 16 ounces, which is but slightly (not quite 4 per cent.) heavier than the English pound avoirdupois (453.54 grams). Gold was not coined in any of the mints. What gold coins were used were of foreign mintage. Payments made in gold are usually by weight in plate or in bars. Even if not required in local trading, gold was at all times a more convenient treasure-hoard than the more cumbersome metal. It is only after the Crusades that the use of the gold coins, first of Byzantine and Saracen coinage, and later the coin of Florence, the florin, became more prominent in trade. The first German gold coins are said to

---

* Inama-Sternegg, ii., p. 403. "12 solidi = 12 denarii + 16 denarii for coinage = 160 denarii is unit of coining weight ; the d. = 1.45 grs. In place of this, by the end of the tenth century already the designation ' Koelnische Mark ' appears, which consequently had a weight of 234 grams and proves itself the half of the old Poundweight of Cologne of 468 grams."

have been struck by Archbishop Walram of Cologne (1333 to 1349). In 1354 the three ecclesiastical Electors, Mayence, Treves, and Cologne, entered into a coinage agreement as follows: "Auch sollen wir eyner gemeiner muntze von golde und von silber in unsern landen zu schlahn eindrechtig werden" (also shall we become united in coining a common money of gold and of silver in all our lands). But the agreement does not seem to have kept them united very long.

The goldflorin of Cologne — the "florin Rhenanus aureus"—maintained its value, but the florin currentis gradually fell to the low price at which we know it to-day, and which is barely one sixth, and in to-day's market value of silver not much over one tenth, its original value.

Mr. Stephan Beissel gives us valuable assistance in his painstaking investigation, *Geldwerth und Arbeitslohn im Mittelalter*, before mentioned. As the building of the church of St. Victor at Xanten embraced fully two centuries of the time of greatest development in the history of Germany and of the world's trade, previous to the discovery of the American mines, we have here valuable material for our purpose. I will not go into the details of the variations of the coins, which would only confuse the reader. But it is necessary for an intelligent reading of prices to understand the value of the money in which they are expressed. For this purpose I will here give the reduction of moneys of certain average periods as carried out by Mr. Beissel, which will fasten the value of the standard of payment, which we shall later on employ in the reading of prices of the same average periods.

The mark of Cologne furnishes the following number of pieces under the name of "Mark current" at the different periods here mentioned in the coins of Xanten.

NUMBER OF PIECES COINED OUT OF ONE MARK FINE.

Periods.	One Mark Silver gave Number of pieces in Mark Current at the named Periods.	Relation of Weight of the Mark of Xanten to its Silver Weight in 1838.
1372–1386	6	13½
1399–1444	7	11½
1454–1464	7	11½
1490	8	10
1551	18¼	4½
1680	26	3¼
1838	80	1

The mark current of the chapter varied but little in value from about 1392 to something near the end of the fifteenth century. From that time to the middle of the sixteenth century, we see it lose over one half in value; up to the latter part of the seventeenth century about one third more, and by the first part of this century it was worth but one twelfth the value of the mark of 1399, and but one fourteenth of the value of 1386. Other German coins current in Xanten experienced much greater debasement.

The Rhenish gold florin intended to govern in the trade of the Rhenish towns and agreed upon to that end by the three electors, stood, therefore, but seldom for a period of more than a few years in the same relation to the minor coins.

With the mark of Cologne and the coinage resulting from it as a guide, we are, however, able to make comparisons with present coins and to read prices, in a measure, within the understanding of to-day.

Reduced to present money in reichsmarks (23.80 cents) the mark of the chapter in 1400 was worth about 7 marks; in 1490 about 6 marks; from 1490 to 1620 between 5 and 2½ marks; in 1680 about 2 and in 1838 but ½ mark.

In France.

The Pondus Caroli suffered still greater vicissitudes. It is not within the aim of this treatise to point out the different changes all the coins underwent in name as well as in the standard. The object is to obtain a basis for price comparisons.

The Livre Tournois finally superseded the other coins and remained the standard in name. Down to the revolution the division of livre, sou, denier remains unchanged. The change in value will be appreciated, however, when we remember that the unit of to-day, the livre of the end of the last century is but the 85th part of the original value of the pound.

The *grands et petits seigneurs*, as in Germany so in France, had acquired the coining privilege and exercised it with the same confusing effect. The crown, however, became gradually the overshadowing power, absorbing the sovereign rights of the feudal lords, and finally the centre of all governmental functions—the very reverse of the historical development in the constitution of Germany. From the days of St. Louis the crown began to exert itself on the coinage. The process was affected partly by confiscation but, chiefly* by purchase of the seignorial rights. Under the third race of kings (the house of Valois) there were only the dukes of Berry, Bretagne, Burgundy, Normandy, Anjou, Lorraine, and Orange, and a few of the minor lords who still possessed the right of coining money. The number was constantly reduced until none was left. It had been the policy and ambition of the kings from the beginning of the fourteenth century to have uniformity of money as well as of measure for the whole of France. Beneficial as unity of coinage was for the trade and development of the realm, it did not pre-

---

* *Cours d'Economie Politique*, par M. G. De Molinari, vol. ii.

vent the constant deterioration of the coins by the kings. We have a unity of name by which we can trace the value back to Charlemagne; the value itself varies on a constantly widening scale. Sismondi says * of Philippe of Valois, that the gold florin of Florence at the beginning of his reign ten sous parisis was worth soon thirty sous, the sou having been debased to that extent.

The Abbot of Bazinghem in the article "Livre" of the Encyclopédie (quoted, see Molinari, *Cours d'Ec. Pol.*), states the number of pieces (livre and its divisions) of the money of his time (1764) which were required to make up the livre and its divisions of the times of the different kings from Charlemagne down to Louis XV. It will show the reader the impossibility of basing comparisons of past periods on the nominal prices as found in the records:

TABLE OF THE REDUCTIONS WHICH THE LIVRE OF CHARLEMAGNE SUFFERED DOWN TO THE YEAR 1764.

		Livre.	Sol.	Den.
Charlemagne to Louis V.	768 to 1113	66	8	—
Louis VI. and Louis VII.	down to 1158	18	13	6
Philippe Auguste	" " 1222	19	18	4½
St. Louis and Philippe le Hardi	" " 1226	18	4	11
Philippe le Bel	" " 1285	17	19	—
Louis le Hutin and Philippe le Long	" " 1313	18	8	10
Charles le Bel	" " 1321	17	3	7
Philippe of Valois	" " 1344	14	11	10
Jean	" " 1364	9	19	2
Charles V.	" " 1380	9	9	8
Charles VI.	" " 1422	7	2	3
Charles VII.	" " 1464	5	13	9
Louis XI.	" " 1483	4	19	7
Charles VIII.	" " 1497	4	10	7
Louis XII.	" " 1514	3	19	8
François I.	" " 1543	3	11	2
Henry II. and François II.	" " 1559	3	6	4
Charles IX.	" " 1574	2	18	7
Henri III.	" " 1589	2	12	11
Henri IV.	" " 1611	2	8	—
Louis XIII.	" " 1642	1	15	3
Louis XIV.	" " 1715	1	4	11
Louis XV.	" " 1764	1	—	

* Sismondi, *Histoire des Républiques Italiennes du Moyen Age*, vol. iii.

The English System.

The English monetary system has remained in its divisions practically the same throughout the centuries as we find it in the earliest periods. The original pound of silver was nearly the same as the Troy pound divided into 20 shillings, the shilling into 12 pence. In following the English price records we have the great advantage of uniform denomination of money and slight variations of the coins up to a late period. The Norman kings as well as the successors of the different royal houses were real kings and knew how to preserve the rights of sovereignty from encroachments on the part of the great feudal lords. The coins remained singularly free from debasement. Up to 1300 the pound contained 5400 grains (12 ozs.) coined into 240 pence. In 1527 the Tower pound was declared by proclamation (5760 grains). The standard of fineness was 11 ozs. 2 dwts. fine and 18 dwts. alloy ($7\frac{1}{2}$ per cent.).

The standard of England was not materially changed down to the time of Henry VIII. It is because of this, as Thorold Rogers says,* " that it is possible to construct an intelligible history of prices in England."

---

* John E. Thorold Rogers, *The Economic Interpretation of History*, pp. 197–198.

" The debasement of the currency was committed only once. The patriot king, after squandering all that he could get hold of, after ruining his people, after pledging that if they gave him the monasteries he would ask Parliament for no more grants, ordinary or extraordinary, began to debase the currency. Mr. Froude, the apologist for this monster, the type of the philosophic historian, and at present the advocate of the Liberty and Property Defence League, has described the transaction as of the nature of a loan. How obliged coiners and smashers must be to him for so courteous a description of their calling ! Most of us are accustomed to consider the coiner of base money as a peculiarly scoundrelly criminal, because the success of his calling depends mainly on his being able to cheat the poor. Except by the

When Elizabeth reformed the coinage, the shilling was given 88.8 grains, about a third the weight in the thirteenth and fourteenth centuries, which was 270 grains fine (the 20th part of 5400 grains).

The Tower pound of 5760 grains was made the basis of the new coinage. Out of it 66 shillings were coined of the weight mentioned. This ratio has remained practically in force to the present day. If we have thirteenth and fourteenth century prices before us, it is an easy matter therefore to compute them to present weight in the coin by multiplying them by 3.

In her proclamation ordering the reform, Elizabeth says: "The loss on the base money falls principally on pensioners, soldiers, and hired servants, and other mean people who live by any kind of wages, and not by rents of land, or trade, or merchandise."

The Virgin Queen deserves the thanks of the world for having given so strong an utterance in favor of honest money, and effecting a reform of the currency at a time and under circumstances by no means free from peril to her. "But she could be courageous and bold when the interests of her people called out her better qualities and made her give the good-by to shuffling and vacillation."

---

magnitude of his crime, Henry is on a level with the meanest of knaves. And the crime is heightened by the fact that it is the first duty of a ruler to keep the currency up to the standard. Such men as Henry the Eighth, and such men as Ernest of Saxe Coburg, who was, I believe, the last European sovereign who issued base money, and repudiated it, ought to be gibbeted in history.

"At first the debasement was not great. The standard is 11.1 in 12. The issue of 1543 was 10 in 12. In 1545 it became only 6 in 12. In 1546 it was 4 in 12, two thirds being alloy. In 1549 Somerset, Edward's guardian, put out an issue of 6 in 12, and in 1551 one of 3 in 12. This was virtually the last issue of base money."

3. The Different Characters of Commodities in Different Price Periods.

It is of great importance in a price review to observe the changing relation of the commodity to other commodities. In primitive countries, such as the most advanced countries of Europe were in remote periods, and some of its countries are still to-day, products of agriculture and articles intended for local trade are very low, while articles of commerce brought from a distance are very high in price. To this latter class also belong the products of local workmanship which commands a high price, by virtue partly of the scarcity of skill and partly of the time required for execution. I find at the beginning of the twelfth century 6 talents paid for a coat of marten skin; for a pallium, 7 talents; 6 glass windows, 9 talents; the same is paid for a church bell. The talent is $1\frac{3}{5}$ mark silver; the mark at 8 ounces makes the talent equal to $12\frac{4}{5}$ ounces of silver. Hence we have 76.80 ounces of silver for the coat; 89.60 ounces for the pallium; $115\frac{1}{5}$ for the 6 glass windows, and the same for the bell. Silver at the ratio of 1 to 9 would make the ounce worth $2.32, and the prices of these three articles, expressed in the gold value of to-day, $178.19, $207.71, and $277.35 respectively. Books were especially dear, and we find a book, *Officium Ambrosii*, in 1024 A.D., at 45 solidi, which is equal to 36 ounces of silver, and, at the same ratio as above, $83.52 present gold value. These must be considered articles of luxury. But we find "camsiles" (shirts?) in the eleventh and twelfth centuries varying between 12 and 20 denarii. In the good old coinage, then still in use, this is equal to a present value of $1.48 to $2.48. A linen sheet is quoted in the eleventh century at 15 denarii ($1.85). These are high prices for common articles. In the lighter denarius even, beginning to appear about that time, and of about half the value of the original heavy coin, these prices are not lower than present prices in Germany for similar home-made articles.

Poultry, butter, cheese, and farm animals are comparatively low; but, as they are not practically articles bought and sold in money at that early period, they would barely be permissible in comparison.

Still their prices were high, little as money was circulating, compared with prices of the present time in equally undeveloped agricultural countries.

A horse was worth from one to two pounds. Walter von der Vogelweide complains of having a horse killed by "the wicked Gerhard Azze," "worth three marks." This is the mark of silver of eight ounces, = half of the pound. According to Inama-Sternegg's researches, this pound is the "pondus Caroli" of 408 grams, and the mark 204 grams fine silver. The mark of Cologne of 144 deniers, with the denier at 1.42 grams (stated in this connection by Inama-Sternegg as the weight), gives us this 204 grams of the mark mentioned above.

If we take the franc, which contains 4.5 grams fine silver as the basis, then this mark is worth in to-day's money 75 francs, and the horse is worth 225 francs, or $44. This is not much below the price of horses in some of our agricultural States, taking the prices from the statement of the Department of Agriculture for the year 1892.*

---

* The average price for horses in the United States is therefore about the same as the price for a common horse in the twelfth century, though the breed is far superior to-day.

The Department of Agriculture has furnished me with tables of the

For a battle horse of fine breed, as high as ten times as much as that was paid.

Expressed in corn, a silk cloak with lining was valued at the time of Charlemagne at 400 scheffel rye, unlined at 200 scheffel.*

English prices of cloth in a much later period show likewise great differences if measured in corn value.

In 1487 it was enacted that "whosoever shall sell by retail a broad yard of finest scarlet cloth above sixteen shillings, shall forfeit forty shillings for every yard so sold."

The usual price was evidently above sixteen shillings, as this law endeavors to reduce the price to that point. In the value of the present money this would certainly be equal to double the amount. Expressed in the wheat price of the time, *i. e.*, 6s. and 8d. the quarter, it would

---

average prices of farm animals. From these I take the value of horses as follows :

	Average Price for	1875.	1885.	1892.
	United States	$68.01	$73.70	$65.01
a.	Texas, New Mexico, Utah, and Wyoming....	32.58	42.16	33.42
b.	Missouri, Kansas, Nebraska, California.......	47.80	67.80	56.91
c.	Ohio, Michigan, Indiana, Illinois.............	70.30	79.57	56.91
d.	Massachusetts, Connecticut, New York, New Jersey..	106.80	102.22	99.05

We notice here the variations which result from progression in economic development. Group *a.* represents the grazing states; group *b.*, the grazing state with agricultural progress; group *c.*, the progressive agricultural stage; and group *d.*, the industrial and commercial state in a stage of highest economic progress. The same stages have been passed through by European countries, though great intervals of time separated one from another.

The state of Germany in the twelfth century was not materially different from that occupied by class *a.*, and for price comparisons would be fairly put half-ways between class *a.* and class *b.*

* A measure of varying contents in the different German states, from one to five bushels.

have taken 2 quarters and 3 bushels of wheat to buy a yard of the cloth. Adam Smith says, "valuing a quarter of wheat at 27 sh., the real price of a yard of fine cloth must, in those times, have been equal to at least three pounds six shillings and six pence of our present money."

Common cloth, such as servants wore, was not to be sold at "above two shillings the broad yard," according to an act passed under Edward IV., in 1463."

"Two shillings was (then) the price of two bushels and two pecks, which at present, at three shillings and sixpence a bushel, would be worth eight shillings and ninepence. For a yard of this cloth the poor servant must have parted with the power of purchasing a quantity of subsistence equal to what eight shillings and nine pence would purchase in the present times." *

It would have to be very fine cloth which could not be purchased in England to-day for the equivalent of four bushels of wheat against the nineteen bushels of 1487. It is also safe to assert that a yard of the cheaper cloth worth the equivalent of one bushel in to-day's low wheat prices, would be of superior quality even to the cloth for which the servant in 1463 had to pay the price of two bushels and two pecks.

On examination we find all articles of manufacture correspondingly high in past centuries.

The same is true of building-materials, nails, metal work of all kinds, etc. Produce from southern countries, pepper, sugar, silk, ginger, currants, rice, etc., were excessively dear. The same holds as to wool, although almost the only article of export. Farm produce, like butter, cheese, eggs, poultry, was cheap, and so were corn and farm animals, apparently. Though if we reduce their prices, in the

---

* Adam Smith, *The Wealth of Nations*, Book I., Ch. XI., Effects of the Progress of Improvement upon the Real Price of Manufactures.

heavy silver pieces of the time, to the gold value of to-day, the difference is not so great. In the case of animals, considering the nature of the breeds and their smaller size, the difference disappears. Meat was very cheap. But this is the case in all undeveloped agricultural communities. It is a sign of a low agricultural development that meat is cheaper than corn. This changes with progressive agriculture and improved relations and communication with the outside world. In many parts of the Highlands of Scotland in the middle of the 17th century, a pound of bread, even of oatmeal, was worth as much as a pound of the best meat. The Union with England, by opening the markets for the Highland cattle, had raised the price by the time of Adam Smith to three times the former value. He says in vol. I., chapter XI., that "in almost every part of Great Britain a pound of the best butcher's meat is, in the present times, generally worth more than two pounds of the best white bread; and in plentiful years it is sometimes worth three or four pounds." In 1887 when flour had not yet fallen to the extraordinarily low price ruling at present, the best quality of butcher's meat was worth fully $8d.$, and of the best wheaten bread $1\frac{1}{2}d.$ to $1\frac{1}{4}d.$, and second quality as low as $1d.$ a pound.*

The prices paid at Greenwich Hospital, quoting from Prof. Leone Levi's *Wages and Earnings of the Working Classes*, compare as follows, per pound:

	Meat. $d.$	Bread. $d.$
For 1740	3	$1\frac{7}{8}$
1750	$2\frac{5}{7}$	$1\frac{3}{8}$
1770	3	$1\frac{5}{11}$
1860	$7\frac{3}{4}$	$1\frac{1}{4}$

* See my reports to the Department of State, U. S. A., in Consular Reports as to cost of living of the working classes and cost of labor in different manufacturing industries, 1886 to 1888 inclusive.

I leave out purposely the intervening decennial years as being either years of war or dearth. The quoted years of the 18th century were distinguished by very low corn prices, and the year 1860 was a year of peace and prosperity and of free trade in corn. The price relations of bread and meat similar in the quotations from the 18th century, and showing about 2 to 1, show for 1860 a difference of nearly 6 to 1, thus bearing out fully the above statements.

Roscher says that "it belongs to the safest proofs of the high grade of economic development of Upper Italy towards the close of the Middle Ages, that the prices of cattle compared with corn prices in the thirteenth and fourteenth centuries show but little variation from those of to-day."

In grazing countries, far away from markets, the meat is of no value whatever.* The wool, the fell, possibly the tallow in a somewhat more advanced economic period, of larger cattle the hide, are the only merchantable parts, and enter into the price region of commodities. Maccann, *Two Thousand Miles' Rides through the Argentine Provinces*, 1853, relates that he bought in the interior of Buenos Ayres 8000 sheep for 18d. per dozen, and after a march of 200 miles to the market sold the fells at 60d. per dozen. The value of the 100 millions of sheep of Australia and

---

* The following statement of the number of animals and the number of inhabitants of the South American, African, and Australasian countries for 1893 will show that the meat supply exceeds any possible demand for home consumption.

Countries.	Horned Cattle.	Sheep.	Inhabitants.
Argentina	22,000,000	80,000,000	4,086,000
Cape	2,000,000	22,000,000	950,000
Australia	10,000,000	95,000,000	2,800,000
New Zealand	831,000	18,000,000	626,000

the 80 millions of Argentina lies almost wholly in the wool and fell, scarcely at all in the meat.

But in the Ireland of 1673, mainly a grazing country, the hide and tallow brought as much in the market town as the ox in the remoter village.

In Russia but a few decades ago, tallow was the chief article of export, and ten times as high in price as wheat, while meat was scarcely dearer than that cereal, weight for weight. Pallas relates that the Cossacks of the steppes hunt their goats solely for the horns and the hide. With the improved conditions, roads and railroads, and a more progressive economy, this has changed. The world always presents the same phenomena in similar stages. Boeckh, *The Economy of the Athenians*, considers it a proof of a high degree of civilization that in the 100th Olympiad an ox-hide was worth 3 drachmas, while the whole animal was worth 77 drachmas.

We can trace the same signs in the United States. The annual reports of the Bureau of Agriculture show variations of the average prices of farm animals extreme enough to prove clearly that the same conditions exist in our remoter states and territories as those mentioned above as characteristic of primitive civilizations. In Texas sheep are worth $1.21; in New Mexico, 90 cents; Arizona, $1.20; Oregon, $1.16; Montana, $1.51. These they breed for the wool, with the fell as an additional profit. The more densely settled states, with meat and other salable products, show prices from $1.65 to $3.43. Milch cows, in Utah quoted at $9.77, are returned for Massachusetts at $32.50. Hogs are $3.80 in Nevada, and $11.58 in Connecticut. Horses, $16.18 in Utah, and $81.21 in Rhode Island. Oxen, $6.77 in Mississippi, are quoted at $28.56 in Connecticut. But taking the highest prices for farm animals, as in the seaboard states, they are yet considerably lower than the prices ruling in England.

Such are the price differences caused by the presence or absence of markets.

4. The Changed Character of Commodities in Progressing Periods.

In examining prices of different periods we have also to take into account the changes in the character of the commodities. If we notice the low price quotations of the Middle Ages, we are inclined to ascribe them to the scarcity of money, and nothing has given rise to the theory here under investigation, so much as these low prices. From what has been said we know that the standard weight of coins was originally very much higher than what it became subsequently through the frequent adulterations. We have shown that prices by no means moved uniformly from a low to a high numerical point. We shall show now that, measured by present value in gold, the price of a time when, on account of the scarcity of money, money transactions could barely have been general, were higher than in the present era with all its vast amount of moneys in circulation. Before entering into this comparison, I must mention, however, that one great item of difference is overlooked if we do not bear in mind that commodities have changed very materially from the Middle Ages to the present day. If we compare cattle, sheep, hogs, horses, and, in fact, all animals, we find quite a different breed in all of them. A wool-fell of to-day has 6 to 7 lbs. of wool. Hardly two centuries ago $1\frac{1}{2}$ lbs. was all it yielded. It is not necessary to go very far back to meet these wretched breeds which would not now be given shelter except in the most backward countries.

In England the weight of an ox, about 1547, was in the neighborhood of 400 lbs.;* under James I. it was 600 lbs.; by the end of last century it had risen to 800 lbs.; and now it is 1200 to 1500 lbs. Sheep weighed about 45 lbs. in the sixteenth century; by the end of the eighteenth, 85 lbs.† The weight of the meat alone was:

	Oxen.	Calves.	Sheep.
1710‡	370	50	28
1845 ‖	800	140	80

The older German writers take the weight of a cow as 400 lbs., while Koppe (1818) speaks of 500 to 550 lbs.; Pabst (1829) 600 to 800 lbs.; and present writers give 1000 lbs. as the normal weight.

Nor was the quality equal to the present. "Wool, judging from the existing specimens of cloth, was coarse, and the fibre was full of hair." §

Woollen cloth made in England as well as the wool had become an extensive article of export. But the cloth was of a loosely twisted yarn, which required shrinking and shearing before it was fit for wear. Hence it became customary to line cloaks and outer garments with fur or other soft material. Thorold Rogers says: "A man in an English winter might as well have dressed himself with a hurdle as with English cloth." The finer cloths were all imported, chiefly from Flanders. When war broke out between Philip II. and the Low Countries, "and es-

---

* "I have opened an account from the Public Record Office of the weight of 40 oxen purchased for the Navy in 1547. The average weight of the oxen is less than 400."—J. E. Thorold Rogers, *History of Agriculture and Prices.*

† Sir Frederic Eden, *The State of the Poor.*

‡ Davenant, quoted by Roscher.

‖ Tooke and Newmarch.

§ J. E. Thorold Rogers, *Hist. of Agr. and Prices.*

pecially when the struggle became desperate, numerous weavers from Flanders crossed over to England, and brought with them the art of manufacturing finer fabrics, in which England had been imperfectly skilled, especially such woollen stuffs as were formed from a tightly twisted yarn." J. E. Thorold Rogers, *Hist. of Agr. and Prices.* *

The manufacture of finer stuffs took its rise from that time. †

The distinctions here mentioned have to be borne in mind when we examine prices. In farming implements, plows, and tools of all kinds they are especially noteworthy.

---

* I have no doubt whatever that tightly twisted yarns, made of combed wool, had their origin in Flanders. Flanders was the seat of a very early wool industry. This is made evident by the fact that we find in the list of articles cited by contemporary writers as tribute received in Rome, woollen cloths from Belgium (and linen from Germany). An active export trade was done at that remote time in these. But English cloths formed articles of commerce at quite an early period, too, as we find Cologne doing considerable trading in them in the thirteenth and fourteenth centuries. I find also in the same period "worsted" mentioned, as imported from England, in German records. See also on this subject Gustav Schmoller, *Die Strassburger Tucher- und Weberzunft.*

† England has always been very fortunate from the time of the Norman conquest in deriving benefit from the folly of her neighbors. There was never a lack of wars, persecutions, and proscriptions to send weavers and other skilled artisans to her hospitable shores, to refine the rather coarse-grained manufacturing skill. I have searched in vain for an alien labor law, making it a crime to bring skilled workers, hired abroad under contract, into the realm.

CHAPTER VI.

Price-Comparisons.—English Prices from the Year 1261 to the Year 1580. The Changes in the Standard of the Coinage as Affecting the Nominal Prices.

HAVING in the preceding chapters paved the way for an understanding of prices in connection with the development and conditions of economic periods, we may now review prices in connection with money. We have noted the different standards and values of money. Subject to constant changes, they have to be reduced to a common basis for each period we have to deal with, to be at all intelligible. We shall first examine prices in England from the middle of the thirteenth century to the time of Elizabeth's reform of the coinage, and thence to the present day, and then adduce some facts from French and German price records in corroboration. We shall then see whether the quantities of money metals put into circulation since the latter part of the sixteenth century have had any effect on prices of commodities.

With England's price history we have easy work. Thorold Rogers' great work not alone gives us a unique price record of five centuries, covering the same localities and records gathered from the same establishments, but also his own interpretation of the price and coinage history of England.

I begin by quoting a few statements from Thorold Rogers' work, *The Economic Interpretation of History*.

Parts of this have been brought to the notice of the reader in a preceding chapter. But they will bear repeating here for the clearer understanding of the coinage relation to the price records.

> "The original standard of weight in the silver penny may be taken at 3. In 1299 Edward I. reduced it to 2.871; in 1344 Edward III. reduced it to 2.622, in 1346 to 2.583, and in 1353 to 2.325. In 1412 Henry IV. lessened it to 1.937; and in 1464 Edward IV. to 1.55. In 1527 Henry VIII. brought it down to 1.378, and in 1534 to 1.163. In 1560, after the restoration of the currency by Elizabeth, it is at 1.033, and in 1601 she brought it to exactly one third of the weight it stood 303 years before."

There is one very important point to be noted: the singular uniformity which rules for nearly the whole epoch of three hundred years in most of the price notations. Thorold Rogers is certain that the English people would not have submitted to the changes in the currency, slight in comparison to continental practice, if payments had not been made by weight but by tale. Rogers says*:

> "I felt convinced then that the view commonly taken of these successive degradations of the currency was an erroneous one, and could not possibly be accepted. To be true, they who manipulated the mint must have been preternaturally wise, or preternaturally foolish, and although the English race is not naturally quick or inventive, it is not incapable of discovering and avenging a grievance. Now the conclusion which I arrived at, and that many years ago, was that payments were made by weight, and not as now by tale, that whatever was the weight of the pieces issued by the Mint, a man who covenanted to receive or pay a pound of silver, for goods, services, or dues, received 5400 grains up to 1527, and 5760 afterwards, and that this system lasted from the earliest records down to the restoration of the currency under Elizabeth. On no other hypothesis could the facts be interpreted, and the question before me was, How could the hypothesis be verified?"

---

* *The Economic Interpretation of History*, p. 194.

On account of the important bearing of the fact on the price history at this juncture, I will state the proofs advanced by Thorold Rogers.

"1. The history of general prices entirely agrees with this hypothesis. They are nearly unchanged for 280 years, if the whole space be taken, though they are affected for a time by such events as the great plague of 1348 and 1361, when the value of an article is mainly due to the labor expended on it. Now, wheat for the first 140 years is 5s. 10¾d. a quarter, i. e., from 1261 to 1400, and 5s. 11¾d. for the next 140 years, from 1401 to 1540. On the other hand, certain prices, notably those of foreign produce and foreign goods, decline rather than increase, especially towards the conclusion of the fifteenth century. Now it is certain that there is no traceable economy in the cost of production, and no discoverable reduction in the cost of freight. And again, English wool is rather lowered than heightened in price, though there is no evidence whatever that any foreign country competed against English wool, or, indeed, could have competed against it.

"2. The price of silver plate. This is very extensively purchased. The purchase of plate, in point of fact, was a very common kind of hoarding. The cost of shaping it was low, and the article was readily pledged or sold. The purchase money is constantly expressed in pounds, ounces, and pennyweights, the raw silver or finished goods being plainly weighed in the scale against coins of all sorts and sizes. Now when the coins in 1462 had been reduced, according to the tale theory, to a little over half what they stood at in the earlier ages, Oriel College, in 1493, bought 33¾ ounces of silver plate, some of which was gilt, at 2s. 9¼d. an ounce, a price entirely impossible by a tale payment, for the pence and farthing represent the cost of workmanship and gilding I might multiply evidence of this kind, for I have it in abundance, and it all points to the conclusion which I have arrived at.

"3. In 1462 gold was bought at 30s. the ounce, the ratio according to Ruding between the two metals being at 11.2 to 1 at the time. Such a price is intelligible if the estimate is taken by weight, quite inconsistent with the facts if it is taken by tale.

"4. We are expressly told that the principal loss of the base which was put into circulation between 1543 and 1553 inclusive, and remained in circulation for nearly twenty years, fell on those who lived by wages. The merchant could weigh it and test it, indeed could not carry on his business unless he did,* and perhaps gain an advantage by his knowledge. But as

---

* It was the practice among merchants in Germany to keep money scales and touch stones up to a recent period. This is within my own recollection.

the issues were of very various degrees of baseness, the man who received his wages, even by weight, would find that one piece went further than another, owing to its being less alloyed, and another was almost a dead loss.

"5. The record of the restoration by Elizabeth is conclusive. The amount of base money which Henry and his son's guardians put into circulation was 631,950 lbs. in weight. The currency value was £638.115,* the difference being no doubt seigniorage, or a charge for coining, to defray mint expenses. The amount of silver in it was 244,416 lbs., indicating a debasement of near 60 per cent. But out of this silver Elizabeth coined by tale £733,248. She said she lost by the process, though there seems a balance to her advantage of £95,133. Whether she spoke the literal truth is a question which some persons who have studied Elizabeth's utterances might very confidently answer. But she had to refine the wretched stuff, and the separation of copper from silver was in that day by no means an easy business, and we know that the adulteration was copper, from stories of the time. Then there was the charge of coining and the seigniorage. It is said that the slag was intractable, and was employed to mend the roads.

"6. There is no reason to believe that the Spanish occupation of Mexico and the discovery of Potosi were followed by any notable influx of silver into England. It is only by the foreign exchanges, *i. e*, by trade, that these exchanges can operate, and in the sixteenth century English trade was exceedingly curtailed. Now the rise in the price of commodities between the date at which the new currency was reformed, and the period at which the new silver unquestionably began to modify English prices, is exactly, or almost exactly, the difference between the old Tower pound with the old prices by weight, and the new prices 2.75 to 1."

I have given in full the statement of facts, by which Thorold Rogers supports the theory of weight, because of the importance of a clear understanding of this point. Without the authoritative settlement and ready acceptance of the fact, that mediæval transactions were made by weight and not by tale, the price history of the past is unintelligible.†

---

* Even for the England of that time a small amount of circulation. But the poor coins drive away the good coins. They are either exported or melted in.

† I will show by an example the impossibility of any other assumption than that payments were by weight.

The uniformity of prices in England from 1261 to 1540 alone is proof of this fact. This would not tally with the gradual reduction of the silver value in the coins from Edward III. down to Henry VIII. had payments by tale been the rule.

The uniformity of average prices here mentioned was, of course, interspersed with years of dearth and famine. The populations were decimated quite as frequently by famine as by the plague. Adam Smith states that "Fleetwood gives us two prices of the quarter of wheat. The one is £4.16 of the money of those times, equal to £14.8 of that of the present; the other is £6.8, equal to £19.4 of our present money." It does not follow that such extravagant prices were the rule for all parts of the kingdom. In undeveloped countries, the abundance in one county cannot be made available to allay the scarcity even in neighboring counties.

The average price of one bushel of wheat, one bushel of barley, and one bushel of oats for the decade 1291 to 1300 amounted to 12s. 11⅝d. The average for the same three bushels in 1351 to 1360 was 14s. 3⅝d., and in the decade 1541 to 1550 the three bushels stood 20s. 10½d.

Now the actual silver value of these three price quotations would have been if paid by tale as follows:

Period.	Price Quotation.	Relative Value of Coin.	Equivalent Price in Silver.
1291–1300	12s. 11⅝d.	3.	12s. 11⅝d.
1351–1360	14s. 3⅝d.	2.50	11s. 10¾d.
1541–1550	20s. 10½d.	1.	6s. 11¼d.

Higher by 50 per cent. over prices of the thirteenth and fourteenth centuries, by weight of silver, prices of the middle of the sixteenth century would have been but one half those of two hundred years before, had they been taken by tale, which, of course, as everybody knows, is opposed by all the facts of history.

We have the sad picture displayed before our own eyes in the famines of Russia, devastating whole provinces of the interior, while the surplus of other provinces cannot be brought to their relief, but goes by adjacent water routes to keep in plenty the teeming populations of England. Granting roads in good condition, as in the England of those days, in the opinion of Thorold Rogers, the frequent feuds of the nobles among themselves or their revolts against the kings would make it difficult to effectually assist in bringing relief. Prices are very variable within one and the same year, and between place and place. This is the case in England well up to modern times.

From 1690 to 1700, the price of coal per chaldron is quoted for Bedford at 21s.; Brecon, 10s.; Brentford, 31s. 6d.; Cambridge, 23s. 4d.; Falmouth, 20s.; Guildford, 32s.; London, 24s.; Monmouth, 30s.; Newcastle, 10s. 6d.; Norwich, 22s.; Nottingham, 10s.; Pembroke, 16s.; Reading, 32s.; Southampton, 43s.; Oxford, 40s. *

Nearness to or distance from the mine made a greater difference to the consumer than it does in our days. Land-carriage of wheat over a hundred miles would have easily doubled the price. But taking out the several years of extraordinarily high prices and averaging the years of extreme cheapness with those of a generally higher level, we find this uniformity of price covering the long period of English history up to the period of the debasement of the currency by Henry VIII. to be an indisputable fact. This was the case not alone in wheat and other cereals, but in live stock, farm produce, metals, and manufactures as well as in southern and eastern produce.

---

* Thorold Rogers, *History of Agriculture and Prices in England*, vol. vi.

There were two periods of a marked rise in the prices of all commodities. The first occurs after the great plague. It ushered in a social revolution. Death cut a wide swath. It made hands scarce and lands cheap. Land could be had for the asking and the tilling. The cloak of feudalism was lifted, and soon torn into shreds. The labor acts of Edward III. did not lower wages, and the broken word of Richard did not help the nobles to bring back the era of serfdom. The latter had outlived its usefulness. The social revolution was brought about by the economic revolutions that preceded it. Changes in economic conditions prepare and make the world's history. As in the cases of John Ball, Wat Tyler, and Jack Cade, it is necessary, frequently, to remind tarrying insistence on mouldy parchments that each generation must carve out its fortunes from the rock of time, with the tools its intellectual status has created for its hands.

The rise in wages was general, the rise in prices only in articles of commerce, while farm produce was little affected. A consequent greater well-being of the working classes up to the time of Elizabeth was the result of it.

This change in prices shows clearly that the cause lies entirely outside of the domain of money influences and fully proves again the positions heretofore explained in these pages.

To make the reader grasp at a glance the price situation, I will give in a collective statement the prices of the chief commodities, as gathered in the great work of Thorold Rogers, for the period beginning with 1261 down to 1582. I shall follow his division of the long space of time into four sections, *i.e.*, 1. 1261 to 1350; 2. 1351 to 1400; 3. 1401 to 1540; and 4. 1541 to 1582, the last period, the time of the great debasement of the currency, and of Elizabeth's change of the coinage, which finally put the stamp of time on the change of 1 to 3.

Not to bewilder the reader with too great an array of figures, I shall confine myself to a statement of the averages for the periods named. The decennial averages of Thorold Rogers's price records vary but little from the general average for an entire period quoted. Where the price average is stated for the time from 1261 to 1400, without separation into the first and second division, the price averages in the decades of the period show no variation sufficiently marked for distinction. I shall put a separate column against each price quotation, with three as a multiplier to bring the nominal price up to the present money price, * in conformity with the facts of the money history of the time.

I.—PRICES OF GRAINS, PER QUARTER, IN THE DIFFERENT PERIODS NAMED, AND THEIR EQUIVALENTS IN MONEY OF TO-DAY.

	1261 to 1351.		1351 to 1400.		1401 to 1540.		1551 to 1580.	
	Price of the Period.	In Present Money.	Price of the Period.	In Present Money.	Price of the Period.	In Present Money.	Price of the Period.	
	s. d.	s. d.	s. d.	s. d.	s. d.	s. d.	s. d.	
Wheat	5.9¼	17.3¾	6.1¼	18.3¾	5.11¾	17.11¼	15. 0	
Barley	4.1¼	12.3¾	4.1	12.3	3. 8¾	11. 2¼	9.10¾	
Oats	2.4	7.0	2.6¾	7.8¼	2. 2¼	6. 6¾	5.10½	
Rye	4.6½	13.6¾	4.2	12.6	4. 7¾	13.11¼		
Malt	4.8¾	14.2¼	5.0½	15.1½	4. 1	12. 3	11. 5	
Beans	4.2	12.6	4.6	13.6	3. 9¼	11. 3¾	11.11	
Peas	3.9¼	11.3¾	3.8¼	11.0¾	3.10	11. 6	10. 0	

* The actual difference would be as 4½ to 1 instead of 3 to 1 as the ratio of silver to gold was 10 to 11 to 1, in the first two centuries of this comparison, against 15½ to 1 of the present coining ratio.

The first column in the last period (1551 to 1580) shows a rise in price over the average which ruled steadily for a period of 280 years almost equal to the changed money relations. The changed relations of the shilling of Edward I. and the shilling of Henry VIII. and of Elizabeth alone are expressed in the price difference; the price in weight of silver has not changed.

In the debasement of the coins by Henry VIII. the adulterations had been practised for quite a while before price changes in domestic produce became very marked. Traders always know how to prevent loss and to protect themselves by taking the poor coins only for their value in silver.

On the whole the change in the coinage did not show its full effect on prices until several decades after Elizabeth's act.

The people become used in a sense to price relations, and when the coinage is limited in quantity, debased coin will for a long time pass for much above its real value in a country whose commerce and industries are restricted, and which has but little communication with the outer world.

The trading revolution of the century barely touched England. The ocean still imprisoned the island kingdom, and it was some time yet before it became England's highroad to power and wealth. What little of foreign commerce there was had been in the hands of the Flemings and the Hansa up to quite a late period. Though Henry VII. and Henry VIII. were active promoters of England's commercial and maritime independence, yet the great uprising under Elizabeth was required to give inspiration and direction to the activity of the country. The inner economy responded to these conditions in pretty nearly the same manner. Hence we shall observe the price relations here noted to continue for quite a time before the change is apparent in the prices collected by Thorold Rogers, and which cover the chief articles of commerce.

In live stock the prices have gone up to the point marked by the new money conditions. In weight of silver they are not changed from what they were three hundred years earlier. I have stated the prices of oxen and of sheep separately. For these animals the weight is recorded in the later quotations. For other animals the weight is not given. The weight recorded, we can follow the price changes in their true relations to the present period, and make quite important deductions. This is impossible where the weight is not given. It is, however, evident that if the mediæval sheep and ox weighed only one third as much as a sheep and ox weigh at present, cows, pigs, and boars were of equally poor breed and equally diminutive as compared to the present stately English herds. And from what we know of the improvement of breeds in subsequent periods, we must conclude that the horse stood, in this respect, on no higher level than his companions of the farmyard.*

---

* In proof of this, take the following statement of Hume, being part of his remarks on the state of agriculture at the time of James I.. "Sir Edward Harwood, in a memorial composed at the beginning of the subsequent reign, says that England was so unprovided with horses fit for war, that two thousand men could not possibly be mounted throughout the whole kingdom. At present the breed of horses is so much improved, that almost all those which are employed, either in the plough, wagon, or coach, would be fit for that purpose."—Hume, *History of England*, vol. iv., appendix iii..

II.—PRICES OF OXEN AND SHEEP IN MONEY OF THE PERIODS NAMED, AND THEIR EQUIVALENTS IN MONEY OF TO-DAY, AND CORRESPONDING VALUE IN WEIGHT OF ANIMALS OF PRESENT TIME.

(Oxen counted in 1st and 2d period as 400 lbs., 3d period 500 lbs., and at present time as 1200 lbs. Sheep at 40 to 50 lbs., 1st to 2d period, and 150 lbs. to-day.)

	1st and 2d Periods.			3d Period.			4th Period.			
	1261 to 1400			1401 to 1540.			1551 to 1580.			1850.
	Price of Period.	In Present Money.	In To-day's Weight.	Price of Period.	In Present Money.	In To-day's Weight.	Price of Period.	In Present Money.	In To-day's Weight.	
	s. d.	s. d.	s. d.	s. d.	s. d.	s. d.	s. d.		s. d.	s. d.
Oxen . .	13.1½	39.4½	118.9½	20.7	61.9	148.0	70.7¼	....	168.5	300.0
Sheep...	1.5	4.3	12.9	2.2¾	6.8¼	20.0¾	6.4	....	19.0	40.0

III.—PRICES OF OTHER LIVE STOCK IN MONEY OF THE PERIOD AND ITS EQUIVALENT PRICE EXPRESSED IN PRESENT MONEY.

	1261 to 1350.		1351 to 1400.		1401 to 1540.		1551 to 1582.	
	Price of Period.	In Present Money.	Price of Period.	In Present Money.	Price of Period.	In Present Money.	Price of Period.	In Present Money.
Animals.	s. d.	s. d.	s. d.	s. d.	s. d.	s. d.	s. d.	
Cows	7.10	23.6	10.7	31.9	....	....	....	....
Cart horses....	18.2	54.6	21.5	64.3	....	....	....	....
Saddle horses..	....	....	....	....	58.11	176.9	144.0	....
Boars	4.7½	13.10½	4.7½	13.10½	8.6¼	25.6¾	23.7	....
Geese	0.3½	0.10½	0.4¼	1.0¾	0.4¾	1.2¼	0.11	....

The prices are here nearly up to the altered relations in the coinage. They have gone through the same process of change as the animals quoted in Table II. It is different in the prices of farm produce. The latter, articles of traffic and of purchase for immediate consumption, still adhere for quite a while to the customary numeral price, before they take rank in the new scale.

IV.—PRICES OF FARM PRODUCE IN MONEY OF THE PERIOD AND ITS EQUIVALENT PRICE EXPRESSED IN PRESENT MONEY.

	1260 TO 1350.		1351 TO 1400.		1401 TO 1540.		1550 TO 1582.	
	Price of Period.	In Present Money.	Price of Period.	In Present Money.	Price of Period.	In Present Money.	Price of Period.	In Present Money.
	s. d.	s. d.	s. d.	s. d.	s. d.	s. d.	s. d.	s. d.
Wool, lb. . . .	0.3¼	0.9¾	0.3¼	0.9¾	0.2¾	0.8¼	0.7¼	. . . .
Cheese, "	0.0⅜	0.1⅛	0.0¾	0.2¼	0.0¾	0.2¼	0.1½	. . . .
Butter, "	0.0¾	0.2¼	0.1	0.3	0.1⅛	0.3⅜	0.2⅜	. . . .
Lard, 10 lbs. . .	1.0	3.0	1.0	3.0	. . . .	. . . .	. . . .	. . . .
Wax, lb.	0.6	1.6	0.6	1.6	0.6¼	1.8¾	0.9	. . . .
Eggs, per 120. .	.4½	1.1½	0.5	1.3	0.6¼	1.6¾	2.6	. . . .

Expressed in the value of the new coinage, wool is lower by nearly twenty-five per cent. than before Henry VIII.'s time. Cheese is but 1½*d.*, while the average price up to 1540, expressed in the new money, would have been 2¼*d.*, butter 2⅜*d.*, against 3⅜*d.*, the equivalent of the old price in the new coins. Eggs, however, are much dearer. They are at double the price, in weight of silver, at which they were in the period closing with 1400, and about sixty per cent. higher than in the early part of the sixteenth century.

Thorold Rogers says on this: "I cannot but think that the peasantry in the growing poverty of their condition ceased to supply the articles and that the stint led to this rise in the price." The explanation is not sufficient in view of the fact that butter and cheese did not even experience a rise equivalent to the monetary changes. In the absence of a more satisfactory explanation, we may, however, accept this one as well as any other. In products of domestic industry used largely on the farm and by the people in general, the same price relations exist. The price has but partly responded to the change in the monetary system.

V.—PRICES OF DOMESTIC INDUSTRIAL PRODUCTS IN MONEY OF THE PERIOD AND ITS EQUIVALENT PRICE EXPRESSED IN PRESENT MONEY.

	1261 to 1350		1351 to 1400		1401 to 1540		1551 to 1582
	Price of Period.	In present Money.	Price of Period.	In present Money.	Price of Period.	In Present Money.	Price of Period.
	s. d.	s. d.	s. d.	s. d.	s. d.	s d.	s. d.
Candles, lb..........					0. $1\frac{1}{4}$	0. $3\frac{3}{4}$	0. $2\frac{3}{8}$
Salt, bu..............	0. $5\frac{1}{5}$	1. $3\frac{3}{5}$	0. $9\frac{1}{2}$	2. $4\frac{1}{2}$	0. $6\frac{1}{4}$	1. $6\frac{3}{4}$	1. $2\frac{1}{2}$
Tar, brl.............	5. $5\frac{1}{2}$	16. $4\frac{1}{2}$	4. $4\frac{1}{4}$	13. $0\frac{3}{4}$	6. $0\frac{1}{4}$	18. $0\frac{3}{4}$	9. 4
Lime, qu.............	0. $6\frac{3}{8}$	1. $7\frac{1}{8}$	1. $2\frac{3}{4}$	3. $7\frac{1}{8}$	1. $2\frac{1}{2}$	3. $7\frac{1}{2}$	2. $9\frac{3}{4}$
Bricks, 1000.........	10.11	32. 9	14. 5	43. 3	6. 0	18. 0	11. 3
Tiles................					5. $5\frac{1}{2}$	16. $4\frac{1}{2}$	10. $1\frac{1}{4}$
Iron, raw, cwt.......	4. $1\frac{1}{2}$	12. $4\frac{1}{2}$	9. $5\frac{1}{4}$	28. $3\frac{3}{4}$	5. $4\frac{1}{2}$	16. $0\frac{1}{2}$	10. $6\frac{1}{2}$
Iron, wrought.......					15. $7\frac{1}{2}$	46.$10\frac{1}{2}$	26. $2\frac{3}{4}$
Board nails, and 6*d.* nails, 1000......	2.11	8. 9	5. 3	15. 9	4. $3\frac{3}{4}$	12.$11\frac{1}{4}$	4. $6\frac{1}{2}$
Lath nails, 1000.....	0. $9\frac{1}{4}$	2. $3\frac{3}{4}$	1. $5\frac{1}{4}$	4. $3\frac{3}{4}$	0.$11\frac{1}{2}$	2.$10\frac{1}{2}$	1. $2\frac{1}{4}$
Lead, pig, fodder....					74. 9	234. 4	159. 2
Rope, cwt...........					13. $2\frac{1}{2}$	39. $7\frac{1}{2}$	29. 8

Here we notice the same relations of prices in the new money but about 100 per cent. higher, while the money represents only one third of the value of the old coin. The manufacturing skill of the nation had not increased nor were the tools improved. The smaller rise in prices than in the changed relations of money values between the two periods is primarily due to the fact that wages did not rise in the proportion that money had been debased. Part, however, is due to the great quantities of building material which had come into the market from the spoil of the monasteries.

VI.—DAILY AVERAGE RATE OF WAGES IN MONEY OF THE PERIOD AND IN ITS EQUIVALENT EXPRESSED IN PRESENT MONEY.

	1261 to 1350		1351 to 1400		1401 to 1540		1551 to 1580
	Rate of Period.	In Present Money.	Rate of Period.	In Present Money.	Rate of Period.	In Present Money.	Rate of Period.
	d.	d.	d.	d.	d.	d.	d.
Carpenter, highest rate	4⅛	12⅜	5⅞	17⅝	6⅞	20⅝	12
do. average	3⅛	9⅜	4⅝	13⅞	5⅞	17⅞	10⅛
Mason.............	3½	10½	5⅝	16⅞	6	18	10⅛
Mason's laborer......					4	12	7⅛
Sawyer.............	3	9	5⅛	15⅜	6	18	9⅛
Tiler or Slater.......	3⅛	9⅜	6	18	6	18	10¼
Bricklayer..........							
Thatcher...........					5¼	15¾	10¼
Thatcher's laborer....					3⅜	10⅛	7⅛
Plumber...........	3	9	6¼	18¾	6½	19½	10
Saddler............	3½	10½	5	15			

The rate of wages in the last named period is practically the same as in the century preceding the great plague. The higher rate of wages dating from that event maintained itself upon the same level, as already mentioned, for nearly two hundred years. Though wages rose nominally, the laborer received only two thirds as much in actual value, as before the debasement of the currency chronicled above.

As seen in Tables I., II., and III., the chief articles of support for himself and his family, the corn for his bread, the malt for his beer—a very important item for mediæval domestic economy, the beans and peas—partly used in his bread and in his porridge, and his meat, so far as he could indulge in it, these were all quickly up to the price made by the new money of 3 out of 1.

No wonder that his condition became more and more depressed, all due to what Thorold Rogers so justly stigmatizes as the greatest crime ever committed by a tyrant against a patient and long-suffering people.

The reader can understand from this fact why, in the face of inert manufacturing and trading conditions, prices of domestic industrial products did not respond to the changes in the moneys.

The price changes are entirely in keeping with the change in the rate of wages. Iron, raw and wrought, extremely high in the middle ages, as well as nails and articles manufactured from iron, responded even less to the changed money conditions than salt, lime, bricks, tiles, rope, and the like. Raw iron, in the period from 1351 to 1401 averaging £28 the ton expressed in the new monetary system, is worth but £16 in 1401 to 1540, and £10 6½s. in the actual money of 1560. Wrought iron, averaging £46 12½s. from 1401 to 1540, is £25 4s., in the later period. Board nails and sixpenny nails, weighing 10 lbs. to the thousand, show little variation from the prices of the two preceding centuries, hence have not at all responded to the revolution in the currency.

But as these articles are quoted at higher prices in the succeeding period, it follows that much of what has been said above on the change taking gradual effect applies also here.

In the seventeenth century nails are quoted by the pound. In 1645 the price paid is 5½d., in 1653 it is 6d., more than six times the present price.

Here I will only say that in the opinion of Thorold Rogers nails were less influenced by the price of iron than other articles wrought from this metal. "The article was in constant demand, was within the skill of every smith, was regularly kept in store by him (as I can well remember before the days of machine-made nails), was a bye-product of his craft when he was not engaged in any definite work, and was manufactured from scrap iron, the better for being old and worn." * This explains well enough the close adherence to the former nominal price, though the price-changes in all other commodities were extreme. In textile fabrics much applies of what has been said concerning other industrial products. The price does not rise in proportion to the changed money relations. Nor does it rise in the next century, as we shall see later on, to the level of average prices of 1400–1540. The work was paid by the piece, and not by the day or week as in the other employments of which I gave the price record in Table VI. We may assume, from analogy, that scattered cottagers and peasants are not more able to enforce their demands for better remuneration than day laborers and craftsmen in towns, who can combine to insist on increase of wages

---

* See my volume *The Destructive Influence of the Tariff*, on the nail-makers of the Taunus Mountains in Germany.

in conformity with the depreciation of money. It is not alone likely, nay, it is a well known fact, that piece workers employed in domestic industry partake more slowly of the advances due to changed conditions here delineated.

I give here the prices of the principal textiles, which had become at an early epoch articles of purchase and sale, as gathered by Thorold Rogers from the records of Merton and Oriel Colleges, Oxford.

VII.—PRICES OF TEXTILE FABRICS IN MONEY OF THE PERIOD AND ITS EQUIVALENT PRICE EXPRESSED IN PRESENT MONEY.

	1261 to 1350.		1351 to 1400.		1401 to 1540.		1551 to 1582.
	Price of Period.	In Present Money.	Price of Period.	In Present Money.	Price of Period.	In Present Money.	Price of Period.
	s. d.	s. d.	s. d.	s. d.	s. d.	s. d.	s. d.
Table linen, doz. ells	3.3	9.9	6.7¼	19.9¾	6.9¾	20.5¼	21.0
Shirting " "	4.1¼	12.3¾	8.4½	25.1½	6.1½	18.4½	13.10½
Canvas "	2.6¾	7.8¼	4.10½	14.7½	4.6	13.6	7.7¾
Sacking "					2.10	8.6	5.3¾
Cloths, Piece of 24 Yards.							
1st Quality..........	79.8	239.0	83.2	249.6	58.8½	176.1½	161.0
2d "	33.2¼	99.6¾	46.6½	139.7½	48.0	144.0	85.0
3d "					34.1	102.3	76.0

In the prices of southern and eastern products brought to the English markets a multitude of causes operate and produce changes. The differences from 1350 to 1540 are so slight that we may call prices almost uniform. Sugar at 1 shilling a pound, equal to 3 shillings in present money, pepper at 1s. 5d., or 4s. 3d. in the present coinage; currants at 3d. = 9d. in the present coinage; rice at 1½d. to 2d. = 4½ to 6d. in the present coinage; high prices in the centuries previous to the change imputed to the influx of silver from the American mines, and declining prices for all of these commodities in the succeeding periods, prove almost anything except the geometrical price-theory of quantity of money covering quantity of merchandise. To this question, however, I shall return, with a retrospective view of the case, after having given descending prices down to our time; and now only refer to prices up to 1582, which in the last named period show only an approximation to the new coin multiple of 3 in some of the items, while in others barely 2 is touched. Sugar is even lower in the new coins than in the full value coin in the second half of the fourteenth century. Pepper again is higher than the average of the preceding 200 years multiplied by three. Of rice, almonds, and some of the spices, other than pepper, the prices do not quite approach the full change. But in raisins and currants the prices are not even 50 per cent. higher than the old prices in the heavy coinage.

That these variations are caused by changed and shifting sources of supply, differences in trade connections, and altered transportation routes could be easily proved. But it would lead to a more extensive treatment of the question under consideration than I have set out to give to this subject, were I to follow the causes of price variations for each article brought under review. I point this out, however, as part of a general effect on prices, with which we shall have to deal more in particular in the sequel.

VIII.—PRICES OF FOREIGN PRODUCE, NOW KNOWN UNDER THE NAME OF COLONIAL PRODUCE, IN MONEY OF THE TIME AND ITS EQUIVALENT PRICE EXPRESSED IN PRESENT MONEY.

	1261 to 1350		1351 to 1400		1401 to 1540		1551 to 1582	
	Price of Period.	In Present Money.	Price of Period.	In Present Money.	Price of Period.	In Present Money.	Price of Period.	In Present Money.
	s. d.	*s. d.*	*s. d.*	*s. d.*	*s. d.*	*s. d.*	*s. d.*	*s. d.*
Sugar, doz. lbs.	10.6	37.6	19.0	57.0	12.0	36.0	12.10¾	
Pepper " "	13.6	40.6	16.9	50.3	17.1	51.3	58.0	
Saffron, lb....	8.5¼	25.5¼	14.2	42.6	11.11½	35.10½	18.4	
Cloves, ".....					4.3¾	12.11¼	8.9¾	
Cinnamon, lb..					3.4	10.0	6.4¼	
Ginger, lb.....	1.6½	4.7½	1.7½	4.10½	2.0	6.0	3.9¼	
Almonds, cwt.	18.8	56.0	30.4	91.0	26.11¼	80.11	70.10	
Raisins, doz. lbs.........					1.9¼	5.3¾	2.5¼	
Currants, doz. lbs.........					3.0¾	9.2¼	4.8	
Rice, doz. lbs.	1.0	3.0	1.6	4.6	1.11	5.9	4.4	

England's Financial Condition.

We have seen now that up to the year 1582 prices had not reached the old level if computed in the new coins. Money certainly should have begun by this time to circulate somewhat more freely, though by no means so abundantly that it could have caused a price revolution. Now England was just about emerging from a mediæval, agricultural state and beginning to take an interest in the affairs of the new era that had opened a century or two before in the advanced states of the continent. A greater amount of circulation under developing conditions in the last decade of the reign of Elizabeth would have been in the nature of things. The small amount of the recoinage of 1560 shows plainly that no extensive trading could have been done unless all large transactions were based on weighing the silver instead of paying in the discredited coin. A large stock of uncoined silver, plate, etc., undoubtedly came into the mint after the determination of Elizabeth not to allow any further cheating of the people by a tampering with the currency had become a settled fact. Still in all the forty-four years of her reign * she coined not more than £4,718,579 in silver and £795,137 in gold. It is plain that this is not an excessive supply for a people beginning to use money more freely in buying and selling than at any previous period of its history. The home stocks of silver had to suffice. There could have been no foreign influx to explain the phenomenon as there was no extensive trading. In the twenty years of James £1,641,004 in silver and £3,666,389 in gold were coined, according to the same authority. Much of these sums, was obtained from recoinages and other melted-in money stocks. During the reign of Charles I. of twenty-four years, £8,776,544 in silver and £3,319,677 in gold were coined. The Commonwealth in eleven years coined £1,000,000 in silver and £154,511 in gold. Charles II. reigned twenty-five years and coined £3,722,180 in silver and £4,177,253 in gold. James II. in four years coined £518,316 in silver and ƒ1,596,799 in gold.

The recoinage under William III., completed in 1699, must have covered nearly all the circulation in existence from the previous coinages.† Still the total coinage under

---

* Ruding, *History of the Mint*.

† No time shows such wide-going adulteration of coins by clipping and sweating, and other means of debasement as the seventeenth century. In Germany we have the *Kippers and Wippers* (the clippers and sweaters), competing with the mint authorities. The writers of the time compare

this reign amounted to £7,093,074 in silver and £3,418,889 in gold. But England's position at the end of the seventeenth century was quite a different one from what it was at the beginning and in the middle of the century. Her trade and enterprise were beginning to give her rank among the first nations of Europe, while in the first half of the century up to the time of the Commonwealth we hear of Sweden and Holland as leading powers, but England is not mentioned and plays no greater part in the world's drama and in the navigation of the seas than Poland or Russia. During that period the circulation was in keeping with the general backwardness of the people. Estimated at about £3,000,000 in silver and gold at the time of Elizabeth's death and £4,000,000 at the end of the reign of James I. (Hume, *History of England*), the middle of the seventeenth century certainly did not see the stock increased to very large proportion beyond that

---

them with the vilest scum, and express themselves in very drastic manner. "All the thieves," says one of them, "that were hanged in a hundred years, have not stolen as much as the Kippers. The Swedes boiled such fellows in molten metal, drowned them in boiling water, or hanged them on high trees. Oh, that such sharp execution would be done on some of these arch scoundrels to-day." This extract from one of the writers of the time gives an idea of the suffering created by the debasing of the coins, and of the feeling of universal hatred and execration created thereby against the perpetrators of this cheating of the people. But this writer consoles himself in the expectation '*Sed nondum omnium dierum sol occidit*,' the punishment can come yet later on."

In France, complaints are not less emphatic and no less well founded.

In England, by the time of the recoinage under William III., things had come to such a pass that serious troubles were apprehended and complaints could not be appeased any longer. No good coins were in existence, either being driven out of the country or thrown into the melting-pot.

That such conditions do not create a plethora of money, such as under any circumstances could create a general rise of prices, ought to be plain to the dullest understanding.

sum, when the money supply is not more than what it is shown to have been under William III., according to the recoinage of all English moneys. The opening of trade relations with Scotland through the Union under the House of Stuart drew that country into the new order developing in England by opening a market for her produce. This coupled with the more active English home trading under James I., would easily have absorbed all the surplus moneys coming into England under the limits set down above for the possible expansion of currency under the first two Stuarts. Under all the circumstances here recorded a price advance could not have been possible on the money-quantity theory.

CHAPTER VII.

The Price-Changes during the Seventeenth Century and the Money-Relations.—The Natural Causes Contributing to the Rise in Grain-Prices.

THE advance in conformity with the change in the coinage, and not yet fully covered in the prices of the period closing with 1583, as shown above, is the only one observable at first. We see prices reach that point only in the last decade of the sixteenth century. From that time on prices advance steadily. But they begin to decline in most of the commodities treated here, to the dire disappointment of our quantity theorists, at a time when the growing importance of England in trade, industry, and colonial extension begins to pour the coveted treasures into her lap.

In order to get a view of the price-changes we have to follow the same manner and sequence as in the preceding tables. Here I will set side by side in parallel columns (1) the prices of the period 1401 to 1540 computed in the new Elizabethan coinage for the assistance of the reader; (2) the prices of the first decade of James I., *i.e.*, 1603 to 1612; (3) the prices of the period of 1613 to 1652; (4) the prices of 1653 to 1702; and (5) the prices of 1693 to 1702, the decade in which occurred the recoinage of the currency, frightfully debased by clipping, sweating, and shaving down of the coins.

I.—PRICES OF CEREALS, PER QUARTER, IN THE PERIODS NAMED, FROM THE BEGINNING OF THE SEVENTEENTH TO THE BEGINNING OF THE EIGHTEENTH CENTURY.

	1401 to 1540.	1592 to 1602.	1603 to 1612.	1613 to 1652.	1653 to 1702.	1693 to 1702.
	s. d.	s. d.	s. d.	s. d.	s. d.	s. d.
Wheat	17. 11¼	34. 10½	35. 3¼	42. 8¼	40. 5	43. 2¾
Barley	11. 2¼	19. 5½	19. 5	23. 4	21. 3	22. 4¾
Oats	6. 6¼	11. 5½	11. 10¾	14. 11	14. 10	15. 1¼
Malt	12. 3	22. 4¾	19. 10	24. 7	23. 5	25. 3
Beans	11. 3¾	19. 10	19. 2	21. 10	24. 5	27. 9
Peas	11. 6	19. 4	17. 5¼	22. 11	24. 6	29. 9

Little besides the destruction of the Armada has happened to give England access to the silver finds by which the sudden rise in prices, which we observe in the second column, is usually explained. True, some rich captures were made. Elizabeth herself did not disdain partnership with the pirates fitted out from her shores. But the wealth gained by buccaneering and piracy is not of a lasting nature. Even the heavy contributions levied on the vanquished by the conquerors in our own days have but a fleeting effect. Prices do not rise permanently through such additions to the money stocks of a country. No other sources of increase of money are discernible in the financial history of the two decades following 1582, and yet prices of corn are nearly as high in the first decade as in the later period of the seventeenth century, when prices have reached their culminating point.*

---

* The limited character of the foreign commerce of Great Britain in the early part of the seventeenth century can be estimated from the fact that in 1610 the imports and exports were £4,628,586. The customs collected were £148,075, of which sum nearly three fourths were collected in London. Yet it is from foreign trading alone that an influx of specie could be

There were, however, causes at work which fully and satisfactorily explain the extraordinary rise in prices in the seventeenth century. The state of agriculture had not made any progress worth speaking of. With some notable exceptions in different parts of the kingdom, the people adhered closely to their old system of cultivation, and were as obdurate to the introduction of improvements as in the fifteenth and sixteenth centuries. Hartlib, a Dutchman by birth, but settled in England, writing in the middle of the century, points out the defects of English husbandry. He says that old men in Surrey remember the time when gardeners first came there and began to plant cabbages, cauliflowers, turnips, carrots, parsnips, early peas and rape, which up to that time were great rarities, but which were seen in England, having come from Flanders or Holland. The gardeners got land with difficulty, though they offered enormous rents for it, the landowners imagining that the use of the spade would spoil the ground. "Even now," he goes on to say, "gardening and hoeing is scarcely known in the north and west of England, in which places a few gardeners might have saved the lives of many poor people, who have starved these dear years." (Here the writer refers to the five years, 1646 to 1650, in which a real famine prevailed.)

Onions and hops were imported from Flanders, and "even plants which grow wild in our own hedgerows, but we are not at the pains to cultivate." Other writers, by the advice they give to farmers, show plainly enough the undeveloped state of agriculture and, in fact, of most of the industries of the country. England had made but slow progress in these, while commerce, trade, and bank-

---

made available to bear on prices. See Thorold Rogers' *History of Agriculture and Prices in England*, vol. v., p. 586.

ing, along with stock-jobbing, began to attain a prominent position in the economic history of the country. By the end of the reign of James I. (1625) foreign commerce had grown to very nearly double what it was in 1604, if the increase in the revenue from customs is a proof.*

The population, which, up to the middle of the reign of Elizabeth, had been rather stationary, grew rapidly. The towns, large consumers but not producers of food supplies, were extending in numbers and population. London, despite its extreme unhealthiness and filthiness, was rapidly filling up. It had 500,000 inhabitants at the end of the century. The increase of population was especially noticeable in northern England. The emigration of religious exiles from Flanders and France made a considerable addition, and the development of the textile industries and the demand for English products stimulated town population, and necessarily increased the demand for the products of agriculture. If to this be added the generally prevailing poor crop years,† interspersed with a number of years of actual dearth, and some of famine and plague, we have an explanation for the prevailing high prices, which is sufficient, and with which the monetary history of the century does not supply us.

---

* "The customs in 1604 yielded £127,000 a year; they rose to £190,000 toward the end of the reign. The customs were supposed to amount to five per cent. of the value and were levied upon exports and imports."—Hume's *History of England*.

† Hume, comparing his time with that of James I., says: "The nation was still dependent on foreigners for their daily bread; and though its exportation of grain now forms a considerable branch of its commerce, notwithstanding its considerable increase of people, there was, in that period a regular importation from the Baltic, as well as from France; and if it ever stopped, the bad consequences were seriously felt by the nation. Sir Walter Raleigh, in his *Observations*, computes that two millions went out at one time for corn."

We find a fair uniformity of average prices from about the year 1610 down to the beginning of the next century. In the prices of animals, meat, and farm products we see the same coincidence.

II.—PRICES OF ANIMALS AND FARM-PRODUCTS FROM THE BEGINNING OF THE SEVENTEENTH TO THE BEGINNING OF THE EIGHTEENTH CENTURY.

	1401 to 1540.	1593 to 1602.	1603 to 1612.	1613 to 1652.	1653 to 1702.	1693 to 1702.
	s. d.	*s. d.*	*s. d.*	*s. d.*	*s. d.*	*s. d.*
Oxen	81.4	103.10	129.8	154.8	143.8	166.8
Sheep	6.8¼	9.0½	9.10	11.5	11.1	11.0½
Saddle and coach-horses	176.9	238.0	236.2	298.0	332.0	332.8
Boars	25.6¾	38.7	40.9	53.0	75.2	99.0
Geese	1.0¾	1.11½	2.4¼	2.3	3.1	3.4
Farm Products.						
Wool, lb	0.8¼	{ 0.10⅞ 0.8		1.0	0.10	0.9
Cheese, lb	0.2¼	0.2¾	0.4	3¾	0.3⅝	0.4¼
Butter, lb	0.3⅜	0.4	0.5	0.5½	0.6	0.6⅞
Beef, stone, 14 pounds	1.6	2.3	2.5¾	2.11	3.5½	3.6
Tallow, cwt		35.4½		32.4	25.2	26.6½
Eggs, per 120	1.6¾	3.7¾	3.3	3.3	3.4	

The rise in prices shown in this table is entirely in accord with the rise in the prices of animals, meat, and farm products with which our own people are familiar in sections of the country going through the same process of evolution as England was then passing through, and it is, indeed, entirely in keeping with the economic history of the world.

The price of oxen in the first column is stated as 81*s.* 4*d.*, instead of 61*s.* 9*d.*, the price in the first table presented by me, for the period 1401 to 1540. This is to bring the weight relation up to average weight of the beginning of the seventeenth century. The various statements as to the size of oxen in the former period and the abundance of testimony as to the size of the animals in the seventeenth century, fully explain this change of price, and show that the prices were nearly equal on the basis of weight. For the other animals quoted weights are not given. Hence, we have to make whatever mental allowance may be found profitable.

Sheep do not seem to have increased in weight. They are still quoted at 38 to 40 lbs. Nor does the price change very much in the hundred years, all things considered. Hogs have grown excessively dear at the end of the period. (The boars of the record are full grown, fat animals.) The carcass is estimated as averaging about 3 cwts. Pork is sold to the navy at 4s. a stone (of 14 lbs.) This is $3\frac{1}{2}d.$ a pound, a rise of something over a hundred per cent. over fifteenth and sixteenth century prices. But as boars are from three to four times as high it follows that the size of the animal has considerably increased in the time.

The prices of cheese, butter and eggs rise on the same scale and likewise remain at a high level all through the century, a clear proof of the existence of a natural cause of general and wide-reaching effect. That it was not the change in the monetary supply is best illustrated by the price of wool. Wool remains almost stationary in price. All the entries collected by Thorold Rogers approximate to the averages here quoted. Now of all articles wool ought to be enhanced in price fully as much as other agricultural products if the rise is due to increase in the money supplies, abundance of the silver finds, cheapening of silver or money or whatsoever else may be used in support of "the natural law." Wool was throughout the

Middle Ages the only article of export. It remained at this more modern period, if not the only, at least the chief article of export. It was in universal demand abroad, and in consequence of the development of woollen manufacture in the north, became of constantly increasing importance in England. If the increasing "abundance" of money had caused the rise of prices, wool ought to have been of fully three times the value it held at the beginning of the century. But instead of this it was not alone not higher, but is about the only article which taken by weight and *value* of silver is actually cheaper than we find it in the average of prices of the 250 years that preceded the reign of Henry VIII. We find it cheaper at the end of the century, in a decade of extremely high prices, than at the end of the sixteenth century, when the prices of other commodities did not yet show even the full effect of the alteration in the coinage.

What Thorold Rogers says on this score thoroughly explains the cause:

". . . The price of wool was lower in the seventeenth century on the whole than it was at the end of the sixteenth. It is very probable that as agriculture improved, or as better supplies of winter fodder were forthcoming, more sheep were kept by the farmers, and that the price of wool fell by reason of greater plenty. So in the last quarter of the eighteenth century wool was cheaper than it was in the seventeenth, ranging from 14*s.* to 20*s.* the tod."* (The tod is 28 lbs., hence from 6*d.* to 8½*d.* the lb.

Considering all the facts, the reader will admit that the money-quantity theory fails here lamentably.

---

* *History of Agriculture and Prices in England,* vol. v., p. 410.

III.—PRICES OF INDUSTRIAL PRODUCTS FROM THE BEGINNING OF THE SEVENTEENTH TO THE BEGINNING OF THE EIGHTEENTH CENTURY.

	1400 to 1540.	1593 to 1602.	1603 to 1612.	1613 to 1652.	1653 to 1702.	1693 to 1702.
	s. d.	*s. d.*	*s. d.*	*s. d.*	*s. d.*	*s. d.*
Candles, lb.	0. 3¾	0.3 11/12	0. 4	0. 4⅝	0.5⅛	0.5½
Salt, bu.	1. 6¾	2.2	1.10	2. 8	*2 6½	†4.9
Tar, brl.	18. 0¾					
Lime, qu.	3 7½	4.4¾	4.11½	4.10	4.9	5.4
Bricks, per 1000...........	18. 0	13.2	14. 7¼	14. 9½	18.8	19.3¾
Tiles, "	16. 4½	13.0¾	13.11	14. 3¼	19.4	17.8
Iron, cwt.	16. 0½	13.6		12. 0		
Iron, wrought, cwt.........	46.10½	33.1	32. 8	39. 3	37.5	38.0⅛
Board nails, 10 lb. per 1000	12.11¼			5. 0		
Lath nails, 3 lbs. per 1000..	2.10½	1.4	1. 5	1. 4¾	1.7	1.4
Lead, pig, the fodder	234. 4			164.10	169.0	
Rope, cordage, cwt.	39. 7½	28.6	30. 0	28. 0	43.0	20.0

The price-changes recorded in this table are entirely in accord with certain economic changes referred to before. I will briefly touch upon the causes to which they have to be traced. Candles would undoubtedly follow the price of tallow. The rise is proportionate to that in meat and live stock. In fact these had but a moderate rise, entirely due to a somewhat greater demand.

Salt is not much higher than in the earlier period up to 1612. It rises, however, to a moderate extent up to the end of the century. This is explained by the fact that salt was obtained from evaporation by solar heat. Thus primitive were the methods yet. The many inclement seasons, which produced the dearth and high prices of corn, interfered with obtaining salt in sufficient supply. Lime, bricks, tiles, and other building materials show a declining tendency up to the middle of the century. They are considerably below the prices ruling in the

*Average of 1653 to 1692 only.

† In 1694 a tax of 16*s.* the quarter was put on foreign salt and of 8*s.* on English salt. This was increased to 53*s.* 4*d.* on foreign and 26*s.* 8*a.* on English salt. The tax remained in force till 1732. This explains the higher price in the last columns.

earlier centuries covered by this inquiry. They rise to about the average prices of the first column (1400 to 1540) in the second half of the century. The rise in wages, as we shall see, explains this rise. Some doubts are raised that bricks and tiles are as carefully made, the materials as carefully selected in the sixteenth century as in the fourteenth and fifteenth.

Iron shows a downward tendency from prices of the first column, though still very high. But nails are very much lower. They were substantially the same at the end of the seventeenth century as in the middle of the sixteenth. In rope and cordage we observe a rise in the middle and a decline at the end of the century. This, taken in connection with the rise in wages over the period 1540 to 1580 or 1600 would naturally indicate an increasing manufacturing skill and a possibly cheaper supply of the raw material, flax and hemp.

The rise in wages from the time of the Commonwealth is apparent in the following table.

IV.—DAILY AVERAGE RATE OF WAGES PAID FROM THE BEGINNING OF THE SEVENTEENTH TO THE BEGINNING OF THE EIGHTEENTH CENTURY.

	1401 to 1540.	1593 to 1602.	1603 to 1612.	1613 to 1652.	1653 to 1702.	1693 to 1702.
	d.	d.	d.	d.	d.	d.
Carpenter, highest rate	20⅝	12¼	14¼	16¼	24⅞	30
" average	17⅞	12	12	13½	21¼	25¼
Mason, highest	18	13½	14¼	19	27⅔	32⅛
Mason's laborer*	12	12	12	14⅔	20¼	28
Sawyer	18	11	11⅜	16½	19¼	19¼
Tiler or slater	18	12	12	14½	19¼	17
Bricklayer		12¼	13¼	13¼	26	30
Thatcher	15¾					
Thatcher's laborer	10⅜					
Plumber	13¼	15	14	17⅝	29⅝	33¼
Laborer to artisan	12	8	8	9¼	13¼	18¼
Women's ordinary work		4	5	4½	5⅜	4½

* In the first column we have recorded the wages of a mason's laborer; in the subsequent columns the wages denote the average rate paid to masons in general.

What with the higher cost of grain, meat, cheese, and malt, everything necessary to his maintenance, and the lower wages he received, the workingman's condition in the first half of the seventeenth century was deplorable in the extreme. It was never so wretched before nor after. All cereals and food supplies were more than double the price of the 1400 to 1540 period. Wages, however, were by one fourth less than in that period, both computed on the new money basis for this comparison.

It is perhaps more than a mere coincidence that about the time of the overthrow of the royalists by the parliamentary army wages begin to rise. In the second half of the century they stand on an average about one fourth above the rate of our first column, and in the last decade from 20 to 25 per cent. more is paid than has been the average rate for the half century which it closes.

With all this, however, the laborer was by no means able to command as much of the necessaries of life as in the period previous to the debasement of the coinage and the change of the currency. Here again I will quote Thorold Rogers, as to the true condition of labor of that time, corroborated by Macaulay, who draws a still gloomier picture than seems warranted by the rates of wages, so carefully collected by Thorold Rogers.*

"All kinds of labor obtained a rise through the seventeenth century, but the rise was necessary, in order that labor should even live. Wages had been driven down to starvation point, and as far as we know, or shall ever know, the mass of the people acquiesced in its misery, and believed, as it was taught from thousands of pulpits to believe, that their degradation was Providential, and must be borne with resignation. The patriots of the first half of the century and the profligates of the last half were equally indifferent to the misery of the poor, upon whose labors they lived. It is no wonder

---

* Thorold Rogers, *Hist. of Agr. and Prices*, vol. v., 662.

that one of those later patriots, Fletcher of Saltoun, who was a republican for the rich and well-born, but had no interest for the fortunes of the workman, should have suggested, as part of the noble edifice of liberty, that the mass of the people should be doomed to hopeless bondage."

The rise in wages, so necessary to enable the workingman to exist, does not show in the price of the products of manufacturing industries, as we have observed in Table III. and see repeated in the annexed table, which gives the prices of textile fabrics.

V.—PRICES OF TEXTILE FABRICS, FROM THE BEGINNING OF THE SEVENTEENTH TO THE BEGINNING OF THE EIGHTEENTH CENTURY.

	1400 to 1540.	1593 to 1602.	1603 to 1612.	1613 to 1652.	1653 to 1702.	1693 to 1702.
	s. d.	s. d.	s. d.	s. d.	s. d.	s. d.
Ordinary table linen,* doz. yds............	20. 5¼	16. 0	16.11½	18. 5	17. 7	16. 8½
Shirting linen, doz. yds.	18. 4½	20. 1½	14. 6	13. 7	14. 4	15. 6
Canvas, " "	13. 6	9. 8¾	8. 8½	9.10½	11. 3	
Sacking, " "	8. 6	8. 0			8. 0	
Cloths, piece of 24 yards.						
1st quality............	176. 1½	147. 4¾	144. 6	219. 3	195. 7	189. 0
2d "	144. 0	114. 0	130. 8	134. 2	126. 6	120. 0
3d "	102. 3	46.10	48. 4	61.10¼	68. 1½	51. 4
Imported cloths.						
Best cloth per yard....		11. 5	16. 7	25. 8	19. 0	19. 0
Velvet per yard........		20. 8	23. 1½	22. 4	26. 8	30. 0
Scarlet cloth per yard..			45. 0			

* There are two qualities quoted in this period (1593 to 1702), second best and ordinary. Considering the progress made in this century in manufacturing industries I adopt for comparison with mediæval prices the lower price column of Thorold Rogers' tables. I am sure the mediæval linens of home manufacture do not lose in the comparison. The finer qualities were imported then, and largely so yet, in the century here in review, mainly from Holland and the Rhine country.

The rate of pay in textiles is by the piece, or the yard, in weaving; by the pound in spinning. The yarn is bought by some, by others made at home in the winter time, and given to the village weaver. The same was the case in Germany within my own recollection and may be found so still, to some extent. The home-spun linens sold at the fairs and found in the shops in Germany give unmistakable evidence of this. Being a by-industry, wages and piece rates remain stationary long after prices in all other directions have gone up. Large quantities of goods are produced in this manner and become collectively a great staple product of trade. The chief processes wherein superior skill is displayed are the bleaching of linen, dyeing and finishing of woollens, and getting them ready for the market. The greater dexterity brought over from Flanders in the earlier period and by the Huguenots in the later period and the low rate of pay in the spinning and weaving, mainly yet cottage industries, undoubtedly explain the otherwise strange fact that prices of domestic textile fabrics are rather lower than higher at the end than at the beginning of the century.

I have included imported cloths and velvets in this table, more with a view of pointing out their high prices as compared to present prices, than their prices at the different periods of the seventeenth century.

In English textiles the width and quality are much better known. Hence, a comparison is more trustworthy. So far as quality is concerned, the tendency is in favor of the later products of the English loom.* Certainly the price

---

* "In so little credit was the fine English cloth even at home, that the king [James I.] was obliged to seek expedients by which he might engage the people of fashion to wear it. The manufacture of fine linen was totally unknown in the kingdom."—Hume, *History of England*.

revolution has so far shown a strange perverseness in producing the contrary effect in almost every instance where rising prices could be attributed to changed money relations. In domestic industrial products, prices certainly do not respond. In produce imported from the tropics, it might be expected that the prices should rise in conformity with the doctrine that the increasing supply of money or money stocks raises prices proportionately, etc. But even this hope is disappointed, as will be seen from the following table.

VI.—PRICES OF FOREIGN PRODUCE, FROM THE BEGINNING OF THE SEVENTEENTH TO THE BEGINNING OF THE EIGHTEENTH CENTURY.

	1400 to 1540.	1593 to 1602.	1603 to 1612.	1613 to 1652.	1653 to 1702.	1693 to 1702.
	s. d.	s. d.	s. d.	s. d.	s. d.	s. d.
Sugar, doz. pds.	36.	19. 1¼	20. 3¼	19. 6	11. 4¼	12. 9½
Pepper, " "	51. 3	46. 5	28. 2½	24. 8	22. 7	17. 8
Saffron, " "	35.10½					
Cloves, pound	12.11¼	8.	6. 1½	9.	7.11	8. 2¼
Cinnamon, "	10.	5.	4.11	5. 1	6. 9	6. 2
Ginger, "	6.	2. 9	1. 5	1. 5¼	0. 9¾	0. 7½
Almonds, cwt.	80.11¼					
Raisins, doz. pds.	5. 3¾	4.10½	4. 1¼	5. 1	5.	4. 3¾
Currants, " "	12. 2¼	5. 9¾	5.11½	5.10	6. 1½	5. 4
Rice, " "	5. 9	6. 0¼	6. 0¾	5. 0	3. 4½	3. 3
Prunes, " "		3. 7	2. 7¼	2. 6	3. 0½	4. 0

Sugar commanded excessive prices in the middle ages and was away out of reach of the common people. Even kings and princes used it very sparingly. Duke William of Saxony, in the middle of the fifteenth century, stands recorded as paying 1 thaler and 8 groschen for one pound of sugar (about $1 of our money reckoned in the value of silver of that time). In England it seems to have been dearer yet, the country being farther removed from the sources of supply, of which Egypt was the chief. In 1440 to 1450 the average price was 24 shillings for a dozen pounds, which calculated in the present coins is equal to 6 shillings.* In the first half of the seventeenth century it was still high, though only one fourth of the above mentioned price, *i. e.*, about 1 shilling 7 pence to 1 shilling 8 pence a pound. But in the second half of the century a great decline takes place. It is but about 1 shilling a pound. New sources of supply, Brazil and the British plantations, begin to make the onslaught on prices which in our days culminates in making sugar nearly as low in price as wheaten flour or bread, pound for pound.

In spices we see the same reversion, due to similar causes, and therefore unnecessary to be given in detail. Prices were kept up for a long time yet by the big profits of traders, and only began to fall when the great monopolies were broken into by new competitors for the trading advantages with the South and the East.

Of this, however, I shall speak more fully in a later chapter.

---

* In the coinage value of silver of the end of the seventeenth century the equivalent would be over 8*s.*, and in to-day's coinage value nearly 9*s.* the pound.

CHAPTER VIII.

The History of Prices in the Eighteenth and Nineteenth Centuries.

It is held by authors of repute that the additions to the money supplies of the world and to the trade of England in particular showed its full effect on prices by 1660. I have pointed out elsewhere that the commercial history of England does not show a road by which the influx of the precious metals could have come into the country. No channel exists outside of commerce, except the British silver mines, by which an increased supply can be obtained. The British mines certainly are not on record for having supplied the invigorating stream. The foreign commerce helps us as little as the mines to account for the reputed wealth, of which there is no record even found in money statistics, or in the amount of the recoinage of 1696, which can be considered adequate. The commerce of England in 1573 shows: imports, £1,650,000; exports, £1,880,000; in 1614, imports, £2,141,000; exports, £2,091,000; certainly not a rapid rise, and in 1687, the last year of James II., and the year before the advent of William and Mary, the imports had grown only to £4,200,000, and the exports to £4,087,000, barely a doubling of the trade figures in the eighty years of the Stuart dynasty and of the energetic rule of the Lord Protector. Truly the stimulus given by Cromwell to a vigorous outer policy was strong enough to have produced a great rising tide in foreign commerce. Though gaining rapidly, undoubtedly, since that time, it cannot be said that the gain was of such a nature as to account for the imputed inflation of prices. However, excepting agricultural products, in which the rise of prices is entirely traceable to natural causes, as explained, no rise of prices is apparent. But even were the facts as stated, that the New World supplies of silver showed their full effect on prices in about 1660, it would be a strange incident in social or physical dynamics if the effect diminished with the growth of the propulsive power.

Surely, things soon began to change. England's commerce grew rapidly in the succeeding century. In 1714, at the time of the death of Anne, the imports were £6,850,000; the exports, £8,000,000. Fifty years later, on the accession of George III., the imports were £10,292,000; the exports, £16,039,000. Another forty years elapse, and at the end of the eighteenth century the imports had grown to £31,420,000; the exports to £36,930,000.

Money, certainly, had become plentiful, compared to the narrow supply of a hundred and forty years before. The guinea had long ago superseded the *louis d'or* as the key to the cabinets of Europe. Frederic had much of the three prerequisites (money, money and once again money!!) which he declared essential to a successful conduct of war, supplied by England. Her fiscal conditions, quite primitive under the Stuarts, soon expanded to more ambitious dimensions under the direction of William III. In 1684, " fourteen hundred thousand pounds had defrayed the whole annual charge of government. More than four times that sum was now required "* (1692). England seems to have borne this heavier rating with ease, judging

---

* Macaulay's *History of England*, ch. xix.

from her generally more prosperous condition. Tradesmen and people in general showed savings and looked for investments. It was still a difficult matter, outside of mortgages on land, to find a place where to put money safely at interest. Banking even was an innovation.

> "In the reign of William old men were still living who could remember the days when there was not a single banking house in the City of London. So late as the time of the Restoration every trader had his own strong box in his own house, and when an acceptance was presented to him, told down the crowns and Caroluses on his own counter. But the increase of wealth had produced its natural effect, the subdivision of labor. Before the end of the reign of Charles the Second, a new mode of paying and receiving money had come into fashion among the merchants of the capital. A class of agents arose whose custom it was to keep the cash of the commercial houses. This new branch of business naturally fell into the hands of the goldsmiths, who were accustomed to largely traffic in the precious metals, and who had vaults in which great masses of bullion could lie secure from fire and from robbers. It was at the shops of the goldsmiths of Lombard Street that all the payments in coin were made."*

On these deposits the goldsmiths issued notes, which circulated unquestioned as money. "A goldsmith's note might be transferred ten times in a morning; and thus a hundred guineas locked in his safe close to the Exchange did what would formerly have required a thousand guineas, dispersed through many tills, some on Ludgate Hill, some in Austin Friars, and some in Tower Street."†

The treasures of plate and of coin, the only expression of movable wealth of the past period, hidden away and closely guarded from the public in dark corners, underground, and in strong boxes, now became integral parts of the money circulation of the country. The addition to the money supply thus given from hoards, now unlocked, was of a very substantial nature.

---

* Macaulay's *History of England*, ch. xx. † *Ibid.*

The additions from the mines to the general supply of the precious metals of the world were also more copious in the eighteenth century than in the seventeenth century. Gold especially became more abundant, and helped greatly in expanding foreign commerce.

Expressed in kilos the finds were in annual averages of twenty year periods:

Seventeenth Century.	Gold.	Silver.	Eighteenth Century.	Gold.	Silver.
1601–20	8,520	422,900	1701–20	12,820	355,600
1621–40	8,300	393,600	1721–40	19,680	431,200
1641–60	8,770	366,300	1741–60	24,610	533,145
1661–80	9,260	337,000	1761–80	20,705	652,740
1681–1700	10,765	341,900	1781–1800	17,790	879,060
Average for century	9,123	372,340	Average	19,121	570,349

The average output of gold was more than double, the output of silver more than 50 per cent. in excess of the seventeenth century, when the great price revolution is said to have occurred.

The causes for a rise of prices on the money hypothesis, wanting in the seventeenth century certainly, were very ample in the beginning of the eighteenth, and continued to increase with its progress. The causes alluded to in a previous chapter, operating on prices in Italy and Germany at the time of their entering into their state of commercial pre-eminence, were now fully developed. England now became one of the Great-Powers, soon to be undisputed mistress of the seas. If anything had been wanting to give sanction to her claim, the rapid growth of the public debt would have easily silenced the scoffer. William III. in 1688 found a debt of £664,264, which at the time of his death had grown to £12,750,000. The interest charge, about which the Stuarts troubled themselves as little as about the repayment of the capital, had grown to £1,200,000, a sum equal to nearly the entire cost of the government barely twenty years before. At the time of the death of Anne in 1714, the debt, through the participation in the wars of the Spanish Succession, stood at £37,000,000; in 1727 it was £52,500,000. Yet the growing burden was borne with comparative ease by the people. The moneys for the great armaments were raised with seemingly greater facility than a twentieth or even a fiftieth part a hundred years before. The nation had fully entered into a state of money economy, and an abundance of money supply and flexibility of commercial conditions had supervened, of which the times previous to 1650 had had no conception.

If ever, therefore, there was a time propitious for a great rise in prices, the first half of the eighteenth century was.

But, as we shall see, the very reverse happened. The only prices that had shown any formidable rise in the previous century were wheat and other cereals and live stock. It is also upon the extraordinary rise in these products that the argument of the money supply was advanced. To the present day a rise or a fall in wheat prices is made the subject of an inquiry by governments, with a view of proving or disproving the altered money supplies as a cause. In the decade of the eighteenth century following the period covered by Thorold Rogers' examinations, prices ruled very high. A number of very dear years, due to poor harvests, occurred. The average from 1704 to 1714 stood at 42s. 9¾d., which is nearly the same as the average of prices that we have noted down for 1613 to 1652, and something over 2s. above the average for 1653 to 1702. The years 1709 and 1710 show an average of 69s.

Tooke, quoting from Evelyn's *Diary*, says:

"1708.—A hard frost which brought on a prodigious scarcity of provisions, more in France than in England. * In general the summer was cold and wet.

"1709.—The queen, in her speech to parliament, complains of corn being exported at such high prices as distressed the poor. Exportation prohibited for one year. There fell this year rain to the depth of 26¼ inches. I think the mean depth of rain falling in England is 19¼ inches.

"1710.—Exportation prohibited for one year."

Price of wheat at Lady-day 81s. 9d. It is unnecessary to seek further for an explanation of the high average price. The decade 1715–24 gives an average of 35s. 4d., a price equal to that of 1603–10; and 1730–39 averages 31s. 3d.; 1740–49 averages 31s. 4d., which is less than the average for 1593–1610; the decade 1742–51 shows only 27s. 6d.; and for 1755–64 an average of 37s. 0d. is the price for the decade.

The years 1742 to 1756 were especially favored with low prices. "In some of those years there was a large export, a great want of corn being experienced in the south of Europe in that interval, and the prices at home were not raised very materially." †

Sir Frederic Eden quotes the January prices of grain at Mark Lane for 1742 to 1756 inclusive, which average as follows:

Wheat.......................... 24s. 4d. to 27s. 8d.
Barley.......................... 13s. 9d. " 16s. 3d.
Oats............................ 11s. 3d. " 13s. 5d.

---

* This we shall see corroborated in the following chapter, devoted to the price-history of France.

† Thomas Tooke, *History of Prices and the State of the Circulation*, vol. i., p. 46.

The average price for this period is 53s. 4d., the three quarters of the three cereals. For the period of 1261 to 1350 the same three quarters averaged 36s. 6½d. ; for 1351 to 1400 they averaged 38s. 4d. ; for 1401 to 1540 they averaged 35s. 8d. (all counted in the Elizabethan coinage). This is but one third below the price of the period 1742 to 1756. But we must not forget that the silver value of the time covered by this 280 years period was, roundly speaking, about forty per cent. higher than in the middle of the eighteenth century. Bringing the prices up to this ratio, they stand 51s. as the average for the period 1261 to 1540; and 53s. 4d. for this fifteen years period of the eighteenth century.

The improvements in agriculture were more varied and thorough all through the eighteenth century than in any other period, and this doubtless has much to do with the cheapness of prices in the period closing with 1765. Though the population of England and Wales had grown from 5,500,000 in 1672 to 7,020,000 in 1754, there was a large balance for export. The balance of exports over imports for the ten years 1742-51 amounted to 8,869,190 quarters in all grains, which is equal to about 7,000,000 bushels per annum.

"There was scarcely a nobleman or country gentleman who did not betake himself to the cultivation of lands, not merely in the sense of keeping a home farm in his hands, which he managed by his steward, but as an overseer of his land, and as an experimenter in husbandry. Writers of the time wrote that country gentlemen talked about land and its properties, the benefit of certain courses, the advantage of turnip fallows, and the economies of agricultural machinery, about breeds of cattle, sheep, and pigs, with the same interest which their fathers and grandfathers used to exhibit on the subjects of the stable and kennel only." *

---

* Thorold Rogers, *Six Centuries of Work and Wages*, p. 470.

Arthur Young, writing in 1772, says:

"There have been more experiments, more discoveries, and more general good sense displayed within these ten years in agricultural pursuits than in a hundred preceding ones, and if this noble spirit continues we shall soon see husbandry in perfection and built upon as just and philosophic principles as the art of medicine."

Thorold Rogers speaking of the great improvements that were made from 1720 to 1760, says that they were due to the eagerness with which landlords strove to improve their estates. This was no mere caprice.

"The truth is, the gains of commerce in the first half of the eighteenth century were very large. In 1750, it is probable that the city of London had a larger commercial income than the rents of the whole House of Lords and the episcopal bench. Their savings supplied the elder Pitt with his enormous loans, the £75,000,000 which he borrowed through his administration, while the whole rental of England, twelve years after the Peace of Paris, was not more than £16,000,000, and the interest on the whole debt was almost one third of the rental." *

But along with the impetus given to agriculture by capital and intelligence turning to the land, at all times the most grateful recipient of their favors, the seasons were favorable in an extraordinary degree.

But, whatever the causes, the effects on the fortunes of the poor were most satisfactory. Wages were somewhat higher than in the last decade of the seventeenth century, after the advance mentioned in the preceding chapter, and more than double the average rate of the first half of that century. The price of corn and bread was about one third below the average of the seventeenth century.

Here the tides change. The seasons become inclement. Not alone in England but on the continent, from Ger-

---

* Thorold Rogers, *Work and Wages*, p. 473.

many and from France, we see reports of failure of crops, scarcity and high prices.

The average price of wheat for the twenty-seven years, 1767 to 1793, was 49s. 5d. a quarter. The whole period shows only one year with the price below 40s., while about one half of the time the price was above 50s. That this sudden turning in price cannot be attributed to any but natural causes, is so evident that an explanation would seem a waste of words.

The enclosures during the century amounted to 3,000,000 acres. The high prices certainly were an encouragement to cultivation. These, under the improvements alluded to above, would surely have created an abundant supply, sufficient to turn the scale in prices again, had nature been at all a factor in the enterprise, as she was undoubtedly in the preceding part of the century.

With the twenty years of war against the French Republic and Napoleon, which the Tories were able to persuade the English people to regard as in their interest, while in fact it was a war carried on by the masses for the classes and against the masses, things came to a terrible condition indeed.

From 1795 to 1820 the average price of wheat was 86s. 10d., which is two and a half times the average price ruling in the fifty years closing with 1765 and fully three and a half times the price of the fifteen years, 1742 to 1756.

In all this distressing time only three years are on record with the yearly average of wheat below 70s. a quarter (60s., 67s. and 69s.), and nine years with the yearly average between 106s. and 128s. The seasons had much to do with this. An example may serve. In January, 1799, the *Gazette* averages for wheat 49s. 6d., barley 29s. 6d., oats 19s. 10d. But the winter of 1799 was extremely rigorous; unfavorable weather continued all through the year, and in June, 1800, the *Gazette* average stands for wheat 134s. 5d., for barley 69s. 1d., and for oats 51s. 1d. The extremest price that I see recorded * is for March, 1801: wheat 156s. 2d., barley 90s. 7d., oats 47s. 2d.

The causes adduced by Tooke in explanation of the high prices of 1799-1801, apply with equal force to the whole war period—" two seasons in succession of extraordinary dearth and taxation,—and impediments arising out of the war to importation of articles which, whether as food or raw materials for our manufactures, were of indispensable necessity." The money movement was rather the other way, more an outflow than an influx. The gold premium, of course, added to the prices of the period. But this is a measurable quantity. Par in 1799, the premium slowly rose to 15 per cent. in 1809, and reached the highest point of about 36 per cent. in February, 1814, which it held for a very brief period only. In 1816 the premium had nearly disappeared.

Wages had been pretty uniformly maintained on the level gained at the end of the seventeenth century. Through the period of low prices referred to above, a rising tendency even is observed. During the harrowing years of dearth and war the rise was small where it did occur. Arthur Young says, in *Annals of Agriculture*†:

"Various statements were put forth by different classes of artisans, setting forth the inadequateness of the rise of wages, including the most recent advance in 1801. Among other statements was one from the journeymen tailors, by which it appeared that their wages from 1777 to 1795 had been £1 1s. 9d. per week, which at the price of 7¼d. for the quartern loaf would purchase thirty-six loaves; while the utmost advance in wages, which in 1795 was to 25s., and in 1801 to 27s. per week, would purchase only eighteen loaves and a half in the latter year."

---

* Tooke, vol. i. † Tooke, vol. i., pp. 226 and 227.

Other statements to the same effect. Factory operatives fared worse still. The distress amongst them was extreme.

By the Greenwich Hospital table the wages of carpenters, bricklayers, masons, and plumbers appear to have experienced little advance. The rate per day is in

	1730–60.	1765–80.	1780–90.	1800.
For Carpenters	2s. 6d.	2s. 6d.	2s. 6d.	3s. 2d.
" Bricklayers	2s. 6d.	2s. 4d.	2s. 4d.	3s. 0d.
" Masons	2s. 7d.	2s. 9d.	2s. 10d.	2s. 10d.
" Plumbers	3s. 0d.*	3s. 0d.	3s. 3d.	3s. 3d.

It was not before the year 1809 that the wages of artisans and agricultural laborers were nearly double of what they had been in the cheap years; while other labor was by no means so well paid.

Considerable numbers of those employed in manufactures were thrown out of employment, chiefly those which depended upon a demand for export. Many of those who were employed and had an advance in wages were working on short time, and thus lost in one way what they had gained in another.

And all this for the glory achieved in fighting for the preservation of foreign mediæval institutions, whose final and complete overthrow would endanger the privileges of the landed aristocracy at home. Victory in such noble cause is worthily thrown into the balance against all the suffering the English millions endured. They received the same reward in recognition of their heroic self-sacrifice as the people to the south of the North Sea. The latter had their chains fastened again, which the French Revolution had loosened. The English had the

---

* 3s. up to 1740; in 1745 = 3s. 6d.; 1750 to 1760 = 2s. 6d.

corn laws continued up to near the middle of the century. The riots and the Chartists' agitation are but the outward signs of the desperation to which the people were driven by their suffering.

The facts are still in the memories of living men. No one attributed the high prices of corn to an over-supply of the currency, to an appreciation of gold, or a depreciation of silver. Upon the abolition of the corn-laws prices gradually declined. We see the gold fields of California and Australia opened and a golden stream poured over Europe within 30 years equal to the product of the 250 years preceding 1850. But excepting periods of war, failure of crops, and scarcity, prices show a downward tendency. Wheat, 1849–52 is 40s. 11d. a quarter. During the period of the Crimean War (1853 to 1857) the average is 65s. 3d. The average for 1858–1866 is 48s.; for 1867 to 1877 the average is 54s. a quarter. The population is growing, and unless the supply from far-off countries increases, or the means of transportation are multiplied and freights are cheapened, there is no reason why corn should not go to prices ruling before the time the corn-laws were abolished. But now prices turn. Wheat averages about 42s. in the decade closing with 1886. In 1886 the average was 31s., a price which maintained itself down to 1892, and from then it has gradually fallen to a point below any ever again reached since 1591. The average 304 years ago was 18s. 1¼d. The price of wheat in November of 1894 stood at 17s. 9d., and at the time of this writing (March, 1895,) it is quoted at 19s. 10d. This is equal to 4s. 6d. the quarter or 6¾d. the bushel expressed in the shillings and pence and silver ratio of the thirteenth century.

We have previously noted the fact that prices of farm products and of meat in periods of limited communication and of production for home supply, do not rise or fall equally with the more susceptible corn products. At a time when wheat, rye, and oats commanded a uniform and moderately high price in the different parts of Germany, and when railroads had been open for some years, farm produce, garden products, eggs, butter, cheese, and meat were extraordinarily low in comparison with contemporaneous English prices. I remember very distinctly the prices paid in Carlsruhe, the capital of the Grand Duchy of Baden, for market produce. There was always a good deal of haggling over the price with the market-women. Butter was 18 to 19 kreutzers a pound. The kreutzer is exactly two thirds of a cent in American money. This then is equal to 12 cents the pound. At that time (1850) butter in England was worth $11\frac{1}{4}d.$, the price paid at Greenwich Hospital, which is about double the German, inland, price. In Mecklenburg, where things, then, were even more mediæval than in Baden, butter was considerably higher, while other farm produce was on a somewhat lower level yet. I compared notes lately with gentlemen of my acquaintance for verification of certain facts relating to this subject. The explanation is that a good deal of butter was being shipped to England. This extra market raised the price in Mecklenburg, while other produce which had to find consumers at home, in an agricultural country, where most people raised their own supplies, kept within the low-price sphere. Eggs were sold at about 8 cents a dozen. The English price at that time was $82d.$ for 12 dozen, or about 14 cents a dozen. Butcher's meat, ordinary pieces, was about 8 to 9 cents a pound. Cabbages were about 1 cent to $1\frac{1}{2}$ cents a head, and other vegetables in proportion. Cherries, prunes, and other luscious fruit from 2 to 3 kreutzers ($1\frac{1}{3}$ to 2 cents) a pound. All this has changed since the towns have absorbed so much population, trade and commerce have developed, and the distribution of products has become more general.

In England in the eighteenth century, we still observe the range of prices in meats, in eggs, butter, and cheese current in the seventeenth century, even in years when corn was dear. They rise in price in the second half of the nineteenth century, while corn was becoming cheaper, because of the growth of industrial pursuits and the collection of large populations in an increasing number of towns. This made the price of the latter articles dearer, not being so fit for transportation from, and cultivation in, far distant countries and opposite hemispheres as wheat.

Prices of Other Commodities.

The prices of live stock would not give an adequate idea of corresponding value at different periods on account of the changes in weight due to improvement of the breeds. All through the seventeenth century the weight in oxen does not vary much from the average of 588 lbs. of the numerous quotations of Thorold Rogers. The eighteenth century notes improvement, while our own time sees the old weight more than doubled. Sheep and hogs are improved no less than oxen.

The wholesale prices of meat and other animal products give a better illustration of the changes in prices in the two centuries now elapsed.

The prices paid at Greenwich Hospital are quoted by the cwt. Thorold Rogers' prices from King's College, Cambridge, are by the stone of 14 lbs. The prices of the quotations of the *Economist,* and of the *Statistical Society Journal* by the tod of 28 lbs. I shall, therefore, for the accommodation of the reader, reduce all prices to the pound weight.

PRICES OF BEEF FROM THE END OF THE SIXTEENTH CENTURY TO THE PRESENT TIME.

(In Pence and Decimals.)

Beef: * {	1593–1632 2.28d.	1633–42 2.53d.	1642–1702 2.97d.	1693–1702 3.d.	
† {	1740–70 3.d.	1770–90 3.71d.	1800 6.8d.	1800–20 7.73d.	1830 4.6d.	1840–50 6.d.
	1860 7.8d.	1865 6.15d.			
‡ {	1856–65 6d.	1865–70 6.63d	1871–78 7.75d.	1879–85 7d.	
§ {	1887 5.5d.	1888–89 6d.	1891 7.5d.	1892–93 7d.	1894 6.6d.

The rise is not very marked in the seventeenth century after the rise in the first three decades commented on before. The rise in the second part of the century is due to causes explained already. In view of the high prices of corn and the growth of trade and population, the price of meat remains rather low. It does not rise during the first two thirds of the eighteenth century, though by 1770 the population had increased at least by 50 per cent. since the death of Elizabeth. The improvements in agriculture must therefore have kept at an even pace with the rapidly extending town population and the development of manufacturing industries.

That live stock was considerably dearer than in propor-

---

* Quotations by Th. Rogers.
† From Greenwich Hospital.
‡ From the *Journal of the Statistical Society*.
§ From the *Economist*.

tion to the rise in the price of beef, mutton, and pork is corroborating evidence of the well established fact of the improved breed of farm animals and the heavier weight of the carcasses.

The rise in the earlier part of this century, the war period, need not be dwelt upon. The known historical facts are sufficient explanation. We see cheaper prices in the thirties. But from about 1840 a rise in meat prices is noticeable which cannot be attributed to any other cause than the difficulty of supplying the increasing demand of population. The industrial state was rapidly stepping into the place of the feudal, agricultural state, obstinately defending its prerogatives, but fighting its battle for existence on grounds becoming rapidly untenable.*

Even the great supplies thrown into England from the western hemisphere, and the antipodes do not change much in this. The English navvy and collier as well as the factory hand, and the high and well-born county people, disdain the meats of animals that are not killed in the British Isles.

The price facts noted above in reference to beef apply fully to mutton, pork, and all hog produce. They apply equally to butter, cheese, and eggs. For these latter I will also give the quotations, taken from the same sources.

---

* By fighting for the preservation of their privileges the landed proprietors in the nineteenth century prevented, or sought to prevent, the growth of the industrial greatness of their respective countries, which gave a value to their land and its products far in excess of anything previously known. The high prices of animal products maintain themselves even in times when all other values fade away under the increasing supplies brought forth from the development which science gave to agriculture and transportation in the second half of the nineteenth century.

PRICES OF BUTTER AND CHEESE FROM THE BEGINNING OF THE SEVENTEENTH CENTURY TO THE PRESENT TIME.

(Per Pound Weight in Pence and Decimals.)

Butter:
- * 1603–52: 5.10d. | 1653–1702: 6.d. | 1693–1702: 6.85d.
- † 1740–70: 5.33d. | 1770–90: 6.40d. | 1800: 11.33d. | 1800–20: 11.50d. | 1830: 6.50d.
- † 1840–50: 10.65d. | 1860: 12d. | 1865: 11.75d.
- ‡ 1849–52: 9.26d. | 1853–57: 11.7d. | 1858–66: 12d. | 1867–70: 13d. | 1871–77: 13.6d.
- ‡ 1878–85: 12.6d. | 1886: 10.7d.
- § 1888–89: 11.46d. | 1892–93: 11.8d. | 1894: 11.11d.

Cheese:
- * 1603–52: 3.5d. | 1653–1702: 3.62d. | 1693–1702: 4.25d.
- † 1740–70: 3.25d. | 1770–90: 3.80d. | 1800: 6.25d. | 1800–20: 7.33d.
- † 1830: 4d. | 1840–50: 4.75d. | 1850: 8d. | 1860: 8d. | 1865: 7.25d.
- ‡ 1873: 9d. | 1882: 8.7d.
- § 1888–89: 8.95d. | 1892–93: 8.56d. | 1894: 7.6d.

The fact that meats of all kinds, butter, cheese, and even eggs follow alike in the same mutation of prices during the eighteenth and nineteenth centuries, is proof that the causes, which operated, were the same. It could not have been any change in the monetary situation that brought prices in the period of 1820 to 1840 from the high range they held from the outbreak of the French wars to about 1820, back, approximately, to those ruling in the twenty years prior to the wars. Nor can the rise in the forties and the fifties be ascribed to any such cause, as the discoveries of the gold fields could not immediately become effective in fulfilling the mission ascribed to

---

* Quotations by Th. Rogers.   † From Greenwich Hospital.
‡ From the *Journal of the Statistical Society.*   § From the *Economist.*

them. The prices from the fifties on show a remarkable steadiness. They remain undisturbed on the high level they had then attained, all through the changing periods of rise and fall of which the last half century has been so prolific. Neither the appreciation of silver, nor the depreciation of gold in the sixties, nor the depreciation of silver and "appreciation of gold" at the present time, has affected them. A sufficiency of evidence that the cause can be no other than the general demand, keeping abreast with, if not being somewhat ahead of, the supply in the new England succeeding the enactment of the reform bill and the abolition of the corn-laws.

The Prices of Wool.

If we examine the price of wool we find the condition the same as in the preceding century. English wool does not rise.

Arthur Young gives the price of English wool for 1765 as 11s. 4d. per stone, which is $9\frac{3}{4}d.$ the pound; for 1776 as 10s. 0d. per stone, which is $8\frac{1}{2}d.$ the pound. It remains at nearly this range up to the time of the wars with France. A singular uniformity of price during two centuries characterized by unexampled changes in the political and economic fortunes of the nation. The price of English wool becomes very high in the period 1850–60 = 21d. the pound, and from then on gradually declines again till it makes its present, lowest level. The price is 1846–52 = 12d.; 1853–57 = 16d.; 1858–66 = $21\frac{1}{2}d.$; 1867–70 = 18d.; 1871–77 = 20d.; 1878–88 = $12\frac{3}{4}d.$; 1892 = 9d.; 1893 = $10\frac{1}{4}d.$; 1895 = $9\frac{3}{4}d.$

Wool, accordingly, is cheaper to-day in the actual money of our time, than it was 300 years ago, long before any emergency arose by which a rise in price could possibly be attributed to an increasing supply of silver or money circulation. Wool of the present breeds is undoubtedly much superior in quality to the growth of that time.

Fine wools, imported from abroad, Spanish, so-called Leonesa wool, was very high in the last and up to the middle of the present century. The decline in these is really phenomenal.

Arthur Young says in a pamphlet to Parliament:

The Question of Wool Truly Stated: "The pound of wool completely dressed and spun costs in Languedoc about 3 lvs. 5 sous per pound, the small pound of 12 ozs." [This equals 85 cents (42d.), our pound of 16 ozs.] "The wool of Segovia costs 5 lvs. 6 sous the pound of 18 ozs. half washed" (= 92 cents or 46d. the 16 ozs.). "Wool in general, washed, costs in France £2 2s. 3d. the tod of 28 pounds (= 18d. or 36 cents the pound); unwashed, 16s. 11d. (7¼d. or 14½ cents the pound); equal, when washed, £2 10s. 9d. (21¾d. or 43½ cents the pound.)."

This must be a wool of great shrinkage as it takes 3 pounds of greasy wool to make up the price of scoured, according to the statement. The Spanish wool is the wool from which our own merino and the fine wools of Saxony and, now, the South American and Australian fine wools take their origin.

The prices quoted by Tooke from 1782 to 1838 for fine Spanish Leonesa wool are as follows:

Average price for ten-year periods:

1782–91	Leonesa wool	3s. 3¾d.	to	3s. 9d.	per pound.
1792–1801	"	4s. 5d.	"	4s. 7d.	"
1802–1811*	"	6s. 0d.	"	6s. 9d.	"
1812–1815	"	7s. 6d.	"	9s. 0d.	"
1816–1819	"	6s. 0d.	"	7s. 0d.	"
1820–1825†	"	3s. 5d.	"	4s. 7d.	"
1826–1831	"	2s. 4d.	"	3s. 4d.	"
1832–1838	"	2s. 6d.	"	3s. 1d.	"

Here, beginning with 1825, we have reached a considerably lower level than existed in the equally normal

---

* I do not include in this statement the years 1809 and 1810. The prices were abnormally high, ranging from 12s. to 22s. the pound. The prices for the other years do not vary much from the average of the decade.

† A duty of 6d. a pound and from 1825 a duty of 1d. the pound.

and peaceful decade before the outbreak of the French Revolution.

If we continue our price comparison to the present time, we have to take Port Philip merino fleece which takes the place of the fine fleeces from Spain:

1846–55 Port Philip merino average fleece,	1s. 6½d. per pound.
1856–67 " " " "	1s. 11d. "
1868–71 " " " "	1s. 7d. "
1872–75 " " " "	2s. 0d. "
1876–84 " " " "	1s. 8½d. "
1885–90 " " " "	1s. 4d. "

In the greasy wools, Adelaide, River Plate, Cape, and similar grades, the rise and fall has been in the same proportion as in the Port Philip prices. The price of Adelaide greasy wool averaged 7½d. in 1848–52, was worth the same—7½d.—in 1893 and 1894, and is now quoted (March 1, 1895) at 6¼ to 6½d. the pound. Low as present wool prices are, the price is not materially different from that of the years 1848–52, which were also years of price depression.*

---

* Wool prices rise and fall according to supply and demand. Certain kinds coming into more active demand than previously obtained for them, gives them for a time a higher proportionate value than is in strict accordance with the general drift of prices. On the whole, the downward tendency of prices is explained by the steadily increasing supplies from the southern hemisphere.

Thus commencing with 1860 we find the five-yearly average of shipments to Europe and North America to have been as follows (in thousands of bales):

	Australasia.	Cape.	River Plate.	Totals.
1860	186	61	40	293
1860–64	234	70	67	371
1865–69	417	126	194	727
1870–74	568	154	300	1,022
1875–79	790	181	273	1,244
1880–84	997	202	326	1,525
1885–89	1,239	252	384	1,875
1890–94	1,676	300	382	2,358
1894	1,896	256	443	2,595

A seven-fold increase of supply taking place in the thirty years beginning

Changes in the Price of Metals, etc.

When we turn to iron, lead, and copper we find even a more marked tendency to lower prices for reasons readily comprehended. Of course, it will be understood that years of war always bring their impress on metals, and I shall confine myself to marking these periods by asterisks.

PRICES OF IRON AND OTHER METALS IN THE DIFFERENT PERIODS FROM THE CLOSE OF THE SEVENTEENTH CENTURY TO THE PRESENT TIME.

(In English shillings per ton.)

	1693 to 1702.	1784 to 1790.	1791 to 1803.	*1804 to 1819.	*1821 to 1838.	1848 to 1852.	*1853 to 1857.	1858 to 1871.	*1872 to 1874.	1878 to 1886.	1887 to 1889.	1893 to 1894.
English pig iron, per ton.	240	70 to 120	103 to 157	140 to 180	114 to 120	41	70	53	102	49	41	42
Finished iron (in bond), per ton....		268	364	298 to 380	308 to 380	119	179	127	220	120	105	100
Copper, per cwt.......	99	80	93	143	91	87	122	99 *74	92	67 †45	90 to ‡39	42
Lead, per fodder (19½ cwt., about 2200 lbs.)..	169	382	441	623	406	340	472	405	430	292	260	180

with 1865 and a doubling in fifteen years of the large product of 1879, was bound to leave its imprint upon prices.

The average price of all the colonial wools imported into Europe and America is given per bale in the circular of Helmuth Schwartze & Co. for each year from 1860. The quinquennial average price, beginning with 1871, is for

  1871–1875............................. £23 15s. 0d.
  1876–1880............................. £18 12s. 0d.
  1881–1885............................. £16 6s. 0d.
  1886–1890............................. £14 6s. 3d.
  1890–1894............................. £12 7s. 6d.
  1894................................. £11 10s. 0d.

* Average of 1867 to 1871.   † Average of 1885 to 1886.
‡ Copper corner in 1888 and collapse early in 1889.

I have only given the raw materials. The decline in price in manufactured articles is so great that a comparison of prices of two hundred, one hundred, or even fifty years ago with present prices would be most astounding if it could be readily put into figures.

Nails may serve as an example. Worth about 5 pence the pound, bought at the smithy, two hundred years ago, they are sold in America now at not much over the tenth part of that price at wholesale, and even after the late rise they are still but one sixth of that price.

I have shown that the price of English wools to-day is not materially lower than it was two hundred years or one hundred years ago. The price of woollen cloth wrought out of this wool, however, is barely one third of the price at which we left it in our price quotations at the end of the seventeenth century.

Eton College pays 250s. as the average price for the piece of thirty-three yards of better grade cloth served out by the college in the seventeenth century, which is equal to 7s. 6d. the yard. St. John's livery cloth is marked down at different periods of the century at 144s. the dozen yards, *i.e.* 12s. the yard. The best cloth is 37s. 6d. the yard in 1633 to 1642, and 19s. in about 1697. These are undoubtedly of imported varieties.

At this present time an English worsted cloth 56 inches wide and weighing 16 ounces is sold to the trade at 2s. 6d. a yard. This cloth is made of much finer wool than the cheaper quality mentioned above could possibly have been made of, as the present worsteds are made of fine merino wools, which cost in former times greatly more than English wools, as we have seen above.

In linen shirtings, table-cloths, napkins, etc., the same price decline has come about, though flax has not changed very materially from the price of the latter part of the seventeenth century, until about ten years ago. It is quoted at 48s. the cwt. in 1695, and at a somewhat earlier period at 36s. The price from 1782 to 1885, excepting the French war period, has varied between 36s. to 52s. the hundredweight.

The great differences in the price of the manufactured product are all in the parts that are added to the value by the art of the manufacturer.

The chief evidence, however, of the indifference of prices to an increasing supply of money in circulation, is again adducible from prices of foreign, *i.e.* colonial, products.

We have noticed their steady decline in the two centuries previously examined. They have come to an extreme of price so low as to be almost astonishing if measured by the quotations of those remote days.

PRICES OF COLONIAL PRODUCTS IN THE EIGHTEENTH AND NINETEENTH CENTURIES, COMPARED WITH THE PRICES OF THE SEVENTEENTH CENTURY.

	1693 to 1701.	1784 to 1790.	1791 to 1803.	1804 to 1819.	1821 to 1838.	1848 to 1852.	1853 to 1857.	1858 to 1871.	1872 to 1877.	1878 to 1883.	1887 to 1889.	1893 to 1894.
	s.	s.	s.	s.	s.	s.	s.	s.	s.	s.	s.	s.
Sugar, white, cwt......	121		60 to 77	62 to 65	35 to 41	$24\frac{1}{3}$	$30\frac{3}{4}$	$29\frac{1}{2}$	28	25	16	$14\frac{1}{2}$
Cinnamon, per lb.....	$6\frac{1}{3}$	$12\frac{1}{2}$	$7\frac{1}{2}$	$8\frac{1}{2}$*	$7\frac{1}{3}$						$7\frac{1}{2}d.$	$7\frac{7}{8}d.$
Pepper, per lb........	$17\frac{1}{2}d.$	16d.	16d.	11d.	$4\frac{3}{8}d.$	3d.	5d.	4d.	$5\frac{1}{2}d.$	$6\frac{1}{4}d.$	$7\frac{1}{2}d.$	$3\frac{3}{4}d.$
Rice, per cwt.	$36\frac{1}{2}s.$	19s.	24s.	35s.	33s.	$14\frac{1}{2}s.$	$11\frac{1}{4}s.$	$10\frac{1}{2}s.$	$9\frac{1}{2}s.$	$8\frac{1}{2}s.$	$7\frac{5}{8}s.$	$8\frac{1}{4}s.$

* The price of cinnamon averages only 4s. 6d. in the ten years for 1799 to 1808, and rises then very rapidly to 7s. and 8s., and reaches in 1814 as high as 15s. the pound.

The price decline is quite natural, and easy of understanding, when we take into consideration the great economies which have become practicable through the achievements in commerce, trade, and manufactures. Of these and their resulting effects upon prices I shall speak in another place. The object of showing the inadequacy of the money-quantity theory is attained by showing that commodities only supplied through commerce from abroad, and wherein a change in the relations of money to merchandise would soonest show results in keeping with the ruling views on the subject, show the very opposite.

Prices of these commodities are lower in the sixteenth than in the fifteenth century. They are lower in the seventeenth than in the sixteenth; lower in the eighteenth than in the seventeenth; and in the nineteenth century, barring years of war and speculative expansion, the consequence of wars and their effects, have made price records, which are, if not lower in the eighties than in the forties, certainly as low as before the great additions to the money supplies were made by the new discoveries.

Of all the tropical products, coffee alone is higher than it was in the ten or twenty years prior to the years when the effect of the American and Australian gold discoveries is said to have become apparent on prices. This is a clear proof that prices are regulated by causes inherent in the commodity. The greater demand on an article that has become an almost indispensable necessity with the working classes in three great industrial states, America, Germany, and France, is explanation sufficient. In England, tea supplies this place. The price is on the same low level as in the years 1845–52. The expansion of cultivation in Ceylon and British India has added so rapidly supplies to the consumer's increasing demands that the effect is as shown in the figures of my table appended below.

PRICES OF FOREIGN PRODUCE FROM THE LATTER PART OF THE EIGHTEENTH CENTURY TO THE PRESENT TIME.

—	1782 to 1790.	1791 to 1803.	1804 to 1819.	1821 to 1838.	1848 to 1852.	1853 to 1857.	1858 to 1861.	1862 to 1870.	1871 to 1877.	1878 to 1883.	1887 to 1889.	1892 to 1894.
	s.	s.	s.	s.	s.	s.	s.	s.	s.	s.	s.	s.
Coffee, East India, (Ceylon from 1848), per cwt.......	80	112	106	80	51	58	67	74	97	83	86	102
	d.	d.	d.	d.	d.	d.	d.	d.	d.	d.	d.	d.
Cotton, American, per pd.	17½ to 28	16 to 28	14 to 16½	7½ to 8	5¾	$6\frac{3}{16}$	7	16¼	8	6⅛	5¾ to 6¾	4½
	s.	s.	s.	s.	s.	s.	s.	s.	s.	s.	s.	s.
Cochineal, per pd.....	15½	19½	28	*7½	4⅔	4	3⅓	3½	2½	1¾	1⅕	$1\frac{1}{10}$
Indigo, per pd.	5¼	7¼	9	7	4¼	5½	6⅔	7¾	6¾	6¾	3⅝	$3\frac{7}{12}$
Saltpetre, East India (Chili from 1848), per cwt....	53	76	63	26	13	18	13½	14	13½	13	17½	17½
Silk, China Tsatlee, per pd........	24½	20¾	27½	17¾	17½	19¼	21	24	21¾	16	13	14
	d.	d.	d.	d.	d.	d.	d.	d.	d.	d.	d.	d.
Tea, Congou, good average, per pd.	46	41	38	39	13½	15	17½	18½	16½	13½	13½	12

In this table the prices of leading products of southern climates are given, the importation of which into European markets, upon a large scale, are of more recent dates.

* Cochineal price quoted in this column is for 1829 to 1838.

Comparisons with mediæval prices are therefore excluded. They begin with the year 1782 with the price quotations from Tooke and Newmarch to 1838. From that time on the official publications of the Board of Trade, etc., supply the data.

The price record of products which lead in a continuous line from the beginning of England's commercial history to the present day, is complete enough a demonstration of our claim in itself. But it will find further support in the next chapter from the price history of France and Germany.

CHAPTER IX.

Corroboration of the Price History of England in the Price History of France and of Germany.—The History of French Prices Beginning with the Year 1201 A. D.

A WORK of great value for our purpose has just made its appearance. Honored with the " Prix Rossi " by the " Académie des Sciences Morales et Politiques " in 1890 and 1892, and published under the auspices of the government, it comes to us with a guaranty of the authenticity of its contents. The work is an economic history of property, wages, incomes, and prices from the year 1200 to the year 1800.* Mr. Emil Levasseur, in a monograph introductory to Mr. d' Avenel's work, gives additional data down to 1891 by adding valuable tables from a corresponding publication by Mr. Zolla.

We have therefore now a continuous price record of France alongside of the price history of England.

The price record is not as complete as that furnished to us by Thorold Rogers. The prices of grain furnish the chief part of the price history. Mr. Zolla's additional tables for a few other articles, however, are very important corroborations of the intrinsic price theory.

---

* Histoire Économique de la Propriété, des Salaires, des Denrées et de Tous les Prix en Général, depuis l' An 1200 jusqu 'en l' An 1800 ; par le Vicomte G. d'Avenel.

What is of greatest value, and has not found exposition before, is Mr. d'Avenel's history of prices of real property for the same long period. The character of the work produced by Mr. d'Avenel is hardly understood by an English reader, who has never had to deal with anything but his pounds, shillings, and pence. In the middle ages, France was not differently situated than Germany in regard to moneys, as already stated. The difficult character of the question as well as the nature of money dealings in the past is best illustrated in a few words taken from Mr. d'Avenel himself:

> "An endless number of disks of gold, silver, and billon were coined by all sorts of people in all kinds of countries, and these the people had to value in livres, sous, and deniers at their true valuation, by weight and fineness. The barons and prelates who coined money regularly in the thirteenth century numbered eighty. There were consequently eighty coining standards but in reality there were a good many more. Besides this there were quite a number of pieces circulating of much more ancient date. In 1420, at Limoges, pieces coined in 817 with the effigy of Louis le Débonnaire were still common. At the same time coins are met with the names of Charlemagne, Eudes, Pepin of Aquitaine, *i. e.* dating from 752 to 890."

All these moneys of different weights, fineness, and denominations had to be reduced to the money of account, as then existing, the "livre tournois," though this was by no means the only livre or money of account.* The "livre tournois" at first was not coined. It only represented a certain quantity of silver, about 98 grammes, a statement being given that the marc (245 grammes) was worth 2 livres 10 sous. This same "livre tournois" in the later coins came gradually to the low standard of about a twentieth part of the livre of the time of Philip Augustus.

---

* The principal ones met with are the *livre parisis* and in the South the *livre raymondine* (Toulouse) all of different values.

It is evident from this that no money payments were possible, nor are quotations of prices at all intelligible, on any other basis than that of weight. Easy as it may have been for those born and bred to the process of computing all sorts and kinds of moneys into the money of account, to the compilers of a price history writing near the end of the nineteenth century, the work is of almost forbidding severity, though he is aided considerably by the fact that payments were adjusted by weight of silver.*

---

* The investigator finds his labor considerably lightened, as most of the ancient amounts are given in the money "forte," or the money of account, *i. e.* by weight of silver. Mr. d'Avenel says on this subject on page 53, vol. i :

"The monetary changes did not have the consequences which one might suppose at first sight and which a majority of historians attribute to them. This is a strange fact, but the study of prices of commodities proves it abundantly. The current value of money does not obey the ordinances of kings. I was myself very much surprised, I admit, to find almost no trace of the troubles one might suppose to have been caused by this action of prices in regard to money. The transactions between private parties do not seem to have suffered seriously. One stipulates to pay in such and such species not changed, or in ' monnaie forte ;' but *the prices of all things, expressed in livres and sous*, remain the same in the years in which the marc of silver suffers, by royal will, an artificial rise over the years that precede or follow.

"This is the case in 1305 when the marc passes quickly from 3 livres 13 sols to 9 livres ; in 1355, when it jumps from 6 livres 15 sols to 18 livres ; in 1360, when it rises to 24 livres, 53 livres, and to 102 livres ; in 1420, when from 7 livres 5 sols it is raised to 26 livres. Under Philip le Bel, the greater part of sales of rentes and realty are by contract stipulated to be paid in good and full money, of the weight and value of St. Louis. Public opinion persists in treating money as a merchandise, and if the government has issued money that is weakened in tale or weight, the people do not accept it except for its intrinsic value, to which they reduce it in their speech as well as in documents.

"Weighing the coins or valuing them in florins, in *écus*, in this or that standard which has remained intact, are the means usually employed in the markets to escape being cheated."

Hence price quotations do not vary with the spasmodic and violent changes in the currency.

Mr. d'Avenel has computed all prices of the periods traversed, into the franc, *i. e.* 4.50 grammes of silver, and the measures and weights, not much less bewildering than the money varieties, into kilogrammes and hectolitres. If we bear in mind that the kilogramme is 2⅕ lbs., the hectolitre 2⅘ bushels, and the franc 19.3 cents, it is not difficult to compare the prices with English and American quotations already stated.

Mr. d'Avenel is of opinion that the increased money supplies coming from the American mines in the sixteenth century caused the rise in prices in the second half of it. He adduces causes of very great moment in the history of France, which are in themselves sufficient to explain the phenomena of the price variations. But he gives no satisfactory proofs that the money increase causes the change. In French prices we also find only grains affected in that way, while other commodities show no changes or declines. We cannot ascribe these views to any other cause than that fixity of opinion which engrafts itself upon the mind by a tradition of authorities coming down from father to son, and not questioned because of their venerable age.

But I will let the facts speak as brought out by Mr. d'Avenel, supplemented by Mr. Zolla, the latter's statements from the brochure of Mr. Levasseur.

I will first give the very interesting review of the value of agricultural land, and the income from land for the three old provinces of Île de France, Normandie, and Champagne; the general average for France, and of meadow land and vineyards with the returns from all of them.

I.—AVERAGE PRICE PER HECTARE (2.47 STATUTE ACRES) OF AGRICULTURAL LAND, MEADOW LAND AND VINEYARDS, AND OF RETURNS FOR LAND (IN FRANCS).

Period.	Île de France.		Normandie.		Champagne.		Average for France.		Meadow Land.		Vineyards.	
	Price.	Revenue.	Price.	Revenue.	Price.	Revenue.	Price.	Revenue.	Price.	Revenue.	Price.	Revenue.
1200–1225..	190	19	130	13	98	10	135	13.50	428	42	387	38
1226–1250..	288	28	236	13	464	46	232	23.50	354	35	600	60
1251–1275..	250	25	204	20	317	31	206	20.60	790	79	340	34
1276–1300..	360	36	290	29	263	26	261	26	376	37	721	72
1301–1325..	243	24	364	36	226	23	222	22	616	61	636	63
1326–1350..	157	15	128	12	82	8	108	10.8	235	23	463	46
1351–1375.	69	6	180	18	53	5	83	8.3	337	33	140	14
1376–1400..	116	11	110	11	62	6	98	9.8	484	48	420	42
1401–1425..	115	11	86	8	78	7	89	8.9	136	13	376	37
1426–1450..	45	4	23	2	75	7	68	6.8	139	13	218	21
1451–1475..	54	5	53	5	22	2	48	4.8	218	21	127	12
1476–1500..	136	11	48	4	67	5	97	8.1	123	10	228	19
1501–1525..	90	7	96	8	101	8	95	8	268	22	191	16
1526–1550..	244	20	109	9	78	6	132	11	237	19	378	31
1551–1575..	426	30	288	20	192	13	241	17.2	524	37	705	50
1576–1600..	371	23	495	30	389	24	317	19.8	448	38	518	32
1601–1625..	400	20	383	19	313	15	277	14	693	34	600	30
1526–1650..	380	19	295	14	412	20	308	15.4	675	33	580	29
1651–1675..	537	21	520	20	500	20	481	19.2	970	48	860	43
1676–1700..	395	19	340	17	478	23	375	18.7	910	45	750	37
1701–1725..	309	12	329	13	323	13	265	11.4	670	27	575	23
1726–1750..	494	20	461	18	402	16	344	13.7	885	35	1125	45
1751–1775..	630	22	600	21	585	20	545	18	1000	35	1380	50
1776–1800..	1092	38	853	30	784	27	764	26	1244	44	1312	47
1890.......	2400	80	2628	87	1145	38	1600	26	2600	86	2600	115

I cannot enter at any length into the question of the high prices for farm land, in the century beginning with 1225 A.D. That transactions of purchase and sale were more limited than in later periods may be averred with full justice. But still the data, so far as they go, cover the question fully as well, as these are the prices actually paid in all the cases brought out from the records of those hundred years.

The prices are extraordinarily high, considering the limited money supply of the time. Farm and meadow land, roughly speaking, rules nearly the same as the average of the period from the middle of the sixteenth to the middle of the seventeenth century.

The average price for farm land in 1225 to 1325 is 231 francs; for 1550 to 1650 it is 286 francs the hectare. Meadow land is 528 francs in the former and 585 francs in the latter period.

Vineyards approximate even more closely. The average for 1225 to 1325 is 575 francs; for 1550 to 1650 it is 601 francs the hectare.

The rise during the succeeding hundred years (1651 to 1750) is not very formidable either. In the face of the general improvement in agriculture compared to preceding periods it cannot be called perceptible even. The average price for farm land is 368 francs, a rise of 60 per cent. over 1225 to 1325, and a rise of 30 per cent. over 1550 to 1650. For meadow land the average is 859 francs, which is a rise of 60 per cent. over the first and 47 per cent. over the second period named. Vineyards are 827 francs the hectare, and show a rise of 43 per cent. over thirteenth- and 37½ per cent. over sixteenth- to seventeenth-century prices. But even these differences disappear when we measure the prices of the medieval period in the silver ratio of the eighteenth and nineteenth centuries.

The returns to the proprietor are decidedly higher than at present, due to the higher rate of interest. The returns from land are 10 per cent.; in the later period beginning with 1550, they are 8 per cent. and then descend to 7; from 7 they soon go to 5 and 4 at the beginning of the eighteenth century, while at present they are but little over 3 per cent. At the end of the nineteenth century, with the great rise in the price of land in France, the low price of money brings the revenue down to a figure not very far from thirteenth-century rates. The great improvements in the economy of agriculture, yielding much higher net results, must therefore give to the cultivator a by far greater return than he ever had before.

A great fall in landed estates and, of course, in the revenue from land sets in with the decade 1350–1360. The depression extends nigh up to the end of the fifteenth century. The misery to which France was exposed by the outbreak of the Jacqueries, the English invasion, and continuous disturbances expressed in the term of "the Hundred Years' War" would explain very easily a great part of the remarkable price decline. Our author says:

> "If the hectare fell to 48 francs in 1451–1475, it is because France, bleeding and depopulated by the devastations of the Hundred Years' War, suffers the last consequences without having found the time yet for repairing the waste. The plaints addressed by the representatives of the provinces to the States-General at Tours, in 1484, show how persistent the scourge has been."

Slowly recovery is made from the very low tide. The fifty years following, it is stated, show no very marked increase on account of the great many new lands then brought into cultivation.

If later on land values rise to the positions held before the beginning of the English wars, is it not as well to ascribe it to the return of permanent peace and the internal improvement to which France could devote herself after the termination of the destructive wars, as to the discovery of silver in America, but little of which found its way into France at that time? With the period of 1675 to 1725 we find a turn to the worse again. Surely silver mining had suffered no abatement. But glory had to be paid for again. It collected its tribute from the generation that was tilling the soil when le Grand Monarque was gathered to his fathers.

But the peace and the improvements in agriculture which characterized the greater part of the eighteenth century showed their beneficial results in higher prices of land and in lower corn prices.

Before entering into a discussion of them I will give in the following table the prices of corn, of bread, and of meals at inns. These three headings do not necessarily come within the same statement.

They form, however, an important measure of money value when used jointly, while each by itself would perhaps not cover so fully the point at issue, that the prices of commodities move entirely independently of the quantities of money in circulation.

The prices of cereals are very variable,—in the turbulent times through which France has passed, but more so yet between the different provinces, than would be the case in more settled periods. Towards the end of the sixteenth century the country was ravaged by robber bands to the extent that a writer in 1585 exclaims: "O le misérable temps pour n'oser sortir des villes!" It will, therefore, be more generally just if I abstain from giving prices of the several departments, and only quote the general average grain prices from the tables of Mr. d'Avenel.

II.—AVERAGE PRICES OF WHEAT, RYE, OATS, AND BARLEY;
OF BREAD AND OF MEALS PER PERSON AT INNS.

Period.	Wheat. Hectolitre.	Rye. Hectolitre.	Oats. Hectolitre.	Barley. Hectolitre.	Bread. Kilogramme.	Meals
	fcs. cs.	fcs. cs.	fcs. cs.	fcs. cs.	fcs. cs.	fcs. cs.
1200–1225.	3.80	1.90	1.53	1.30		
1226–1250.	4.12	3.76	1.35	1.60		
1251–1275.	5.80	5.00	1.28	1.93		
1276–1300.	6.41	6.11	1.32	3.49		
1301–1325.	8.66	6.00	2.30	4.00	0.20	
1326–1350.	6.70	5.00	3.00	4.00		
1351–1375.	9.00	5.00	2.66	3.30	0.26	
1376–1400.	4.66	2.80	2.00	2.00		0.70
1401–1425.	7.20	3.50	1.90	3.00	0.17	0.65
1426–1450.	6.70	4.60	2.35	3.15		0.80
1451–1475.	3.25	2.30	1.05	1.55	0.08	
1476–1500.	4.00	3.00	2.00	1.62		0.45
1501–1525.	4.00	3.30	1.60	2.85	0.07	0.55
1526–1550.	7.00	4.00	2.40	3.70		0.90
1551–1575.	12.00	9.00	4.25	6.00	0.16	0.70
1576–1600.	20.00	15.70	6.00	8.75	0.31	1.20
1601–1625.	14.25	10.00	3.75	4.60	0.27	0.52
1626–1650.	19.00	13.00	5.40	9.00	0.26	0.69
1651–1675.	16.00	8.00	4.50	5.70	0.23	0.68
1676–1700.	13.50	9.00	3.50	6.50	0.23	1.06
1701–1725.	14.80	9.00	4.00	8.70	0.29	0.93
1726–1750.	11.00	6.70	3.00	4.80	0.18	0.61
1751–1775.	13.25	10.50	4.40	7.34	0.20	0.56
1776–1800.	15.00	10.50	6.90	7.60	0.16	1.28

Considering the many vicissitudes France had to go through from the beginning of the thirteenth century to the second half of the sixteenth, the prices of grain show comparative evenness in these averages.

At the middle of the sixteenth century a great change springs into prominence. Prices are about double the average for the preceding three hundred years. The next period shows a still further increase. Here we note the highest range in the six hundred years, the subject of the researches of Mr. d'Avenel. The next quarter of a century shows much lower prices again, succeeded by a range nearly as high as in the previous quarter, and then constantly declining prices, till the lowest price level is reached in 1725-50. The average here for all the four grains is barely 50 per cent. higher than for 1525-1550. We have here a price condition corresponding with that of England. The rise in prices in France begins at a somewhat earlier period than in England. The abatement from the high-price range in the seventeenth century antedates the English abatement by about the same length of time.

France, no more than England, could possibly avail itself of the treasures from the New World when they actually began to make their appearance in the circulations of the trading communities of Europe. There was no trade or commerce which could bring them over the border. A hundred and fifty years after this epoch, in 1715, the foreign commerce of France amounted only to 71,000,000 francs in imports, and 105,000,000 francs in exports. How insignificant a figure must the foreign trade have cut under Henri IV. and Louis XIII., when at the end of the glorious reign of Le Roi Soleil the foreign trade was still in so primitive a state as these figures indicate.

The excess of exports over imports did not, however, enrich the treasure chests. The imports show only the legitimate trade. Smuggling was conducted on so great a scale, in spite of the risks and dangers to those who carried it on, that the contraband trade fully absorbed the credit balance shown in the official figures.

From these facts alone, it is natural to infer that the money stores of France could by no possibility have received an augmentation by which the great rise in grain prices could be explained.

I think that I have made this point plain enough to dispense me from offering any further proofs of the inadequacy of the money-quantity theory to explain the price phenomena of the sixteenth and seventeenth centuries.

The Inner State of France in the Seventeenth Century.

Safer grounds remain from which to explain the rise in corn prices. As one of the reasons, we may point out that the town population in France was being increased by the great ravages suffered by the country. This growing town population certainly made a greater demand on the produce of the soil, with agriculture in a most deplorable condition and production decreasing.

The population, according to the careful estimate of Mr. Moreau de Jonnés, numbered about twelve millions and a half. Moreau de Jonnés, on the authority of Bodin and Boulanger, two writers of the time, gives the following picture of the state of the country. He says:

"Two facts impress themselves; one is the immense extent of forest and waste lands which cover half of France; and the other the great extent of arable land, at least four times the land actually under seed. Of the three hectares and a half to each inhabitant, only a fifth part bears crops. Double fallows, it must be admitted, gave to the land two years to rest, and made it possible to dispense with all manure, and reduced the cost of production to half the cost at the present time. When the year was good, grains were at a price which ruined the agriculturist and determined him to lower the acreage under seed, which resulted in dearth the following year."*

The twelve years from 1589 to 1600, according to Moreau de Jonnés and Mr. d'Avenel, vary as follows in

---

* Moreau de Jonnés, *État Économique et Social de la France*, 1867.

the price of the hectolitre of wheat: 1589, 12 francs; 1590, 16; 1591, 55; 1592, 26; 1593, 16; and 1594, 44. Mr. d'Avenal gives us for 1597, 27; for 1599, 12; for 1600, 8.35 francs.

The next period shows much lower prices, beginning in 1601 with 11 francs; 1602, 12; 1603, 14—the average for the twenty-five years being 14.25 francs. These greatly varying years were all under the same monetary influences, but differently affected by the great price-maker, the sun.

The condition of the people was one of extreme misery throughout the seventeenth century. The ruling powers had more important matters to attend to, in the first half of the century at least, than to care for the prosperity of the people and to promote progress in agriculture and industry.

Henri IV. and Sully exerted themselves energetically in this direction to the extent that the weak power of the crown allowed. Sully traced a plan for a general draining of the marshes which still abounded all over France, and began on a large scale the construction of canals and roads. But after him and after Olivier de Serres came a complete reaction, and, on the whole, "the seventeenth century occupied itself far less with agriculture than the sixteenth." *

The turbulent times, the wars of the Fronde, and the many insurrections, which were always rudely suppressed by force of arms, made the agricultural situation one of worse character than it would otherwise have been under all the forbidding circumstances already noted. The open country was always subject to pillage and destruction.

---

* Dareste de la Chavanne, *Histoire des Classes Agricoles en France.*

The disbanded soldiery, as well as the great multitudes of dispossessed burnt, plundered, and murdered without restraint. It required something more than the edicts of Richelieu and Mazarin to enjoin the military forces from pillaging the country districts, as if in the enemy's country, and the publication of instructions to the soldiery to pay for what they took from the poor, unfortunate peasantry. As the money-quantity theory of prices has found its chief support in France from the rise in these grain prices, I may perhaps not be found unnecessarily prolix if I give a few illustrations delineating the political and economic aspect of the country and the condition of agriculture and the agriculturist.

"Crushed under the load of arbitrary taxes of all kinds, tailles, tithes, capitation taxes, twentieths, aides, capitaineries, salt tax, etc., etc., which robbed him of all the fruits of his labor, and the forced road building, which took from him the greater part of his time, the unfortunate inhabitant of the country had to endure in addition the still harder blows of the many civil and foreign wars of the seventeenth and eighteenth centuries with the invasions which came in their train." *

Conditions were of a nature that "they led our poor peasants to kill themselves after cutting the throats of their wives and children, and furnished examples of mothers who, in the delirium of hunger, ate their own children, as happened in France in 1639." †

An eye-witness states that the soldiers were so accustomed to burn down the villages, that around Lons-le-Saulnier he could not anywhere find a roof standing.

"And as if all these accumulated evils were not sufficient, as if Heaven had wished to join itself to all these enemies, against whom the peasant,

---

* G. Saunois de Chevert, *L'Indigence et l'Assistance dans les Campagnes.*
† *Ibid.*

crushed as he was, did not even try to defend himself, famine, hideous famine, was almost permanent, with the full train of calamities which always follow in her tracks."

Dearth and the plague in 1583 to 1587; famine in 1623; of which a writer says:

"It brought contagious diseases and, the plague following it, death carried away no fewer than a million people." *

"In the train of the Swedish invasion under Gustavus Adolphus, with whom Richelieu had signed a treaty of alliance, the plague appeared, commencing Easter, 1630, not to disappear before the spring of 1637. The wolves came to complete the catalogue of calamities, and more than six hundred thousand Lorrainians perished from famine, the plague, the sword, cold, and the teeth of wild beasts. Villages disappeared to the last man, others had but a hundredth part of the inhabitants left, and parish priests were seen harnessed to the plow with their parishioners so as to obtain food for their own support."

The ruling powers were interested in these calamities only so far as they interfered with the collection of their revenues, which, however, were not the less ruthlessly extracted because the exhaustion was so complete. Richelieu and Mazarin were, in regard to the interest they took in the common people, no better than their masters, Louis XIII. and the execrated Anne d'Autriche, the regent up to the time of Louis XIV. reaching his majority.

It was part of the continental statecraft of that time to keep the people in a depressed condition. Richelieu's own words express it as a maxim of state. "The people ought not to enjoy too great a degree of prosperity else they become indolent and inclined to revolt." †

---

* Bonnemère, *Histoire des Paysans.*

† "Il ne faut pas que les hommes aient trop de bien-être, sans quoi ils deviennent indociles et sont disposés à la révolte."

Under Louis XIV., thanks to the wise councillors he collected around him, some progress was made in agriculture as well as in industry. The result shows in the annual average yield in all grains. At the beginning of the seventeenth century it is given by Moreau de Jonnés as 49,000,000 hectolitres. The population at twelve millions and a half gives 3.92 hectolitres per head (inclusive of seed). In 1700 the population had increased to 19,000,000, including the new territorial acquisitions, and the grain production to 93,000,000, which is 4.85 hectolitres per head. The condition of the people was wretched enough still. How miserable they must have been, and how this must have affected grain prices is seen at one glance when we make comparison of this larger product with that of the present time. The average annual product for all grains is a rising one. The ten years' period, 1834–1843, gives 198,980,000 hectolitres; 1876–1885 gives 251,852,000 hectolitres for the same number of departments constituting present France. (From the report of the Minister of Agriculture, *Statistique Agricole de la France*, published in 1887.) The returns for the five years ending with 1893 show an average of 261,000,000 hectolitres.

Taking the population at 38,000,000, we get an average return of 6.87 hectolitres per head. If we add to this (roughly estimated from the value), an average of 25,000,000 hectolitres annually imported, we have a gross of 7.53 hectolitres per head of the population, against 3.92 hectolitres at the beginning of the seventeenth century, and 4.85 hectolitres at the beginning of the eighteenth.

But this is not all. The people were then far more dependent on bread for their daily subsistence than at the present time. Potatoes were not introduced until much later, and the consumption of meat was nil with the poorer classes, while now it forms a very important and increasing part of their diet. Mr. Moreau de Jonnés, quoting from the work of Scipion de Grammont *Le Denier Royal*, published in 1620, says that compared with the price of labor a sheep was worth five times as much as in our time (1867).

"It can be seen that mutton, though the least expensive of meats, was an impossible luxury under the reign of Louis XIII., not alone for the peasant, but for the middle classes. The high price of things proves their scarcity; consequently, the animals which furnish meat to the butchers were then in very limited supply." *

From a careful analysis of the statistics of annual production and of the wages earned by a peasant, aided by the labor of his wife, Mr. Moreau de Jonnés finds that under the best of circumstances, *i. e.*, grain not exceeding the average price, a peasant could not have bread enough to feed himself and family for more than ten months in the twelve. John Locke,† travelling in France in 1677, gives figures to the same effect, which contrast very materially with the statements of many of the contemporary writers. They are proved by the researches of Mr. Moreau de Jonnés to be substantially correct as to both the net and the gross product. Vauban's carefully prepared statistical statements are to the same effect. Moreau de Jonnés points out the noteworthy fact that "every third year showed incomparably worse conditions;" because then the price rose one half above its decennial average, and this proved a state of scarcity which occurred fifteen times in seventy-two years. By a much greater

---

* Moreau de Jonnés, *État Économique et Social de la France*.
† J. Locke, *Journal of Travels in France*.

and more terrible fatality the price rose to double the average price ten times during the reign of Louis XIV.

" Hence, during this reign, the memory of which is perpetuated among us by the magnificence of so many monuments, there were twenty-five years of scarcity and famine; and if one considers years of scarcity those in which the annual earnings were inferior to the value of corn necessary to the support of life, there were no fewer than thirty-four, that is to say, almost as many as the years of plenty."

The Burdens of Taxation.

Whatever improvement Louis XIV.'s rule may have introduced to raise the inner conditions of the kingdom over those of the preceding reign, the wars he carried on heaped burdens upon burdens upon the poor, so that the annual exactions for the benefit of the crown trebled in the space of sixty years. Moreau de Jonnés shows the following figures of net revenue and cost of collection for the year 1700:

Tailles	90,000,000
Capitation (Head-tax)	41,000,000
Dixième (Tenth)	50,000,000
Gabelles (Salt-tax)	41,000,000
Domaines	40,000,000
Customs duties	25,000,000
Sundry taxes	50,000,000
Cost of collection	122,000,000
Total francs	487,000,000

These enormous burdens were, however, considerably exceeded by the exactions of the nobility and clergy. The consumption (octroi) and other communal taxes are not included in any of these.

If all these are added to the budget of the state then it

is surprising that the nation could at all exist and propagate itself in view of the limited productive capacity of the soil, as proven above, and which did not exceed a gross total of 1,500,000,000 francs according to the careful investigation and well sifted estimates of Moreau de Jonnés, taken from Vauban and other trustworthy sources.

The worst part of the oppression, however, was in the ruthless manner of collecting the taxes. To read the description reminds us of the barbarous scenes reported to us from the last days of the Roman empire. It sounds almost incredible to our ears to be told by Boisguillebert that "it is nothing uncommon to demolish a house worth 10,000 *écus* to draw from it the lead—twenty or thirty pistoles—which the proprietor owes to the fisc and which he cannot pay." Extreme as this may appear, yet, at most, it is an aggravated case, descriptive of the scourge under which the people were made to suffer the agonies of despair, drove the cultivator from the land and filled the country with beggars and robbers, who under a more enlightened system would have been active creators of the country's wealth and prosperity.

But if the taxes and burdens were increasing and the ability to contribute was declining, the contributors themselves were reduced in numbers by an act of folly so stupendous that an advanced age looks in vain for extenuating terms.

No example in history exists, outside of Spain, of a king's divesting himself of the services of his most intelligent subjects by driving them into neighboring countries. Louis XIV. by his own folly made these able to become formidable competitors of his own suffering and impoverished people. It is said that 1,500,000 of the population of France were expatriated or killed by this glorious ruler because they did not wish to hear mass and preferred to worship their God in their own manner and in their own language. By this act of fanaticism much of the good created by Colbert's intelligent institutions was lost again. From all this it is no wonder that by the time of Vauban France was in a condition which impelled him to the following words:

"The populations are impoverished by the excess of taxes to the privation of the nutriments necessary to sustain life. Numbers, thrown into despair, desert their country or perish from want. These evils exist at the time I write this, and are even constantly increasing. They are much greater than is usually supposed, and may lead to most disastrous consequences for the body politic. They are of a gangrenous nature, and corrupt by degrees all the parts of the body till they reach the heart. This comparison ought to be well considered. It gives room to deep reflections.

"The highways and byways are filled with beggars driven from home by hunger and the loss of all they possess. They are the tenth part of the population, and it is out of the power of half of the rest to give them alms, because it is reduced to nearly the same condition."

In another place of the same memoir, *Projet d'une Dime Royale*, he adds in illustration of the onerous system of taxation then existing:

"Things are reduced to such a state that he who could avail himself of his ability to exercise the art or trade in which he is skilled and which would put him and his family in condition to live a little more at his ease, prefers to do nothing; and he who could keep a cow or two and some sheep, with which he could improve his lands, is obliged to deprive himself of them, so as not to be crushed by the taille the following year, which he would be sure to be if he made something and his returns were seen to be somewhat more abundant than usual. It is for this reason that he not only lives very poorly, he and his family, goes almost naked and has but the meagrest subsistence, but also lets the little land he has go to destruction, working it by halves only, for fear that, if he made it yield all it is capable of producing by fertilizing and cultivating it, it would be made an occasion for imposing double taxes. It is evident therefore that the first cause of the declining returns of the land is poor cultivation, and that this neglect results from the manner of imposing the taille and of collecting it."

With such a calamitous history of the land and its cultivators from the latter part of the sixteenth century down to the end of the reign of Louis XIV., the price history of grains, the chief product of agriculture, for that long period is easily explained, without recourse to stilted and far-fetched theories.

Vauban's enlightened views to which he gave utterance in the memorable work in which he recommended the abolition of all taxes save the single tax, "la dime royale," on all products and on all incomes, brought upon him the bitter persecution of the court. His work was condemned, and he himself died from chagrin and despair, while concealing himself from the searching pursuit of the powerful enemies his free utterances had made. His ideas, however, lived and bore fruit in the more enlightened treatment of agriculture and the general improvement of the internal conditions of the country.

Fortunate seasons aided in bringing about better and better results in the years of the seventeenth century succeeding the death of Louis XIV., results shown in the prices of grain.

The general average for the period of 1726–1750 in the table is

For wheat, fcs. 11.00 ; for rye, fcs. 6.70 ;
" oats, " 3.00 ; and for barley, fcs. 4.80.

This makes an average of fcs. 6.38 a hectolitre for the four grains; a considerably lower price than the average for the four grains for the period 1551–1575, which is fcs.

7.81 a hectolitre. The cheapest years in the prices recorded by Mr. d'Avenel are the ten years 1727–1736. They show a much lower range:

> Wheat, fcs. 8.40; rye, fcs. 3.78;
> Oats, " 2.72; barley, fcs. 3.46.

an average of only fcs. 4.59 for the four grains. This is as low as the average for the long period of two hundred years, 1250–to 1450, and for the twenty-five years, 1526 to 1550, the period still belonging to the time preceding the opening of the Peruvian and Mexican mines.

If we express the price average of the long period, 1250 to 1550, in the lower silver value of the eighteenth century the price difference is decidedly in favor of the time of 1727 to 1736. The average price for the four grains per hectolitre, counted in the ratio of 1 : 15 against 1 : 11 (as the general average for the 300 years), is 5.12 francs, while the average for 1727 to 1736 is but 4.59 francs. (Expressed in American measure and money this is 34.74 cents as the medieval price, and 31.27 cents as the price of the eighteenth-century period of lowest prices.)

What lends peculiar interest to the comparison of the seventeenth-century and eighteenth-century grain prices, upon which alone the assumption can be based of the decline in the purchasing power of money, due to the increase in the money stocks, is the fact that the gold and silver production of the eighteenth century exceeded very largely that of the seventeenth century.*

But this is not all. Aside of the fact that the effect of the imputed cause exhausted itself at the start in grain

---

* See tables in Chapter II. and table of Chapter VIII., page 151.

prices, remains the important consideration that it has no force left to make even passing impression on prices of other commodities, nor on labor either, as we shall see. Bread even, which in general follows the price of grain, shows a greater uniformity throughout the six centuries, down to recent years, if we except the low range from 1451 to 1550, than is noticed in grains.

That wages and other expenses did not follow in the rise with the price of grain, except to a very limited extent, as will be seen further on, undoubtedly accounts in a large measure for the smaller increase in the price of bread than in that of grain.

The prices of meals at taverns show the same remarkable uniformity, if we except three periods of a higher range interspersed with lower prices, *i. e.*, 1576–1600; 1676–1725. The causes for these higher ranges may not be far to seek. The prevailing dearth in the 1576–1600 period might easily explain the one; the depression caused by the wars of Louis XIV., the other. After that the price falls back again to as low a figure as in the cheapest of times.

It is plain that the prices of meals and of commodities for the laborer's subsistence must keep within possible reach of his wages. The commodity may deteriorate in quality, but the price will accommodate itself to his purchasing ability. Bread in the dear years changed quality, as is well known. This, in connection with the other cause stated above, would explain the less violent fluctuation in its price than that of corn. How little wages were affected in France by all the violent economic and political convulsions the country experienced in these six centuries I will show in the following table. The rates are all "without board," except 7, 8, and 9.

III.—GENERAL AVERAGE OF WAGES FROM THE YEAR 1201 A.D. TO THE YEAR 1800.

Periods.	1. Agricultural laborer, per day. Male.	2. Agricultural laborer, per day, Female.	3. Vintner, per day.	4. Mason, per day.	5. Carpenter, per day.	6. Painters and Plasterers, per day,	7. Farm hands, per year.	8. Male domestics, per year.	9. Female servants on farms, per year.	10. Annual income of male help calculated per 250 working days.
	Francs	Francs	Francs	Francs	Francs	Francs	Francs	Francs	Francs	Francs
1201–1225	..	..	..	..	..	..	..	..	..	135.00
1226–1250	0.65	..	..	..	..	..	..	..	..	125.00
1251–1275	0.60	..	..	1.09	..	..	..	..	..	125.00
1276–1300	0.60	..	..	0.95	0.77	1.15	45.00	..	..	147.00
1301–1325	0.67	..	..	0.90	0.92	1.00	47.00	75.00	..	167.00
1326–1350	0.80	0.55	1.04	1.02	1.06	1.10	55.00	..	24.00	200.00
1351–1375	0.90	..	..	1.15	1.17	1.15	80.00	..	..	225.00
1376–1400	0.73	0.55	..	1.04	0.93	1.10	66.00	72.00	37.00	182.00
1401–1425	0.70	0.50	0.75	1.10	1.08	1.13	70.00	50.00	40.00	175.00
1426–1450	0.65	0.46	0.87	1.00	0.99	1.05	75.00	45.00	36.00	162.00
1451–1475	0.60	0.40	0.90	0.87	0.95	1.00	57.00	..	24.00	150.00
1476–1500	0.58	0.32	..	0.80	1.06	0.95	50.00	46.00	28.00	145.00
1501–1525	0.60	0.33	..	0.81	0.82	0.86	51.00	47.00	19.00	150.00
1526–1550	0.70	0.37	0.96	0.98	1.14	0.88	48.00	45.00	30.00	175.00
1551–1575	0.75	0.41	0.86	0.96	1.01	1.00	44.00	40.00	20.00	188.00
1576–1600	0.78	0.43	0.91	1.20	1.19	1.17	60.00	50.00	29.00	195.00
1601–1625	0.76	0.45	0.98	1.00	1.06	1.10	63.00	63.00	42.00	190.00
1626–1650	0.74	0.53	1.25	0.90	1.25	1.15	69.00	66.00	49.00	185.00
1651–1675	0.80	0.55	1.07	1.16	1.00	1.30	80.00	70.00	45.00	200.00
1676–1700	0.80	0.50	0.89	1.03	1.20	..	68.00	54.00	40.00	200.00
1701–1725	0.70	0.37	0.90	0.98	1.00	1.04	71.00	55.00	37.00	175.00
1726–1750	0.68	0.45	0.80	0.94	0.96	0.90	55.00	46.00	30.00	170.00
1751–1775	0.75	0.47	0.86	0.90	0.92	1.12	63.00	50.00	35.00	188.00
1776–1800	0.82	0.50	1.01	1.15	1.20	1.25	80.00	77.00	42.00	205.00
1890......	2.50	1.50	..	3.40	3.70	3.50	350.00	369.00	210 on farm; 300 in house.	750 for 300 days.

The Laborer and his Subsistence.

To give graphic proof that the high prices of grain in the period of about 1560 to 1725 were due solely to the bitter causes illustrated, we need only compare the rate of wages with the prices of corn.

To make this clear, I will draw the average of wages

for the period 1351 to 1550 and the average for 1551 to 1750, and put these averages against the averages for the four grains per hectolitre. This will show us at one glance that the statements of the preceding pages as to the suffering of the working classes were by no means exaggerated.

IV.—STATEMENT OF THE AVERAGE OF DAY WAGES OF THE WORKING CLASSES, COMPRISED IN THE SIX FIRST COLUMNS OF TABLE III., AND OF THE AVERAGE OF FOUR GRAINS PER HECTOLITRE IN THE PERIODS 1351 TO 1550, 1551 TO 1575, AND IN THE PERIODS 1576 TO 1725 AND 1726 TO 1750.

Occupations.	Average Rate for 1351 to 1550.	Average Rate for 1551 to 1575.	Average Rate for 1576 to 1725.	Average Rate for 1726 to 1750.
	Francs.	*Francs.*	*Francs.*	*Francs.*
1. Agricultural laborer, male...	0.68	0.75	0.76	0.68
2. " " female.	0.42	0.41	0.47	0.45
3. Vintner....................	0.87	0.86	1.00	0.80
4. Mason......................	0.97	0.96	1.05	0.94
5. Carpenter..................	1.01	1.01	1.12	0.96
6. Painter and Plasterer.......	1.02	1.00	1.15	0.90
Average of the six occupations..	0.83	0.83	0.92	0.79
Average price of the four grains, per hectolitre..............	3.48	7.80	9.70	6.37
Rise (+) or fall (−) of wages over 1351–1550 period.......	*Per cent.*	*Per cent.*	*Per cent.* +11.0	*Per cent.* −5.0
Rise of price of grains over average 1351–1550.		94.0	178.0	83.0
Purchasing power of six days' wages, in hectolitres, of average of four grains	*Hectolitres.* 1.43	*Hectolitres.* 0.64	*Hectolitres.* 0.57	*Hectolitres.* 0.77

It will be seen from the above how infinitely better the condition of the working classes was in the mediæval period than at any time since the middle of the sixteenth century. At no time, excepting the low-price period of the eighteenth century treated above, was the workingman able to buy with his wages more than half as much grain as he could in the time preceding the discovery of the new silver mines.

The abrupt change dating from 1550, nearly doubling grain prices in the average of the next twenty-five years, and almost trebling them in the long term of one hundred and fifty years from the average for the two hundred years preceding 1550, gave no increase in wages in the first twenty-five years of the great rise at all, and only 11 per cent. of increase after 1575, to offset an increase in grain prices of 178 per cent.

The happy interval in the eighteenth century, referred to above, made conditions supportable again, but the dear years succeeding in the century, dating as in England from about 1765, very soon threw matters back to where they were during the early part of the eighteenth century. Much of what followed in the history of France is explained by these price-facts.*

---

* The portraiture is made more impressive yet if we discard the method of averaging grain prices by regular, set periods of twenty-five, fifty, or one hundred years, and separate the dear years and cheap years in periods implying historical changes, such as I delineated in the preceding pages.

Thus beginning with 1561, and following the tables of Mr. d' Avenel, we have up to the year 1600 but three years with the price of wheat at less than 10 francs—the hectolitre. These are the years 1561, 1564, and 1600 with an average of 8.35 francs. The thirty-eight dear years 1562 to 1599 average the famine price of 19.46 francs.

The forty years' period preceding 1560, *i. e.*, prior to the Huguenot wars, show but six years with grain above 10 francs—the hectolitre, an average of 16.66 francs; while the average for the thirty-four cheap years is but 6.76 francs.

The period of 1601 to 1668 shows not a single year in which the average for wheat was below 10 francs. The average for the whole long period is 17.30 francs.

From 1669 to 1715 we count twelve cheap years giving an average of 8.33 francs and thirty-four years averaging 16.96 francs.

Thus we see that in the one hundred and fifty years dating from the outbreak of the Huguenot wars to the end of the reign of Louis XIV. only

The Prices of other Commodities.

The change in the prices of other commodities is equally illusory and gives no other showing than what we found in English prices in the preceding chapters.

In this class we find the same conditions expressed as in English prices. There is no where any indication that at any time prices were raised by the reputed price revolution. Iron is very irregular and very high in comparison

fifteen years are under the high-price average, and one hundred and thirty-five years of scarcity and famine prices.

The longest succession of dearest years and the highest average, we find in the time of smallest money supply, but in the time characterized more than any other by a long succession of inner disturbances and civil wars.

The period of 1716 to 1765 gives us twenty-four years with an average of 8.07 francs and twenty-six years averaging 12.62 francs, thus showing an average of 10.45 francs for the fifty years as against 8,24 francs for 1520 to 1560. Counted in the ratio of the eighteenth century brings the average of 1520–1560 to 11.23 francs, a somewhat higher range than the average for the fifty years in 1716 to 1765.

We see by this showing that the averaging of prices of fixed-time periods, which I followed in the text from Mr. d'Avenel's procedure, gives by no means so full a demonstration and so impressive a picture of the price situation of the past as this division into periods measured by historical events.

The period 1766 to 1800 has but a single year when the average fell below 10 francs, and shows 15.10 francs as the average for the whole time of the other thirty-four years.

I will add here the statement of prices of wheat divided into historic periods in tabulated form.

STATEMENT OF PRICES OF LOW AND HIGH PRICE YEARS; AND THE NUMBER OF YEARS OF LOW AND HIGH PRICES IN THE NAMED PERIODS:

Period.	Price under 10 Francs per Hectolitre.	Number of Years with Price under 10 Francs.	Price over 10 Francs per Hectolitre.	Number of Years with Price over 10 Francs.
1521–1560	6.76	34	16.66	6
1561–1600	8.35	3	19.46	38
1601–1668	—	—	17.30	68
1669–1715	8.33	12	16.96	34
1716–1765	8.07	24	12.62	26
1766–1800	—	1	15.10	34

with modern prices. It certainly does not show any general tendency to a rise from what may be called the general mediæval average.* Lead is more steady. The average for 1351 to 1550 is 51 centimes; for 1551 to 1750 it is 52 centimes the kilo.

V. PRICES OF METALS, WOOL AND WOOLLEN CLOTH.

Period.	Iron. Kilo.	Lead. Kilo.	Wool— Raw. Kilo.	Woollen Cloth. Per Meter.		
				1st Qual.	2d Qual.	3d Qual.
	Francs.	*Francs.*	*Francs.*	*Francs.*	*Francs.*	*Francs.*
1276–1300........	"	0.40	..	20.58	12.33	5.83
1301–1325........	0.34	0.20	"	32.11	13.27	6.36
1326–1350........	"	0.78	0.91	25.48	13.50	4.58
1351–1375........	0.43	0.67	"	29.18	14.06	3.22
1376–1400........	0.64	0.45	"	37.80	13.63	5.49
1401–1425........	0.78	0.38	"	"	11.82	5.12
1426–1450........	0.75	0.54	"	20.60	10.98	4.19
1451–1475........	0.45	0.34	"	"	10.18	2.62
1476–1500........	0.41	0.64	0.70	"	"	4.14
1501–1525........	0.82	0.61	"	24.61	"	3.65
1526–1550........	0.30	0.46	1.00	"	12.96	4.72
1551–1575........	0.50	0.36	0.90	45.36	10.86	4.64
1576–1600........	0.61	0.52	1.30	20.90	15.96	3.42
1601–1625........	0.61	0.54	"	21.00	8.80	3.20
1626–1650........	0.84	0.54	2.50	42.00	9.20	2.75
1651–1675........	0.32	0.64	1.30	28.00	6.50	2.70
1676–1700........	0.40	0.53	2.80	"	"	"
1701–1725........	0.31	0.53	0.80	25.00	6.00	4.50
1726–1750........	0.47	0.50	1.70	26.00	9.10	2.60
1751–1775........	0.28	0.50	1.10	"	"	2.45
1776–1790........	0.51	0.76	1.90	15.00	6.60	2.80

The manufacture of finer woollen cloths up to the middle of the seventeenth century had no existence at all. The finer cloths were all imported and the home manufacturers

---

* The average for the period 1331 to 1550 is 57 centimes; for 1551 to 1751 it is 51 centimes the kilo, which is equal to 5 cents and 4½ cents respectively the pound. Allowing for the higher silver value for the period the price is equal to 7 cents. At present the best raw-iron is not over a tenth part of that price.

in the coarser makes, had not developed even to a state of efficiency. At the end of the fifteenth century there were but fourteen towns in all France (outside of Rouen, St. Lô and Montivilliers in Normandie) engaged in the manufacture of woollens.* With Colbert, the manufacture of the finer cloths was started in Carcassonne and in Sedan where Spanish wools of the finest quality were employed. The reduction in prices follows as a natural consequence of the industrial progress. The high prices of the preceding period are but natural. But they demonstrate clearly the economic fallacy of the money theories. The wool prices are too sparingly given for the time preceding the middle of the sixteenth century for use in this discussion. The prices vary considerably from one period and another. Wool was never the great staple in France that it was in England, and it would be very bold to draw comparisons from these records, as wool is a very variable quantity so far as quality is concerned. But even if we were to take 1.80 fcs. the kilo as the general average price for the period 1600 to 1800, this would be a low price. It would be equal to 16 cents the pound and below the price of English wools which held about the same price at the end of the eighteenth century it held at the end of the sixteenth ; but was considerably below the fourteenth century prices, not counting even the altered ratio of silver.

Arthur Young, in "The Question of wool truly stated," says :

"That in 1787 unwashed French wool cost 16s. 11d. the tod of 28 pounds = (14½ cents the pound) which is, washed, equal to £2 2s. 6d. (36½ cents the pound)."

The wool of Berry he gives as £3 0s. 0d. to £3 5s. 0d.,

---

* See *Moreau de Jonnés, État Économique*, etc.

"half washed." This is undoubtedly a higher grade and, certainly, far superior to the kinds of wool raised previous to 1550. To these latter the lower-price wools mentioned by Arthur Young can be fitly compared, which would give then an equivalent in French money of about 1.50 fcs. the kilo. (13 cents the pound).

The French price comparisons which we have conducted to this point show the same general points which we found in our English records. The prices vary, but on the whole show no material rise from middle age prices, reduced to money of our time, up to the end of last century, to which period Mr. d'Avenel has led them down. The only great difference is in grain prices. The proportionate rise is nearly the same and covers also the same stretch of time. We shall find the same occurrence in German prices, to which we shall turn presently. But even this difference becomes very much reduced when we remember that mediæval prices, *i. e.*, up to the latter part of the sixteenth century, are given in a much higher value in ratio of silver to gold. Mr. d'Avenel is of opinion that giving prices in silver value in relation to gold would be creating an ideal money standard, that the payments were made in the silver equivalents of the time, and have to be considered as such. This may be correct so far as corresponding comparisons of the time are made. But when we measure values of another period, when these very altered relations of ratio, *i. e.*, the cheapened price of silver, have admittedly caused altered price conditions, this changed value of the paying medium, has necessarily to be considered. I have refrained from applying this change in the ratio to my tables of prices, intending to reserve the statement for the reader to give it the weight which it undoubtedly deserves in the whole record of English and

French prices. In the German grain prices, tabulated in the following pages, I have added two columns, giving the prices of wheat and barley up to 1600 in the coinage value of to-day. The reader can see from that illustration how much nearer to mediæval prices our present prices and even seventeenth century prices come if reckoned in the present coinage value of silver.

It is impossible to give an exact statement as to ratio in the past, varying as it was as to time and place. The statements of contemporaneous writers disagree very materially for the same country even. The average ratio prior to 1500 may be taken around 1 : 11. From after 1501 Soetbeer gives it for Germany, the Netherlands, and France, as follows :

```
1501 to 1520 = 1 : 10.75
1521 to 1540 = 1 : 11.25
1541 to 1560 = 1 : 11.30
1561 to 1580 = 1 : 11.50
1581 to 1600 = 1 : 11.80
1601 to 1620 = 1 : 12.25
1621 to 1640 = 1 : 14
1641 to 1660 = 1 : 14.50
1661 to 1700 = 1 : 15
1800         = 1 : 15.50
```

Prices, if read in the lower silver value, would therefore have to be counted as follows, taking 1800 as "100":

```
1501 to 1520 = 144 ;   1521 to 1540 = 137½
1541 to 1560 = 137 ;   1561 to 1580 = 135
1581 to 1600 = 131 ;   1601 to 1620 = 127
1621 to 1640 = 110 ;   1641 to 1660 = 107
1661 to     = 103 ;   1800         = 100
```

A Page from the History of Prices in Germany.

I have referred in another place to the history of prices and money in Germany and to Mr. Stephan Beissel's investigation of the records covering the building of the

Cathedral of Xanten. This is the only German publication known to me in which a continuous history of prices and moneys at one place is carried to the nineteenth century. Xanten lies on the Rhine, not far from the Dutch frontier. It was part of the archbishopric of Cologne, and had within easy reach a number of sovereignties, all of which minted their own money. It is evident from this that quite a variety of moneys circulated in the town and were handled by the chapter.

The money of account into which all of these had to be translated, their weights and values varying at different epochs, was the mark of Xanten. Of this enough has been said to dispense me from again going over the ground. Mr. Beissel gives us the decennial average prices of wheat and barley from 1350 down to 1838; the wages of a master carpenter and his man from 1350 down to 1680; and the prices of some building materials and metals down to the beginning of this century. These he all gives us in the Mark, Solidus, or Denier of the Chapter. By this he has made it a comparatively easy task for us to read the price history of nearly five centuries of very varied money relations. All we have to do to make the figures intelligible is to apply the change in the value of the coins which the different periods have experienced, a somewhat incomplete statement of which has been supplied in a preceding chapter.

The treatment is not as satisfactory as if the values had been figured in the money of to-day, as was done by Mr. d'Avenel in his *History of French Prices*. We have in Mr. Beissel's statement only general periods for which the relation of the money of the period to the mark of to-day is given. He leaves it somewhat in doubt when the change took effect. But as the prices are quoted in decennial averages, and these decennial average prices agree with the figures of the long periods, it is safe to accept the ratio given for the period which is marked by corresponding prices, but which fails of close identification of money ratio. To leave the least possible room for doubt, I have given only the consecutive figures up to 1550, and left out some of the intervening decades of the later periods on account of certain omissions in the statement of my authority. I shall, however, fill in the prices also to show the general coincidence of the averages with the averages for which I have supplied the values of the moneys.

I.—PRICE OF ONE MALTER (OF XANTEN) (4⅝ BUSHELS) OF WHEAT, AND ONE MALTER OF BARLEY, GIVEN IN THE MARK OF THE CHAPTER; IN THE MARK OF TO-DAY; IN THE EQUIVALENT IN BUSHELS AND IN AMERICAN MONEY; PERIOD 1372 TO 1838.

(Columns 8 and 9 give prices of 1372 to 1600 in the average ratio of the modern period.)

Periods.	Prices in Marks of Chapter.		The two Malters.	Value of Mark of Chapter in Rmks.	Prices of the two Malters in Rmks.	Equal per Bushel in Dollars.		In Ratio of to-day. *i.e.* 11 = 15½	
	Wheat per Malter.	Barley per Malter.				Wheat.	Barley.	Wheat.	Barley.
1361–1400	1 4⁄12	10⁄12	2 2⁄12	7	15 2⁄12	$0.50½	$0.30½	$0.70½	$0.43
1401–1450	2	1 1⁄12	3 1⁄12	6	18 6⁄12	0.61	0.32	0.86	0.45
1451–1480	1 10⁄12	1	2 10⁄12	6	17	0.56	0.30½	0.78	0.43
1481–1520	1 11⁄12	1 7⁄12	3 6⁄12	5¾	18 7⁄12	0.56	0.36	0.78	0.50
1521–1550	2 2⁄12	1 5⁄12	3 7⁄12	5½	20 1⁄12	0.62	0.41	0.85	0.64
1551–1580	5 2⁄12	3 1⁄12	8 3⁄12	4	39 2⁄12	1.05	0.70	1.42	0.95
1581–1600	11 3⁄12	6 7⁄12	17 10⁄12	3	53	1.64	0.91	2.11	1.17
1601–1620	11 2⁄12	6 5⁄12	17 7⁄12	3					
1621–1680	14 7⁄12	8 7⁄12	23 2⁄12	2¼	56 4⁄12	1.72	1.01	1.82	1.09
1681–1720	15 8⁄12	8 5⁄12	25	2					
1721–1750	14	7 7⁄12	21 6⁄12	1½	32 8⁄12	1.04	0.59	1.07	0.61
1751–1780	25 2⁄12	13	38 2⁄12						
1781	26	13 7⁄12	39 7⁄12	⅞	26 8⁄12	0 88	0.48	0.90	0.47
1838	34⅓	16⅔	51		25⅞	0.86	0.43	0.86	0.43

II. WAGES OF A MASTER CARPENTER AND A JOURNEY-MAN SAWYER PER DAY IN DENARS (144*d*. TO THE MARK) TRANSLATED INTO THE RMK. AND PFENNIG OF TO-DAY ACCORDING TO THE RATE IN TABLE I. (1350 A. D. to 1680.)

(Reichsmark 23.80 cts.)

Period.	Wages per diem		Relation of Money as in Table I.	Wages in Rmk. of to-day.		Price per bushel of		Per cent. of rise of the two Grains over price of 1400-50.*	Per cent. of rise of wages over 1400-50.*
	of Master.	of Journeyman.		Master.	Man.	Wheat.	Barley.		
			m	*Rmk. Pf.*	*Rmk. Pf.*				
1360–1399	37	26	7	1.80	1.26	$0.50½	$0.30½		
1400–1450	43	34	6	1.80	1.42	0.61	0.32		
1451–1480	38	25	6	1.58	1.04	0.56	0.30½	− 9	−12
1481–1520	33		5¾	1.32		0.56	0.36	− 9	−27
1521–1550	36	32	5½	1.34	1.24	0.62	0.41	+15	−20
1551–1580	54	53	4	1.49	1.47	1.05	0.70	+70	−11
1591–1620	125	129	3	2.58	2.68	1.70	1.02	+196	+65
1621–1650	189	164	2½	3.27	2.85	1.90	1.10	+220	+90
1650–1680	200	189	2	2.78	2.62	1.52	0.88	+155	+66

In Table I, I have calculated the prices of the two grains, reported by Mr. Beissel in the mark of the chapter, in Reichsmarks and carried this into American money and measure for the convenience of American and English readers. I have also added two columns giving the prices in the new relations of silver to gold, which gives to prices expressed in silver a very different value in the periods previous to the beginning of the seventeenth century from those succeeding the change in ratio. This is only to show the nearer approximation of mediæval prices to the more modern prices, if both are expressed in the inferior silver value of the later time. We find the same rise in grain values in the latter part of the sixteenth

---

* Rise is marked +; Decline is marked −.

century, which we noted in the French price-history, and going all through the seventeenth century as in the price-history of England and France.

It is hardly necessary to dwell upon the history of Germany of the seventeenth century. The Thirty Years' War is perhaps one of the most appalling chapters in the history of human savagery. Since the days of the migrations of nations no such thorough destruction was wrought in any other European country. Not one third of the population of Germany was left when the Westphalian Treaty arrested the destroying hordes to whom friend and foe were equally inviting prey. That tillers were few and prices were high, famine and disease the characteristics of a considerable period after the close of the war, are facts so well established that folk lore is full of reminiscences of them. The horrors of the time are to this day the theme of the fascinating stories which help while away the winter evenings in villages and towns.

But no sooner had the wounds begun to heal than the borders of the Rhine were again made the seat of sanguinary war. The horrors of the wars of Louis XIV. were mainly felt there. Whole sections were laid waste. The atrocities of the Thirty Years' War were re-enacted. It is easy of comprehension from all this that grain prices would show the effect of the conditions which characterize the history of Germany from the latter part of the sixteenth to the second or third decade of the eighteenth century.

With the beginning of more prosperous times after the close of the war of the Spanish succession, we witness also here the appearance of a new price era. Grain prices show now the same lowering tendency which we find in French and English prices. I need not dwell to any extent on this phenomenon here, as I have dealt extensively with the subject when treating of French and English prices. That the three leading countries of Europe all experienced a rise, covering nearly the same period under a sufficiency of natural causes, and that a decline followed when these causes had abated, is abundant refutation of the theory that the quantity of money in circulation causes the rise and fall in prices.

The German prices after the high-price period show a very near approach to the prices of the period closing with the middle of the sixteenth century, the time from which the decadence of Germany begins. But even this is but a repetition of the coincident facts in English and French price-history.

In Table II. the wages show the history of the times in a graphic manner. It is the same sad story told by Thorold Rogers of England, and in the French price-history given above. Wages rise, in round numbers, but 65 per cent. over mediæval rates, while grain prices are about 200 per cent. higher.*

The most highly colored description of the effect of high prices of corn, whatever the cause, on the fate of the working classes, would pale alongside of the eloquence of these figures.

---

* Next to the war the deterioration and debasement of the coinage had much to do with this. I have referred to the state of the debasement of the currencies of Germany in the seventeenth century in preceding pages. Prices advance rapidly under such debasement but wages creep up very slowly and seldom, and then only under very favorable conditions, work up to the standard of altered prices. These favorable conditions, however, were entirely wanting in the seventeenth century in Europe, a century in which all the refining and redeeming features of the Renaissance period became lost and the freedom and independence of the community were submerged in a general sweep of absolutism and oppression.

With the help of these facts the few prices quoted in Table III. will also find an explanation. Destructive wars would necessarily show their effect first on bulky materials as a rule brought from a considerable distance.

III.—PRICES OF CERTAIN BUILDING MATERIALS IN DENARS OF XANTEN AND IN THE MARK OF TO-DAY.

(One mark = 23.80 cents.)

Period.	1000 Bricks or Tiles.		1 Malter Lime.		1 Load of Slate.		1 Pound of Lead.		100 Lath Nails.		1 Pound of Wax.	
	Deniers.	Rmk.	Deniers.	Rmk.	Deniers.	Rmk.	Deniers.	Rmk.	Deniers.	Rmk.	Deniers.	Rmk.
1361–1400.........	177	8.60	50	2.10	135	6.56	3½	0.17	3	0.147	30	1.46
1401–1450.........	220	9.17	65	2.70	170	7.08	6	0.25	4	0.166	20	0.83
1451–1480.........	170	7.08	52	2.15	180	7.50	5	0.207	3½	0.147	34	1.42
1481–1520.........	170	6.80	48	1.91	192	7.50	4½	0.173	4	0.16	40	1.60
1521–1550.........	230	8.80	48	1.83	178	6.77	4	0.152	4½	0.17		1.71
1551–1580.........	500	13.87	95	2.60	290	8.05	10	0.27	8	0.20	50	1.47
1581–1600.........			270	5.60	445	10.12	15	0.31	13	0.26	108	2.25
1601–1620.........	1700	29.60	335	5.65	865	15.10	23	0.39	18	0.30	165	2.80
1621–1680.........	2050	28.14	620	8.61	1900	26.40	26	0.36	25	0.35	180	2.50
1681–1720.........	2500	25.00	690	7.18	1600	16.80	32	0.33	26	0.27	180	2.08
1790–1799........			1320	6.10	2200	10.28			63	0.29	350	1.65
Average, 1360–1550		8.18		2.16		7.08		0.20		0.16		1.39
do. 1601–1720		25.38		6.01		15.40		0.32		0.29		2.41
Average, 1360–1550 in silver value of 1621–1720.......		10.90		2.86		9.40		0.28		0.23		1.89
Percent. 1601–1720 over first period..		131		138		65		14		26		28
Percent. 1790–1799 over first period..				115		9				26		— 8

The rise in prices is smallest in small articles, produced near the place of consumption, such as nails and wax, or in articles of small bulk relatively to value, such as lead. These show but little above the percentage of difference which wages show in excess of mediæval wages. Workmanlike dexterity, inventiveness, and flexibility of organization had experienced very decided decline from the high development which distinguished the German industrial world of the two centuries closing with 1550. With no improvement in the system of labor the price of industrial commodities must closely conform to the ruling ratio of wages.

Expressed in modern silver value these latter articles in the two price divisions show so close an approximation, that little remains upon which could be based even the most strained argument for proving the money-quantity theory.

Compared with the prices of 1790–1799, these differences become so minimal that they disappear in some instances.

Before closing this chapter I will give a comparison of a few prices of meat, poultry, and farm-produce, quoted by Mr. Beissel. These I shall state in present money only, with the original quotation of deniers in parenthesis. The prices are not in equally continuous quotations.

	1370–79.	1420–99.	1540–59.	1790–99.
Ham, per pd..		(5) 4.78 cts.	(12) 8.25 cts.	
Pork " "		(5) 4.78 "	(8) 5.50 "	(45) 5.14 cts.
Beef " "			(11) 7.20 "	
Capon, one...		(20) 19.12 "	(23) 15.55 "	(170) 18.6 cts.
Chicken, "	(7½) 8.35 cts.	(6) 5.95 "	(14) 9.60 "	(60) 6.66 "
Eggs, 100....	(29) 33.25 cts.			(300) 33.32 "

Few as the quotations are which I can give in the last column, they are very significant when compared with the mediæval price columns. They show conclusively what has been already pointed out in another place, that prices of farm produce and meats are rather stable, and change only when altered economic and commercial conditions make an inroad into the old economy, and open up markets which had no existence previously. These conditions, however, were not present in the Germany of the first half of this century and neither were prices of this class of commodities higher in 1850 than they were in 1350 to 1550.*

The prices of home manufactured articles, cloths and wearing apparel, which I find quoted, point the same information as in table III.

Year.	Article.	Denars.	Ratio of 1 : 15½.	
			In mark of to-day.	In dollars.
1370	An ell of good cloth	84	6.52	1.55
1380	An ell of good linen	15	1.00	0.24
1390	A coat	432	29.40	7.09
1420	An ell of black cloth	108	5.85	1.40
1430	An ell of medium cloth	52	2.90	0.70
1440	An ell of coarse grey cloth	48	2.80	0.68
1440	An ell of fine grey cloth	120	7.00	1.70

* The few illustrations cited, on the contrary, point to higher prices in the period 1350 to 1550 than in the last decade of the eighteenth century. If we contrast the industrial activity and general prosperity of the time closing with about 1550 with the stagnant conditions in the latter period, these prices are but natural exponents of the conditions prevailing in the Germany of that time, during which the purchasing power of the industrial classes was reduced to the lowest possible minimum.

In giving these prices their proper value, we must not overlook the fact that the economic development of the lower Rhine country, at this period, was quite in advance of the England of the seventeenth century even; Cologne was especially reputed for its cloth industry. The cloth weavers were its most powerful guild. Linen was a prominent industry of the surrounding country. The trade of Cologne rested largely upon these two staples. Yet who would not see at first glance that the articles quoted could be easily procured to-day, or at any previous time, at the prices named?

The kind of ell is not mentioned. But the ell of commerce in use in the lower Rhine country up to very recent times was the ell of Brabant = 69 centimetres, or 27 inches. The ell of Cologne did not differ much from this. The number of ells accounted for a coat agree with this presumption.

With this allowance to bring the ell up to our yard measure, we can quickly see the high character of these prices. It will be admitted that at no time within recent experience would these prices not have been considered very dear. It is needless to go into fuller detail. I could have added, perhaps, more extensive data for illustration. But as the price-history of England and France so completely demonstrates the same facts, any more proofs would be useless and tiring amplification.

In view of all the facts introduced, any argument on my part would be filling space without adding to the fulness of the demonstration brought out in these chapters, that prices are not the effect of the accidental relations of money quantities to merchandise.

In the succeeding chapters I shall show the actual factors which make the prices of commodities.

THIRD PART.

THE TRUE PRICE-MAKING FACTORS.

CHAPTER X.

Relation of the Share of Labor to the Cost of the Product.—Comparison of Wages and of the Corresponding Cost of Labor in the Product in Different Countries.—There is no Connection between Time-Wages and Labor Cost.—Fall in the Cost of Labor and Rise in the Rate of Wages in Industries, Manufacturing, Mining, and Agricultural within the Century.—The Cotton Industry as an Illustration—The Iron and other Industries.

FOREMOST among the elements that make prices stands the cost of labor. A real rise in wages started in England at the time of the Revolution, and has progressed, with interruptions and even retrogressions at certain periods, until it has reached the maximum figure of the present time. In France the rates have always been lower than in England. But a progressing rise from the time of the French Revolution * to the present day can be demonstrated with absolute certainty. In Germany the wages in the first half of this century were painfully small. Only after the half-successful Revolution of 1848 removed some of the worst encumbrances of mediævalism which the Congresses of Vienna and of Laybach had fastened again on the unfortunate country, did things begin to mend. From 1870 on a considerable turn to the better is observable. In America, wages, always higher than in European countries, the rise from 1850–1860, down to the present time, varies from 50 to 100 and even 150 per cent.

---

* Mr. Yves Guyot, in his valuable work *La Science Économique*, has collected the wages paid in various occupations at different periods in Paris and

Rise of Wages and Decline of Cost.

But the steady rise in wages has gone hand in hand with an equally steady decline in the cost of labor in the product. It is not a bold assertion, but quite in keeping with the facts in the case, as we shall see, that the rate of wages is in an inverse ratio to the cost of labor. It is a demonstrable fact that in countries where the wages are lowest the cost of product is highest, and *vice versa*.

Where we meet with such contradictions of what is usually assumed as a well-settled theory, *i. e.*, that the rate of wages determines the cost of production, it cannot surprise us that so much confusion should still prevail on

in the provincial towns of France, for both male and female labor. The same proportionate increase is noticeable for Paris as for the rest of France, and in male labor the same as in female labor. For briefness, I quote only the table referring to the building trade:

AVERAGE RATE OF WAGES PER DIEM OF WORKINGMEN ENGAGED IN THE BUILDING TRADE IN PARIS.

	1805.	1840.	1853.	1865.	1875.	1883.	Rise.
	fr. c.	fr. c.	fr. c.	fr. c.	fr. c.	fr. c.	Percent.
Cellar digger.............	2.25	2.25	3.00	4.00	4.00	5.50	100
Stonecutter...............	3.35	3.50	5.00	5.50	5.50	7.50	110
Stuccoworker			6.75	8.00	9.00	12.50	88
Stonesetter	3.25	4.00	5.25	6.00	6.25	7.50	105
Mason.....................	3.25	3.25	4.25	5.25	5.50	7.50	130
Limousin [1]..............	2.50	2.50	3.00	4.25	5.00	6.25	150
Laborer...................	1.70	1.90	2.50	3.35	3.50	4.75	179
Carpenter.................	3.00	3.25	5.00	6.00	6.00	8.50	183
Cabinet maker............	3.50	3.25	4.00	4.50	5.00	7.50	115
Blacksmith................	5.00	5.00	5.00	6.50	7.00	7.00	40

According to J. B. Say, *Traité d'Economic Politique*, wages had risen about 50 per cent. in the time of the empire from the time before the Revolution. They kept on the same level until into the forties. From then only the steady rise is noticeable, as seen in the figures here quoted.

[1] The Limousin goes in the season to Paris and other large towns, and returns to his country home when building operations stop during winter.

this question of first importance in a rational price theory.

The most fundamental errors have been propagated by confounding the wages of the laborer with the cost of the labor in the product. Writers always have the day rate of wages in view when they deal with the question of relative cost. The rate of wages is one thing, the pay for a certain amount of work done is quite another. Wages concern the workingman as a consumer, and are of importance to the producer, inasmuch as the workingman is, by the larger or smaller amount he receives, either enabled to keep the human machine in condition or forced to let it run down for want of sufficient nutriment. High wages are an element of strength to the producer. The payment for the work, however, is quite another thing. This, the cost per piece, concerns the employer, and is the only element that has to be considered as one of the price-making factors. Had the propounders and defenders of the old theories gone into factories and workshops to gather their information, instead of formulating them from preconceived notions, much bitter warfare could have been saved to the world. The employers of labor still can not free themselves from the notion that a high rate of wages necessarily involves a high cost of production.

The wage theories referred to have been accepted by the employing classes, and were as readily taken up as axioms by those who have striven for the elevation of the working classes, and have undoubtedly been animated by the most humane considerations. The so-called iron law of wages is the theory upon which all the socialistic and communistic leaders rest their argument.

But there is not a scintilla of truth in the doctrine of an iron law of wages. Wages usually are highest when profits are highest. Both are regulated by the demand for the product of labor.

And wages rise in direct proportion with the rise in the productiveness of labor, whatever may augment this *sine qua non* of all wealth, profit, and wages.

This will be seen from the consideration of the neglected element in the question; the mode of payment of the labor. In all employments engaged in the production of salable articles the work is directly paid by the piece rate or the day rate gauged by the output. Wherever it can be applied the piece rate prevails. When a day rate is established it is gauged on a fixed daily output. In some of the silk mills of Crefeld I found the maximum day rate of weavers fixed at 3 marks. The number of yards of the daily output was regulated by the quality, the number of shoots to the meter. Where this maximum was not reached corresponding deductions were made. As an excess of earnings, from higher exertion, leads, in the experience of workingmen, to reduction in the piece rate, it is plain that few are anxious to make their superior ability an instrument for their own discomfort.

In the old system of work in vogue at the time of Ricardo the pay by the piece was very general. The house industries supplied the manufacturing merchant with the supply of goods. The weaver received his yarn and returned the woven goods, and received his stipulated pay per yard. A great deal of the German textile trade to-day is conducted on the same basis. The yarn, before the great inventions were put into operation and enabled the introduction of the factory system, was spun in cottage homes, and certainly could not be paid at any other than piece rate.*

---

* Arthur Young, in *Travels in Ireland*, tells us of the large exporting trade

Up to very recent years the peasant girls of Germany, and the town-bred girls, too, were in the habit of procuring their marriage outfits from the fruit of the spinning wheel.

---

of Ireland to England[1] in worsted yarns on account of the lower wages paid to spinning girls, saying that they received from $2\frac{1}{2}d$. to $3d$. a pound (5 to 6 cents). In England $5d$. to $6d$. was paid (10 to 12 cents). Sir Frederic Eden, in *The State of the Poor*, gives the daily earnings of a spinner girl in 1787 as $7d$. Arthur Young in another place quotes them for about the same time as $6\frac{1}{4}d$. At the present time the spinning, doubling, and twisting of a fine combed yarn, so-called 2 fold 40 yarn, costs 4.20 cents in Bradford, England, 4.92 cents in a mill in Pennsylvania, the accounts of which I examined in 1887, and 5 cents in a Rhode Island mill, taken from the mill accounts by me in the summer of 1894.

The wages of a spinner girl in a woollen factory in England are to-day about $2s$. (about 50 cents) per diem, and in America 75 cents.

The yarns here mentioned by Arthur Young bear no comparison with the yarns quoted by me as present product. This yarn is of fine Botany wool and greatly finer than any spun out of Irish or English wool a hundred years ago.

But putting them side by side, with this mental reservation, then even we have the remarkable fact here illustrated:

	Per diem. Wages. Cents.	Yarn, per pd. Labor cost Cents.
1767–1778, England	$12\frac{1}{2}$	11
1767–1778, Ireland	6	$5\frac{1}{2}$
1887, England	50	$4\frac{1}{4}$
1887–1894, America	75	5

In the summer of 1894, while officially engaged with the Finance Committee of the Senate in Washington in collecting statistical information bearing on tariff legislation, I received from Mr. Elijah Helm, the Secretary of the Chamber of Commerce of Manchester, valuable information which he procured for me, among which the following data on wages and labor cost in a spinning mill. He writes as follows:

"It may perhaps be of further interest to you to have the following particu-

---

[1] The total of exports in woollen yarns and worsted yarns averaged
From 1764–1770, 8,458 stones 170,038 stones
" 1771–1777, 1,459 " 101,964 "
(The Irish stone is 16 lbs.).

Whatever the amount of wages, the output was dependent on the tools employed and the time devoted to the work. The piece rates were at all times small. But at the time when handwork supplied the rising demands of an expanding trade the result would be the same—rather a rise than a fall in pay, concurrent with higher profits.

Sir Frederic Eden, in 1797, speaks of a rise in wages over 1787 in all employments where piece rates were the mode of payment, "which," as he says, "ten or twelve years ago was not nearly so plentiful as at present."

lars of actual *earnings* of mule spinners at a well-appointed Lancashire cotton mill, which I have received this morning in response to an inquiry.

"The average gross earnings of all

	£	s.	d.		$
The spinners are per week........	3	12	11	=	17.85
Less paid to piecers	1	6	6	=	6.37
Net........................	2	6	5	=	11.48

"In some cases the net earnings—deducting the same rate for piecers—reached £2 14s. 5d. = ($13.40) per week. These earnings are all for 53¼ hours of actual spinning.

"On ring frames the average earnings—for girls—are 18s. 5d. ($4.47) per week."

The wages for ring spinners in American cotton mills are about 85 cents a day. But as the week in Massachusetts is, even now, after the late reduction of the working time, one of 58 hours or 10 per cent. more than the English time, the wages of the spinners are as high in England as in American mills rated on working hours.

The mule spinners in America earn at a higher rate than the English spinners. This is explained by the fact that the mule spinners have no piecers, but employ a back-boy between two of them. It follows that the spinner has to work harder. The average wages for spinners in the King Philip mill are given me by Mr. Robert Howard, the Secretary of the Mule Spinners' Association, at Fall River, as $15.00 gross—less $2.00 for the backboy = $13.00 net. With the greater exertion necessary on account of the absence of the piecers and considering the longer working hours, the spinning in Fall River ought not to be higher than in Lancashire, in the higher num-

A reduction in the rate of pay could occur only consequent upon the introduction of new methods. Adam Smith does not yet mention any of the improvements in spinning which were destined to revolutionize the textile industry, and with it the industries of the world. Still, wages had risen considerably from the beginning of the century to his time. With the introduction of the spinning machine wages rose in the spinning industry, which became a factory industry thereby.

bers even. And this is practically the case, as I had occasion to find out by comparing the wage lists of the mule spinners' associations as then in force at Fall River, Mass., and at Bolton in Lancashire. The prices are gauged on the number of spindles in the mule in Lancashire. In Fall River, in the lists sent to me by Mr. Howard, the prices are all rated on 720 spindles.

Taking the same number of spindle rate for Bolton I find the numbers to be paid at the following price per pound of weft yarn spun:

MULE SPINNERS' PRICES PAID AT FALL RIVER, MASS., AND BOLTON,* ENGLAND, PER POUND OF WEFT YARN.

Yarn number.	Fall River. Cents.	Bolton. Cents.
36	1.17	1.10
40	1.368	1.294
48	1.8	1.614
52	1.944	1.82
60	2.37	2.256
64	2.56	2.466
72	2.995	2.966
80	3.56	3.476
84	3.805	3.739
92	4.351	4.287
96	4.538	4.47
100	4.85	4.86
108	5.346	5.45
116	5.647	6.066
120	6.098	6.38

* I have computed the English penny price into cents and the Fall River price which is paid per 1,000 hanks in the pound, so as to get to an even basis.

But for a long time the weaving remained a house industry, and what is here to the point was in the time during which Ricardo was forming his views, receiving increased wages, because of the greater demand for the piece goods and the freer supply of yarn. Before the introduction of the spinning machine the weavers could frequently not supply the goods in demand for the want of yarn. Sir Frederic Eden, Adam Smith, and Arthur Young give the rate of earnings of a weaver at about 8s.; in 1818, the time of Ricardo's writings, they were about 15s.

Examples from the Cotton Industry.

A manufacturer, Mr. Houldsworth, gave before a parliamentary committee, in 1837, from the books of his firm, the wages of spinners : *

Year.	No.	Mule spinners. s. d.	Assistants. s. d.
1804	180	32 6	27 6
1804	200	36 6	31 0
1814	180	44 6	27 6
1814	200	60 0	30 0

These high rates were to an extent counterbalanced by the prevailing high price of bread. But they were so much in excess of the rates in vogue before the introduction of the inventions, referred to, that a mere mention of this fact would show the error of the generally diffused views.

The weekly earnings of fine yarn spinners at Bolton were given to me in 1887 as averaging 50s. a week, and spinners of medium numbers at Salford told me that they received about 2 guineas a week. But 50s. a week in 1887 was quite a different thing from 50s. in 1814, and even in

---
* Quoted by Thomas Tooke, History of Prices.

1818. If we measure the value of money in these different years by the price of bread, then the value of wages is three times as high now as then, in the time of the Napoleonic wars.*

But with the rising wages a constant reduction in the cost of labor had gone on, and consequently a reduction in prices. This also showed itself in steady progression from the beginning of the century to the present day.

The price of No. 40 twist per pound was:

	1797	1812	1822	1832	1877
	s. d.	s. d.	s. d.	d.	d.
Price of yarn......	7 6	2 6	1 4¾	11¼	8¼
Deducting cotton, including waste....	3 4	1 6	9	7 ¼	6
Leaving for wages, expenses, and profits.	4 2	1 0	7¾	4	2⅛

* Expressed in the price of flour, following the statement from the wage-book of Thomas Houldsworth, Manchester, and adding for comparison present earnings computed by the price of flour of to-day, we have this result of the exertions of a fine-yarn spinner in the progress of time:

	Wages of mule spinners. Average per week.	Hours of work per week.	Price from Greenwich Hospital records. Flour per sack.	Quantity which a week's net earnings would purchase.
	s. d.		s. d.	lbs. of flour.
1804................	34 6	74	83	121
1814................	52	74	70 6	207
1833................	38 6	69	45	233
1894................	46 6	53½	20	652

Low prices of food and raiment may not be found satisfactory by the classes immediately concerned in their production and distribution, but the wage-earner will not look with displeasure upon such results of recent development. If he and the farmer do not get all they are entitled to, it is due to the appropriation of an over-large part by the middleman, reduced by competition, however, to smaller and smaller proportions.

The cost of labor per pound and the average of wages earned per annum, per hand employed, is given by Mr. Ellison in his book on *The Cotton Trade*.

Nothing is more instructive than this table for our purpose:

	Product per head, lbs. of yarn.	Cost of labor per lb. of yarn.	Average earnings per head.
		d.	£ s.
1819–1822	968	6.4	26 13
1829–1831	1,546	4.2	27 6
1844–1846	2,754	2.3	28 12
1859–1861	3,671	2.1	32 10
1880–1882	5,520	1.9	44 4

We find the same results in the weaving industry. Print cloth shows:

	Weekly product, yards.	Labor per yard.	Weekly earnings per weaver.
		d.	s. d.
1814	130.7	1.3	14 0
1832	221.2	.6	12 0
1890 { 3 looms	540	.13	17 2
{ 4 looms			22 5

The conditions of the weavers in 1832 were deplorable. The reduction in the pay was in consequence of great pressure exercised on the weavers by the encroachment of the power loom. In 1890 we see the labor cost reduced to about one fourth that of 1832, the wages increased by 50 to 100 per cent., and the cost of bread reduced to less than one half the old price.

Ellison shows about the same progression in woven cotton goods as in the yarns:

Year.	Lbs. product per head.	Cost of Labor per woven lb.	Average of yearly earnings.
		d.	£ d.
1819—1821	322	15.5	20 18
1829—1831	521	9.0	19 08
1844—1846	1,658	3.5	24 10
1859—1861	3,206	2.9	30 15
1880—1882	4,039	2.3	39 00

We see by this illustration that there is no connection whatever of the rate of wages and the cost of labor in the product. The cotton industry is not equalled by any other in importance. No other industry outside of agriculture employs the number of hands, sets so many wheels in motion and has exerted such an influence on the mental development of the age. No other is, therefore, so well adapted for our demonstration. It is only necessary now to make a few comparisons with the development in the industry in Germany to show once for all that higher wages depend on nothing else than the free exercise of the intellectual faculties in the economy of production, and that there is nothing more detrimental to the interests of the employers themselves than the application in practice of the objectionable theories referred to.

My own inquiries, as published in the Consular Reports of the State Department at Washington,* and in my book *The Economy of High Wages* have lately found most complete corroboration in the work of an eminent German economist, Dr. von Schultze-Gaevernitz, Professor of Political Economy at the University of Leipsig, in his book, *The Factory System (Der Grossbetrieb) as an Economic and*

* See Consular Reports, No. 93, on the cost of Manufacturing Print Cloth, also the Prefatory Letter to the Secretary of State of the author to his Report on Industrial Education in France.

Social Progress, a Study in the Cotton Industry. (Leipsig, 1892.) The relative state of the industry in England and Germany was the especial object of his examination.

With wages not more than one half, and with 10 more working hours in the week, he finds the cost of direct labor in spinning mills a fraction higher in Germany than in England. The total cost, however, is considerably higher on account of the many overseers and other auxiliaries employed in German mills, who are almost entirely absent in English mills.

Everything is done more quickly with fewer hands in England than in Germany.

He compares the efficiency of an establishment in Mulhouse and one in Oldham, both employing self actors; the Oldham mill with 70,000 spindles, the Mulhouse mill with 32,000 spindles. The former employs 167 hands, the latter 185. Oldham has 2.4 and Mulhouse 5.8 hands per 1000 spindles.

The number of yarn is 36s to 40s in Oldham, 20s in Mulhouse. With the same number of yarn the difference would be greater yet.

In spinning of No. 40s twist he finds the number of hands employed per 1000 spindles to be 2.3 for Oldham and 6.2 for Switzerland.

In the weaving the cost of labor is higher on the Continent than in England, in England higher than in America, as I have previously stated in my reports, and is here confirmed by v. Schultze-Gaevernitz. The number of looms tended by one operator, the number of yards of the weekly output, make the rate of wages. It is not necessary to recapitulate the statements, the matter ought for all time to stand as *res adjudicata*. It may, however, serve my present purpose to mention the case of the hand-loom weavers still engaged in their old trades and homes, earning wages not higher than those which made the English weavers of 200 years ago sing out their plaintive wails as reported to us by Macauley: "Six pence a day; if justice were done us, a weaver would earn his shilling a day."

The result of an inquiry published in 1890 by Dr. Carl von Rechenberg, and cited by Prof. Brentano in his new edition of his *Relations of Wages and Working Time to the Product of Labor* refers to the incomes and the mode of living of the poor hand-loom weavers of Zittau. Rechenberg investigated the cases of 28 families. All the members of a family work together. Outside of school-time the children are engaged in spooling; the wife assists in the weaving. The time at work is 14 to 16 hours in winter and 13 to 15 hours in summer, if the efforts of their feeble frames can be called work. The incomes from weaving vary between three and seven marks per week.

It is surprising to learn that some of them are still engaged in weaving shirtings and print-cloths. Here the daily earnings of one weaver engaged on this cloth are given as low as 37 pfennigs—about 9 cents (almost incredibly low) with a product of about 8 yards of 30 inches wide. Several other cases cited have earnings per day of 48 to 60 pfennigs—*i. e.*, 12 to 15 cents.

Of course, it is an uneven struggle, this attempt of keeping up the contest, in countries of low economic development. But low as the earnings are, they are by no means so very much different from those ruling in the same regions in the good old times, when mechanical weaving was yet unknown. Dr. Louis Bein, in his *Industries of the Voigtland* (Saxony), gives us the weekly wages of hand weavers and machine spinners in Plauen and neighborhood. They are:

Year.	Weavers.	Spinners.
1816	$0.76	$1.75
1819	0.93	....
1827	0.75 to $1.35	0.70 to $1.40
1834	1.40	....
1863	0.70 to 2.10	....

For the convenience of the reader, I here again set down the earnings of the English spinners and weavers from the data given above side by side with the earnings of these contemporaneous workers in one of the earliest cotton manufacturing districts of Germany.

AMOUNT OF WEEKLY WAGES OF WEAVERS AND SPINNERS IN PLAUEN (SAXONY) AND LANCASHIRE, ENGLAND, EXPRESSED IN AMERICAN MONEY:

	Saxony. Weekly Wages.		Lancashire. Weekly Wages.	
	Weavers.	Machine Spinners.	Weavers.	Spinners.
1804	$0.82 to $1.00			$7.40
1819	0.76 to 0.93	$1.40 to $2.10	$2.00	10 48
1832	1.40	1.05 to 1.75	1.86	8.37
1862*	0.70 to 2.10	2.10 to 2.40	3.26†	7.00‡

The fine-yarn spinner's wages may be reckoned at about 25 per cent. above the average of mule-spinners' wages in England. Even with this allowance made, what an enormous difference in the rate of wages at contemporary periods between the two countries. §

---

* Power-looms.

† Women.

‡ The average rate for mule-spinners; the three preceding lines in the fourth column represent only fine-yarn spinning wages.

§ The German rates in the first half of the nineteenth century are a good way below the wages of the fifteenth century, expressed in the same money equivalents, and not making any allowance whatever for the changed value of silver.

This under-payment of the spinners and weavers of Plauen and the Voigtland against English-men and women gives its true showing only when we hear the story of the effect of English competition upon the industries of this poor country with its imputed advantage of a low rate of wages.

At the time of the Napoleonic decrees the spinners and weavers were comparatively prosperous. But no sooner were the ports opened to English yarns and manufactures, after the downfall of Napoleon, and the demand of the world following a return of peace had been satisfied, than the wail of distress is heard. The markets become glutted with the cheaper English yarns and goods. The 104,964 spindles running in 1816 become reduced in 1817 to 86,500 spindles. The time of 12 hours is reduced to 6 hours.

"The English competition, which had become so disastrous upon the (German) fairs, made itself equally felt in the direct trade from home. Wherever the Voigtland turned with its manufactures it found the markets filled with English cotton goods. Turkey, which had become during the continental embargo a chief customer of England, did not suffice to the powerfully expanding British industry, especially as there were in Constantinople in the neighborhood of 2000 looms in operation. She needed new fields for export, so that now in all the Mediterranean ports, closed so long a time, English ships entered again. From now on the English flag endeavored to make its preponderance felt upon all the seas, and English commerce began to occupy the first place in the world. Following the condition of things in the year 1814, the dealers in muslin of the Voigtland, who had their consignments in Vienna side by side with the English goods, found themselves constrained to take their unsalable stocks back to Plauen and seek other markets for them, though the expense amounted to no less than 100 florins ($40) in freight and duty per case."*

This brief quotation suffices to illustrate the history of the trade of this and other German manufacturing dis-

---

* Dr. Louis Bein, *Die Industrie des sächsischen Voigtlandes*.

tricts during the nineteenth century in competition with the higher paid labor of England. At every turn of the wheel English competition threatens to break down the feeble reed upon which they lean, which the ignorance of ages has been extolling as a staff of iron, safe at all times to rest upon.

The Bugbear of Indian and Japanese Competition.

It has of late become the fashion to raise the cry of alarm at the threatening danger from Japanese competition in the manufacture of cotton goods, the same as it was for some years previous to the starting of Japanese mills the fashion to become hysterical at the sight of the expansion of the Indian trade. The fact is that India spins only low counts, not above No. 20. The labor cost in these numbers is very small. The fall in the price of silver only affects the difference in the labor cost. The cotton is the same to the Lancashire spinner as to the Bombay spinner, plus the freight from Bombay to Manchester. But, on the other hand, coal and machinery, superintendence, and wear and tear, are higher in Bombay. The advantages, therefore, are limited, and consist in the difference in the cost of labor, and in the saving of the freight from Bombay to Manchester on the raw cotton, and of the freight charges from Manchester to Bombay on the spun yarn.* But allowing all that is claimed, the mere fact that only the lower numbers can be spun successfully in India, where the cost of the ma-

---

*A statement of Mr. T. Comber, of Liverpool, submitted to the Royal Commission on Gold and Silver in 1887, shows the differences on which the fall of exchange would operate against the Lancashire spinner and favor the Bombay spinner.

The number of yarn is No. 20. The rate of exchange at 1s. 5d. per

terial stands highest and the labor lowest in the proportionate parts of the cost, contradicts the low-wage theory totally. In anything requiring higher proportions of labor the English hold the field. This is the same in rupee, about 30 per cent. discount, gives the following account for the time the statement was made.

Comparison between cost to English and to Bombay spinners of producing and laying down in Bombay 1 lb. of 20s yarn:

	Cost to		Advantage to	
	English Spinner.	Indian Spinner.	English Spinner.	Indian Spinner.
	d.	d.	d.	d.
Cotton...........................	5.69	5.	....	.69
Depreciation and interest on mill and machinery.....................	.42	.64	.22	....
Coals............................	.05	.16	.11	....
Wages...........................	1.11	.99	....	.12
Stores...........................	.28	.46	.18	....
Sundries.........................	.40	.25	....	.15
Cost at mill.....................	7.95	7.50	.51	.96
Packing and carriage to Bombay...	.50	....	....	.50
Delivered at Bombay..............	8.45	7.50	.51	1.46
Net advantage............				.95

It takes 1¼ lb. of cotton to spin a pound of yarn from Surat cotton. The .69 d. for freight to Lancashire of the cotton and .50 for freight of the yarn express the natural advantages which remain to the Bombay spinners under all possible circumstances, and cannot be removed whatever the rates of exchange may be. The other advantages are of very small significance against this great factor, and are more than counterbalanced by the advantages enjoyed by the Lancashire manufacturer, as is demonstrated in the above table.

In finer numbers the advantages are reversed. Surat cotton cannot be spun advantageously in higher numbers than 23s or 24s. American cotton has to be used in these, and the freight advantages enjoyed by India on her

Plauen as in India, in Moscow, or in Tokio. The Moscow spinner is not more enabled to compete with England at home on account of his depreciated paper rouble, than the Austrian was when his paper florin was but half its own cottons become lost to her. Here on a quasi-equal footing with England, so far as the cost of the raw-material goes, the advantages accruing to her from the low value of the rupee, in the other items of cost, could be put to a test. But so far no capitalist has yet been willing to take advantage from the alluring outlook, presented by bi-metallists and free-coinage advocates. Nor does British trade to India and the East suffer a very keen setback, as is usually proclaimed, although she has lost her trade in the coarser yarn numbers. Excepting years of depression, the trade of cotton-goods has been expanding ever since mills were started in India in about 1872.

A list of exports shows this:

QUANTITIES OF COTTON PIECE-GOODS AND COTTON YARNS SHIPPED TO BRITISH EAST-INDIA AND TO CHINA, JAPAN, AND TO DUTCH EAST INDIA IN THE FOLLOWING YEARS:

	Piece-Goods in millions of yards.		Yarns in millions of lbs.	
	British East India.	China, Japan, and Dutch East India.	British East India.	China, Japan, and Dutch East India.
1870	923	478	31	10
1878	1,295	478	35	5
1880	1,813	632	47	6
1884	1,791	600	49	31
1886	2,237	620	49	20
1888	2,196	839	57	44
1890	2,189	806	52	38
1891	1,964	790	53	28
1892	1,974	765	42	31
1893	1,981	605	40	28
1894	2,419	670	43	25

A comparison of the first line of figures (1870) representing the time before the East-Indian mills were started, and even 1878, with the last year's figures, demonstrates the futility of the arguments, which these pages have endeavored to controvert.

present value and wages were as low as they are now. In Bohemia, in 1884,* in one of two cotton factories investigated by Dr. I. Singer, the wages ranged from 40 cents to $1.20 a week for 63 per cent. of all employed, and from $1.20 to $2.00 for the remaining 37 per cent. In the other factory the earnings were higher, that being a better organized mill. Still they ranged only from 60 cents to $1.80 for 62 per cent., and from $1.80 to $2.80 for the remaining 38 per cent. The highest rate in mill A fls. 4 to fls. 5 ($1.60 to $2.00), was earned only by 47 per cent.; and in mill B the highest rate fls. 6 to fls. 7 ($2.40 to $2.80), by 2.8 per cent. of the total employed. The average earnings of mill A were $1.20 per week, *i. e.*, 20 cents per day, about 1¾ cents per working hour; and in mill B $1.50 per week, *i. e.*, 25 cents per day, 2¼ cents per working hour. The value of the paper florins in gold was then 36 cents, or near 20 per cent. less than the full valued money in which American and English operatives received their wages, higher by four or five hundred per cent. than these pittances.

It is barely necessary to go to the far East for a low rate of wages paid in a debased coin or a depreciated currency. We find the Hindoo, the Chinese, and the Japanese in Europe. They are found in the south and the west of Ireland, in the mountain districts of Eastern Germany to the Carpathian mountains, and from these to the Ural. But though their wages are almost stagnant, the wages of the intellectually advanced industrial nations have been all the time rising in the ratio shown above. Neither the depreciated money nor the low rate of wages have been able to stop the triumphant progress of the

---

* See my statement in *The Industrial Situation*, G. P. Putnam's Sons, 1885.

high-wage countries (America and England) in industry and commerce. The ten-cent-a-day wage of a Hindoo spinner, of which we hear so much as the cause of real or simulated apprehension, has risen to a higher figure with his increasing efficiency. But let us offset this increase by the decline in the rupee value, then we can easily find duplicates in the far more muscular individual of Northern Europe, working for a much smaller wage than this, and too anxious to have a ten or a fifteen-cent rate a day for every working day in the year.

During my travels in Ireland, in Kerry and in Donegal, I found women and girls in profusion who would have been only too happy with steady earnings at sixpence to a shilling a week. I found them sitting in clusters on the road or walking barefoot, their shoes, with their stockings stuffed in, hung over their arms so as to save the wear and tear, knitting away eagerly. In some few places offices had been opened by London people, half for charity and half for trade, to make use of their work and find some employment for their latent talent. The peasant women walk fifteen miles to Glenties, where two London houses have opened stores, to dispose of their finished work and get their yarn. For long worsted stockings four shillings is paid a dozen pair. It takes all an expert knitter's time to finish six pair in a week. The men tramp in gangs of ten and twenty to the nearest port to cross over to Scotland to bring home three or four pounds as the net results of their labor in harvest work.

Yet England does not avail itself of this cheap labor begging for work at her very doors. According to a Parliamentary Return of 1879, there were only 1620 persons of both sexes employed in the cotton industry in Ireland, while England's cotton operatives counted up 451,508 persons. When I asked after this industry in 1889, I was informed that the cotton mills, as well as many of the woollen mills, had been forced to give up as they could not compete with England.

The Low Level of Russian Wages.

I doubt whether any examples can be brought from the East of wages that are lower than what Russia shows. I have before me "*Landwirthschaft und Gewerbe in Mittel-Russland*," by Alfons Thun, and the "Report to the Russian Government of the Commissioners to the American Exhibition at Chicago."

Thun describes the condition of the peasantry and the trades which give employment to this great multitude comprising still the working population of the Empire. He spent a number of years in the middle and western provinces. The governments of Moscow, Smolensk, Vladimir, Nischni-Nowgorod, St. Petersburgh, etc., were the field of observation. It is my object only to show the miserable pittances at which the European sells his work, anxious to find even such earnings, of which we shall here give a few instances. At the opening of navigation a very active time sets in in the shipping trade. Vessels are to be loaded and unloaded, taken down the river, helped over bad places in the river bed. Frequently a vessel gets stuck, and the cargo has to be transferred to another boat. It is a hard time for the poor peasant, who by such arduous toil hopes to earn and take home a sum of money with which to pay at least some of the expense necessary to tide over to the next harvest, or to pay off some of the dues and arrears hanging heavily over him. Thun gives the following statement as to these earnings: From 1571 contracts made in 1875, in the district of Orlow, it appears that a workingman averages 13.88 roubles in money, and 3 roubles in provisions for three months, or 18 kopecks (12½ cents) a day. He receives from 6½ to 8½ roubles, money down to bind the bargain, which, of course, is included in the total stated. This is about the only money that he can call earned. The balance, partly, has to defray various expenses of his own and partly to remunerate the headman of the artel and the leader of the gang, who procured him the job.

The raftsmen on the Dnieper earn about 35 kopecks. (25 cents) a day.

Carpenters and builders hire themselves out to contractors in artels of eight to fifteen men. The province of Waetka is especially famed for its carpenters and builders, whose number is given at the high figure of 10,000. They go to great distances under the charge of contractors. They are found by the contractors. The earnings are given for the Orlow district as ranging from 30 to 95 roubles for nine months. (From 8 to 27 cents a working day.)

Four hundred and eighty-nine contracts for another district, that of Urschum, divide the earnings as follows:

7½	per cent.,	100 to 160	roubles	($70	to	$112.)
29	"	71 " 100	"	(50	"	70.)
35	"	50 " 70	"	(35	"	49.)
23	"	31 " 50	"	(21.70	"	35.)
5	"	15 " 30	"	(10.50	"	21.)

Five eighths of the number, earn less than $50 for the period of work, *i. e.*, nine months.

Brickmakers by machinery or hand in the district of Moscow, at the time of great speculative movement in the building trade, earned in three months from 75 to 87 roubles (without board), *i. e.*, about 70 to 78 cents a day.

The average for other governments is about half a rouble=35 cents. Laborers at the brick-works for the season (five to six months) 55 to 70 roubles (27 cents a day) in the Moscow district.

I illustrate some of the leading trades only which employ large numbers on full time, at least as long as the season lasts. I omit the many occupations which we class as house-industries, and wherein earnings cannot very well be gauged on a time basis. We can estimate from the earnings quoted for occupations requiring an uncommon amount of endurance and strength, as well as considerable skill, the standard of wages in the lighter industrial employments.

But as these wages relate to a period of some twenty years ago, and twenty years, it may be said, contain the possibility of great changes in these rapidly moving times, we can here take up the thread spun for us by the Russian Government itself in the Report of the Department of Agriculture of the Ministry of Crown Domains for the World's Columbian Exposition held in Chicago, in 1893.

I will give a few extracts from this very elaborate and highly instructive report, touching only upon some of the chief employments of the agricultural classes, which, be it remembered, are mainly the working classes of Russia.

Starting with cooperage and wood industry barrels, tubs, carts and sledges are made in the villages. About 24,000 families are occupied. A workman earns about 30 to 40 kopecks (21 to 28 cents) a day.

Cabinet-making gives occupation to about 10,000 peasant families. Some masters employ hired workmen, who get 40 to 50 roubles (28 to 35 dollars) per year (with board), according to skill. Working time 13 to 14 hours a day. The profit of the master is 90 to 100 roubles a year.

Village locksmiths earn about 2 roubles ($1.40) a week, and the most skilful only 5 roubles. The wares are generally sold to middlemen, who spread them throughout the Empire and to countries in Asia beyond the Russian domain.

In pottery an average potter makes a cartload of pots a week, which he carries to the neighboring fairs or bazaars for sale. The price per cartload varies according to the season from 2.50 to 3.50 roubles, this being the total weekly earnings of a potter out of which the cost of the fuel and sometimes that of clay, not unfrequently bought, have to be deducted. Thus a potter earns no more than from 2 to 3 roubles per week. Spinning is still done on spindles—the wheel is not known. A good weaver, man or woman, can make a piece of linen 50 arshines (28 inches) long, a week, and can earn in the working season from 70 to 100 roubles.

Cotton weavers work at their homes or in small factories where from 10 to 20 looms are placed. The warp and the weft, both machine made, are received by the peasants from the manufactories through the intermediation of commissioners found in the linen cloth industry; the goods are forwarded to the orderers as soon as they are finished. In the cotton weaving an ordinary weaver receiving from 1.5 to 2.5 kopecks per arshine of tissue (1.05 cents to 1.75 cents per arshine, or 1.35 to 2.25 cents per yard), earns during the winter not more than 15 roubles; good workmen earn from 40 to 50 roubles. In the government of Saratov, where the Sarpinka is mainly worked, weavers earn from 33 to 45 kopecks per day or from 50 to 60 roubles per year.

By comparing these rates with those stated by Mr. Thun, it will be seen that labor could be hired as cheaply in 1893 as in 1873 in the dominions of the Czar.*

In addition to this advantage of a very low wage-rate, Russia has had all along and still enjoys the advantage of a depreciated silver rouble, and up to recent years an even more depreciated paper currency. Wages are paid in this latter rouble, as it is about the only money in circulation.

"For budget purposes the official value in 1891 was 1.60 paper to 1 silver rouble, or 22.43*d*. (44.86 cents)." † (The value of the gold rouble is 77 cents.)

If we compute the wages given above at this rate of exchange—as of course we have to do for this comparison—then I doubt whether there is much to choose in the standard of wages, and in the advantages which a debased currency is said to give to a country's industries, between Russia on the one hand and India and Japan on the other. If these are advantages, then Russia would not need great armaments and vast plans of conquest to

---

* I have frequently shown that low wages are always found in countries of undeveloped economic conditions and advance with the progress to a higher stage of development.

An interesting proof I found recently in an address by Alfred Krupp, the father of the present owner, to his workmen, who had asked for an increase of wages. I will not repeat the self-complacent speech in which he details the part of benefactor he played in the early critical years of the works. The significant part is his own statement that in about 1827 smiths and casters were given then, after a rise in wages had been granted by this earthly Providence, *one thaler and fifteen silber-groschen* (one dollar and five cents, = sixteen and one half cents a day). Mr. Krupp was of opinion that the higher wages paid in 1870 were due to his generosity, and not in obedience to a general economic law. How far this rate of wages falls behind mediæval wages, ruling in the same neighborhood, can be seen by consulting Table II. of the Xanten price records of the preceding chapter.

† *The Statesman's Year-book*, 1894.

revenge herself on England. All it would require would be to set her millions to work at wages one third to one fifth those of England, and further reduced some 40 per cent. through a depreciated currency, and thus destroy the commercial and industrial greatness of the Island Empire at one sweep.

Comparing Output of Labor.

Very interesting results are derived from a comparison of the output of different countries working under such different rates of wages in the same industrial employments, and of the cost per piece in the same fabrics. We have noted above the cost of spinning fine yarns in Alsace, England, and America.

Like effects appear in weaving. We have mentioned the cost per yard and daily output of hand-loom weavers in Zittau and the labor cost of weaving cotton cloth in Russia. The output of a hand-loom weaver in Zittau is about nine to ten yards of cloth thirty inches wide, at a labor cost of about one and a quarter cents per yard.

In Russia we find a cost of $1\frac{1}{4}$ to $2\frac{1}{4}$ cents per yard of weaving according to fineness. Reducing the paper rouble to a gold basis, the average would remain the same as in the Zittau example. The lower rate in the Russian account is undoubtedly on a coarser kind than the one in Zittau. The weekly output here is about sixty yards. The average output per loom per week in Burnley, Lancashire, in cloth of the same width is about two hundred yards. But as a good single weaver runs four looms in Burnley, and in Fall River and Lowell six to eight, the output is from eight to twenty-two times as great as in these low-wage countries. I found the complete cost of labor and expense of weaving and finishing, including general expense (which has to be counted in as an offset against hand-loom weaving where the weaver returns the finished cloth against the yarn received), to be in Burnley 6.182 cents and in Lowell 5.071 cents per seven yards, = 0.883 and 0.724 cents per yard, or about one half the cost at which the poor hand-loom weavers keep up the struggle for existence.

But the difference between hand-loom weaving and power-loom weaving shows no less pregnant variations when we compare earnings, output and labor cost in power-loom weaving in the different countries which now are engaged in industrial competition. It is always the low-wage country which comes out second in the race, *i. e.*, where the people toil the longest number of hours and produce at highest cost.

Von Schultze-Gaevernitz in speaking of the relative productiveness of labor and its effect on wages and labor cost says:

" I confine myself here to the following example, which rests on statements of Schoenhof, which were corroborated to me in Lancashire. It relates to print-cloth 64 x 64.

	Weekly product per weaver. Yards.	Cost of labor per yard.	Working hours day.	Weekly earnings. $ c.
Germany	466	0.606	12	2.74
Switzerland	466	0.606	12	2.67
England	700	0.55	9	3.90
America	1200	0.4	10	5.10

Professor von Schultze took these figures from a pamphlet *Influences Bearing on Production* published by the State Department in Washington in 1888. This formed part of my report on Industrial Education in France. I gave there, in brief outline, the general industrial situation as I found it from my travels and observations made in 1887.

The wide scope of my commission and the brief time at my disposal made it necessary to go quickly over a vast field, and leave for another opportunity a closer examination of very important detail. I took up in 1888 the examination of manufacturing cost in different countries of textiles, iron, and steel and other industrial products. Print cloth was one of the first items of my inquiries. The data for America, Switzerland, and Germany were taken from mill accounts by me. The English rate was obtained for me by friends, themselves large manufacturers in Lancashire, but not making this particular kind of print cloth in their own mills. Not satisfied with any information not obtained by personal inquiry on the spot, and from the mill accounts, I visited Burnley, the chief seat of print cloth-making for Lancashire the same as Fall River for America. There I obtained exact figures from the work accounts, which I made the subject of my report to the State Department " On the Cost of Manufacturing Print Cloth in Massachusetts, Lancashire, and Switzerland." * The price paid in Burnley at the time was $25\frac{3}{4}$ cents per 50 yards, *i. e.*, 51 cents per hundred yards. The statement given above has to be corrected to that extent.

Last summer, having to deal with these questions in Washington in connection with the tariff legislation then pending, I wrote to England for information as to changes made since 1888 in the piece rates paid to operatives.

I received the following answer from one of the principal concerns:

---

* See *Consular Reports of the United States*, No. 93, May, 1888.

"Below we give a few examples. We rise or fall $\frac{1}{8} d$ per pick and $\frac{1}{8} d$ for each 4 inches in width per piece of 24 yards. For instance:

28 inch, 16 x 16 (American, 64 x 64) $5\frac{1}{2} d =$ 44 cents per 100 yards.
32 "   "   "   "   "   " $5\frac{3}{4}$ "   48 "   "   "
28 " 18 x 18 (American, 72 x 72) $6\frac{7}{8}$ "   56 "   "   "
32 "   "   "   "   "   " $7\frac{1}{2}$ "   60 "   "   "
36 "   "   "   "   "   " $7\frac{7}{8}$ "   64 "   "   "

This is a considerable reduction since 1888. But the American price has also been reduced to such an extent that the difference is still nearly as great as I found it in 1888 between America and Lancashire. In answer to an inquiry, I received this reply from my friend, Mr. Robert Howard, the Secretary of the Fall River Cotton Mule Spinners' Association:

"In reply, etc., I will inform you that the price for weaving 64 x 64 regular print cloth (28 inches wide) in Fall River is 16 cents per cut of 45 yards."

This is equal to 36 cents per 100 yards against Burnley, Lancashire, 44 cents per 100 yards. Hence the American weaver gets 8 cents less pay for weaving a hundred yards of cloth than the English weaver, although the American earns from 25 to 33 per cent. more wages. This is made possible, as has been explained, by the American weavers attending nearly twice as many looms as the English. English wages are so much higher, and English labor is so much cheaper than Continental for the very same reason. In the light of such facts, it must always remain an amusing spectacle to see the American cotton manufacturer become excited and threaten to close his mills when a reduction is suggested of a 60 tariff to a 40 per cent. basis.

Examples from Other Industries.

Similar examples can be supplied *ad infinitum*. I will give two, collars and cuffs and white shirts. These two items were very important factors in the legislative history of 1894, and deserve brief illustration. I am also here possessed of the facts through personal investigation.

In 1887 I obtained in Berlin the cost of manufacturing these articles from the leading firm there, which is also a large exporter to America. Before making use of the data then obtained, I procured in 1894 a statement of the firm's present manufacturing cost through their selling agent at New York, who wrote for it to his firm for presentation of the facts to the Committee on Ways and Means.

I found these figures to be the same as those given to me in Berlin. Little had changed in the seven years. The American figures are those submitted by the collar manufacturers (or rather by the foreman of one of the firms) to the Ways and Means Committee. The correctness of the figures was corroborated to me by leading manufacturers.

Without entering into detail, I state here the labor cost for making a dozen linen collars in Berlin and in Troy:

COST OF MAKING A DOZEN LINEN COLLARS.

	Berlin. Pfennige.	Cents.	Troy. Cents.
Cutting.................................	7.50	1.78	1.50
Cutting button-holes..................	2.50	.60	
Machine sewing, turning, banding, etc..	72.50	18.00	21.00
Button-holing.........................	33.00	8.00	2.88
Laundry and ironing..................	60.00	15.00	13.00
	174.50	43.38	38.38

The cost is higher in Berlin than in Troy. The buttonholes in the Berlin collars are hand-made, though of a rather inferior kind. The button-holes in the American collars are machine-made. If we allow the five cents to equalize this difference to the credit of the Berlin collars, then the cost is exactly alike. Yet the time wages of collar-makers, laundresses, and cloth-cutters are fully double what they are in this very well-equipped factory in Berlin, which I found to be paying higher wages than is the ordinary rate for like work.

In shirts with linen fronts I found the same conditions and facts, of which I will also here give the comparative figures :

COST OF MANUFACTURING ONE DOZEN SHIRTS IN BERLIN AND IN NEW YORK.*

	Berlin. Pfennige.	Cents.	New York. Cents.
Cutting	100	23	18 to 20
Making shirt	355	84.50	} 1.00
Making holders	30	7.00	
Stamping sizes	5	1.25	†
Making button-holes	130	30.85	25
Washing and ironing	360	85.75	1.25
		$2.33.15	$2.70

The difference is trifling. The cost of laundrying is higher in the New York statement because shirts are laundried by steam laundries. The cost statement for New York, therefore, includes an extra profit and separate expense. The Berlin amount covers the mere labor outlay for washing and ironing only, which being done in the factory carries all extra charges over to expense and profit and loss account.

We have the proof here so full and so complete of the confusion of ideas resulting from confounding wages and cost of labor that little needs to be added in illustration. The low labor rate by the piece follows the industrial progress, the intellectual and material development of the age. The rate of wages keeps in a progressive ratio with

* For New York statement obtained from leading shirt houses.
† Part of cutting expense.

this development. If in the treatment of the question of wages we had separated it and dealt with the piece rates when we meant to determine the cost of labor and the competitive positions secured thereby, we should have come nearer to the facts and to a mutual understanding, though we might have seen fewer learned treatises on the principles of economic science.

The extent to which this paying by the piece is carried in manufacturing industries is seen from a statement relating to the working force of a cotton weaving mill in North Lancashire, which is as applicable to America as it is to textile manufacturing in general.

The 225 hands employed in the mill divide:

	In piece rates.	In weekly rates.
Spooling............................	16	..
Beaming.............................	2	..
Sizing...............................	..	1
Dressing............................	..	5
Warping.............................	5	..
Weaving.............................	180	..
Overseers...........................	*6	..
Cloth examiner......................	..	1
Laborers............................	..	3
Others..............................	..	6
Totals.............................	209	16

The Progress in Metallurgy.

The progress in the technical development in the iron- and coal-mining industries shows the same general results. The lowest labor cost goes hand in hand with the shortest hours and the highest wages, and the price declines in conformity. In mining and in many branches of the

---

* Paid at the rate of 1s. 4d to the £. of the weavers under their supervision.

iron and steel industry the men are paid by the tonnage handling. Of course, where, as in pig-iron, the labor processes are mainly manual, like the handling and barrowing of the ores and fuel, the labor cost is influenced by the higher wages. But even this is not carried to the extent that the higher wages make equally high cost. It is a demonstrated fact that English iron is produced as cheaply, as far as the furnace labor goes, as German iron, although English wages are higher by at least one third. The better feeding and living of the Englishman fully make up for the difference, on a footing of equally improved plant, in increased efficiency.

A particularly low cost of labor in pig-iron making, considering the nature of the ores, has been supplied to me from the working accounts of the Tennessee Coal and Iron Company. The account relates to the output of three furnaces for the month of September, 1894. It shows a total labor cost per ton of iron of 78.6 cents. This includes all labor items at and around the furnace, and salaries and office expense connected with the works. The cost in England, covering the same items, of iron requiring, however, a somewhat smaller tonnage handling of ores, I found at Middleborough, to be $3s.=73$ cents, and the same at the Duke of Sutherland's furnaces in Staffordshire.

In both the English accounts the ore is a 50 per cent. ore, while in the American account a 40 per cent. average appears. Making allowance for the difference in labor arising therefrom, the cost in either case comes to about the same rate per ton of finished iron.

In America we produce the ore, the coal, and the coke cheaper than in England (and England does it cheaper than Germany), although the daily wages are higher. The beds are deeper in like kinds of ores and coals, therefore easier workable. But on the whole the higher rate of wages, the higher standard of living, ruling here, causes a more thorough working organization than elsewhere. The application of labor-saving machinery and appliances is carried to an extent in the mining and metallurgical industries unknown in countries where a lower rate of wages prevails.

The costliness of these alone is a bar to their introduction except under conditions as ruling in America. With the progressing application of these methods the rates of labor by the piece (the ton) have fallen, the earnings have risen. We need only refer to the census returns of bituminous coal mining where 1890 shows this progressively over 1880, as 1880 shows it over 1870.

	Cost of labor per ton.		Yearly earnings per head.		Value per ton at the mine.	
	1880.	1890.	1880.	1890.	1880.	1890.
Kentucky...............	73	70	$261	$334	$1.20	99c.
West Virginia...........	72	60	295	391	1.20	82c.
Ohio....................	86	69	320	352	1.29	94c.
Illinois.................	99	69	382	357	1.44	97c.
Pennsylvania............	65	63	337	391	1.02½	85¼c.

Iron-ore mining shows for Michigan, where nearly all the Bessemer ores were mined:

	1880.	1890.
Labor cost...............	$1.40	$1.19
Earnings................	413.00	535.00

The recent developments in the Mesaba range in Minnesota in iron-ore mining are familiar to the reader. Inexhaustible stores of a superior kind of ore have been found. Being surface ores they need no sinking of costly shafts, no laborious and expensive mining operations to bring them forth. They are put on board cars by means of steam shovels at a total labor cost of 6 to 7 cents a ton. The ores are laid down at Pittsburgh furnaces now at less than one half the cost of three years ago. Bessemer iron can be produced at a cost of $9.50 a ton, which cost $16 to $17 some six or seven years ago at the same furnaces, from no other cause than this cheapening of the supplies. The day-rate of wages has not changed either at the furnaces or at the mines.

The cheapening of production by scientific progress is nowhere else so apparent as in metallurgy. This applies to mining operations in all the branches. The laborer's lot is made less arduous, the dangers become more circumscribed, and his pay advances with the progress that cheapens his product to a point at which the labor cost is but a nominal charge, compared to former times.

A very graphic illustration of this has lately been printed by the *Iron Age*, from the records of the Quincy copper mine on Lake Superior. They cover a period of forty years. I take the statement in full from the pages of the *Iron Age*:

"The following table shows the product for a series of years, together with the yield of the rock, in ingot copper, and the cost of production:

Year.	Product. Pounds ingot.	Yield per cubic fathom. Pounds copper.	Cost per pound. Cents.
1864	2,498,574	562	26.71
1870	2,497,500	528	14.90
1875	2,798,300	485	15.79
1878	2,868,500	397	14.01
1881	5,703,000	767	10.03
1885	5,848,530	710	7.50
1890	8,064,253	769	6.51
1894	15,484,014	584	5.68

"It will be observed that the yield in 1894 was nearly the same as that 30 years ago, and that the cost of production fell from 26.71 cents per pound, currency, in 1864, to 5.68 cents in 1894. In 1875, when the yield, it is true, was considerably less per fathom of ground, the cost was 15.79 cents. In 1874 it was 15.13 cents on a yield of 577 pounds of ingot copper per cubic yard, so that the figures are more directly comparable.

"The managers of the Quincy Mine have been in the habit of reporting annually the wages received by miners on contract. Here are the figures for a series of years:

WAGES OF QUINCY MINERS ON CONTRACT.

1870	$46.09	1879	$38.76
1871	47.08	1880	49.70
1872	60.62	1881	48.54
1873	62.92	1882	48.83
1874	48.38	1885	44.00
1875	46.74	1889	49.15
1876	47.13	1890	52.60
1877	43.79	1894	50.70
1878	41.50		

"With the exception of the two years, 1872 and 1873, better wages have been paid in the last few years than ever before. Evidently labor has not been the sufferer from the decline in prices which our silver friends attribute to 'the appreciation of gold.' In fact, wages were very low long before that calamity occurred, and when gold was still very 'abundant' soon after the California discoveries. Thus at the Cliff Mine, in 1853, the average monthly earnings were $39, when the product of the famous old mine sold at 27.32 cents per pound. In 1894 the Quincy paid $50.70 per month to its miners on contract and got about 9.5 cents for its copper. Yet it paid $400,000 to its shareholders. We might multiply examples from the Lake Superior copper region to prove the very large reduction in cost of production, but this single one may suffice."

The same scientific levelling process has operated on the cost of production in gold-mining and silver-mining, be it remembered, all the time, and a fiat of the State cannot make water run up from its source.

In manufactures of the cruder sort, no less than in those of a finer and complicated nature, the same effects are noted—higher wages and lower cost of labor.

Some fifteen years ago Sir Isaac Lowthian Bell found the cost of labor in the conversion of pig-iron into steel rails higher in America than in England by the difference in the rate of wages ruling in the two countries. He found an average difference in the daily rates of about 100 per cent. I found the difference in the average of earnings in 1888 to be about 50 per cent. higher in America, but the labor cost about equal. This has since been corroborated by other investigations. All this is due to the great improvements and inventions, which find quicker application in America than elsewhere on account of the high rates of wages ruling here.

In the spring of the present year Bessemer steel billets were sold at two to three dollars less a ton at the works in Pittsburgh than in Barrow-on-Furness or in Middlesborough.*

---

* In 1887 and in 1888, already, I found the cost of labor in a ton of steel rails practically the same in Bethlehem and Pittsburgh, from the ore and coal and coke up to and including the finished steel rails, as in England (Darlington and Middlesborough).

The Commissioner of Labor, Mr. Carroll D. Wright, in a report on the same subject, makes the labor cost in America $3.78, or about 50 per cent. higher than in England. This results from the employment of strange methods of computation on his part.

He uses in his computation two and one fourth times as much coal for turning iron into steel rails with two processes in American practice as it takes in England with three processes. I should do violence to the understanding of my readers were I to tell them that it does not take more fuel in American than European practice.

He averages the cost of coke from a great number of coke works in the Union, and makes this statistical compound the basis of his calculations. This product of the imagination is rated at fully twice the labor cost at which Connellsville coke is put on board cars. Connellsville coke, however, is the only coke used in Bessemer iron, as Connellsville, producing cheapest, has also the advantage of lying nearest the Bessemer-iron-making centres. The remainder of the difference is made up of items of a similarly visionary character. Removing these and putting in the place of statistical quantities

Under the old methods working with hand tools, such as are still universally employed in the black country in England and in the Taunus mountains in Germany, a nailmaker's weekly earnings would be stated at a high rate as averaging $3, but his labor per pound of nails would cost for ordinary sizes, 1¼ cents. An American nailmaker in Pittsburgh earns in two thirds of the time of a hand nailer $5 a day. His work, counting helper and all, does not cost one half the price which one of the old-time workers is paid. Indeed the nails are sold in America at a considerably lower price than these nailers receive as pay for their work.* In composite products the divergence of time wages and labor cost shows still more distinctly.

The average of wages in the Waterbury Watch Company works was given me for men, women, and young persons as averaging $10.50 per week. The labor cost in a watch was 50 cents. In a watch factory in the Black Forest in Germany the average wages are less than 10

---

the actual quantities upon the basis of cost of the materials actually used, we have the same cost of labor remain over for America as for England.

Were a manufacturer to conduct his business upon such a basis as is imputed in the report of the Commissioner, he would bankrupt himself very quickly and deserve the derision of the commercial world.

Manufacturers do not use statistical materials at "scientific" average prices, but employ commercial materials at commercial prices. They make use of every stratagem and invention for the purpose of saving materials, and these they always obtain from the cheapest place of production from where it can be transported to the works at the lowest possible freight charge.

* The following price quotations are taken from the *Iron Age* of April 20th: "Wire nails for carloads at mill may be named at 85 to 90 cents (100 lbs.); small lots from store at New York $1.10 to $1.15. Cut nails at Pittsburgh: carloads at mill 70 cents; less than carloads 80 cents; small lots on dock or from store at New York, 90 cents." These are the lowest prices ever reached in any country. Since then a considerable rise has set in.

marks, $2.40, but they admit that they cannot compete with America in the lowness of the labor cost.

In a Lynn factory the wages average for men, $12; for women, $7. A particular kind of ladies' button boots made there costs 35 cents in the aggregate of all the labor parts in the boots. In England I found the earnings of men between $5.76 and $8.40, and that of women between $2.83 and $4.32; but the cost of labor in the same class of boots aggregated about 64 cents.

We could follow this *ad infinitum*, and we should always find that labor cost cannot at all be computed from the wage rate known to exist. In all these higher developed occupations the piece rate prevails. The remarkably low cost (and consequent decline in price) goes hand in hand with the high rate of wages, because of the minute division of labor, the employment of highly perfected machinery, and the fullest employment and intense exhaustion of the working time, which the best conditioned labor alone is capable of putting into the work.

CHAPTER XI.

Other Causes of Price-Decline—The Neglected Element in Political Economy—The Intellect as a Creative Force and Destroyer of Values.

I HAVE shown with great fulness and, it seems to me, conclusively in the last chapter that that part of the price of a commodity which is the chief element of cost, and is expressed by the word *labor*, has followed a downward tendency throughout this century. It follows from this with certainty that the cost of labor cannot have been influenced by the quantity of money in circulation. The labor cost was highest when the stocks of the circulating mediums were at the lowest; a rise in wages and the decline in the labor cost were simultaneous with the increase in the money stocks, from the quantity-theory view, utterly irreconcilable facts. If this principal element in the cost of production has occupied a smaller and smaller part and has fallen constantly in price while the money quantity has risen in a formerly unheard of ratio, then it is plain that the price-decline cannot be caused by the influences as assigned by the advocates of free coinage of silver.

Quite on the contrary, if the rate of wages determined the cost of production, if a day's labor in one place and at one time were worth as much or produced as much as at another place and at any other time, and if prices had to be measured by to-day's rate of wages in comparison with prices of fifty and a hundred years ago, then prices would naturally be two, three, and five times as high as they were then.

If the money quantities in existence were instrumental in making prices, then the vast accumulations of treasure the world over ought at least to have raised prices in the proportion in which labor is better remunerated. But if on the contrary prices are all the way from 50 to 75 per cent. lower, in many of the commodities of chief importance to mankind, while wages are much higher, then there must be other influences at work than those so readily accepted, to cause this remarkable coincidence of a rise in wages and the fall in the labor cost, the chief cause of the fall in prices.

It is a fact of no small significance that this rise in wages, which is so satisfactory an evidence of progress, can only be found in the gold-paying countries, *i. e.*, the countries which accepted for their standard the metal of highest value.

With this is connected the equally well established fact that the decline in prices is most noticeable in the advanced, gold-paying, countries. Bi-metallists, or rather silver mono-metallists, deduce from this ever-present fact, that gold has appreciated in purchasing power, meaning that prices have fallen, because gold alone has to perform the functions now which the two metals exercised before. Of course, this is again the money-quantity theory, the mechanical theory of prices.

But the causes of the phenomena lie deeper than a mere accident of money supply, silver depreciation, or gold appreciation.

Because the causes are of an inherent and not of an extrinsic character, the effect—low prices of commodities

—will remain the impressive exponent of the higher civilizations, comprehending the gold-paying nations of the world.

The gold-paying countries are the great progressive nations. There all the great industrial revolutions have taken their rise. No wonder that there the effect was most marked in this decline in prices, so astonishing to those who have omitted to take this feature, the natural result of an era of scientific development, into their calculation. Let us take up an item which is pre-eminently a product of gold-paying countries—pig-iron. It serves well as an illustration of a thing hardly considered worth examining as an element in price making—brain power.

Let us see what havoc this overlooked element has produced. We can see thereby what a value maker and a value destroyer the laboratory has come to be alongside of which the silver and gold mines of the world play a very small part indeed.

We have left the price of raw iron at the end of the seventeenth century in England at £12 10s. 0d. a ton. The weekly output of a furnace was about 10 tons. Charcoal was the only fuel used. Mineral coal, though abundantly supplied for other purposes, and an article of commerce as far back as the fourteenth century, called "seacoal" in the records of Merton College, because brought by sea from the mines, was not put to use in iron-making until long after. A law was promulgated against iron-making at the time of William III. on account of the devastation of the forests by the extensive consumption of wood and charcoal in the few iron-making districts. Yet the whole annual output is estimated as not exceeding 10,000 tons a year. A great deal of the iron consumed was brought from Spain.

Within a hundred years the price of iron came down considerably. But still, compared to our time, when in Alabama iron is made as low as $5.85 cents * a ton, the lowest cost ever reached in any country, the price must be considered extraordinarily high, although it is not much over one half of the price in 1694.

Tooke quotes the prices of pig-iron from 1782 to 1838 :

	£	s.	d.		£	s.	d.
In 1782 (Tooke)	6	0	0	and	7	10	0
In 1794 (Tooke)	5	0	0	and	8	0	0
In 1806 (Tooke)	7	0	0	and	9	0	0
In 1822 (Tooke)	6	0	0	and	7	0	0
In 1837 (Tooke)	6	0	0	and	6	10	0
In 1852					2	10	0
In 1857					3	10	0
In 1887	†1	8	0	and ‡	2	5	0

Neither appreciation of gold nor depreciation of silver can have had any effect on the steady price decline from 1837 to 1886, when, as I well remember, pig-iron sold in Middlesborough at 26s. a ton. But the laboratory, or what stands in its name, technical improvement, had.

The prices varied considerably in every year, and more so, naturally, between years of war and years of peace. But, on the whole, an average of £6 to £7 a ton marks the price of pig-iron for the fifty years previous to 1837, which are covered by the investigations of Thomas Tooke.

In 1850 the lower price level was existing. Since then the great change in the money stocks has made little difference in the price of coequal periods. All changes in

---

* This price is from the pay-rolls for the month of September, 1894, of the Tennessee Coal and Iron Company mentioned in the preceding chapter.

† Cleveland iron.

‡ Bessemer iron and Scotch iron. 1887 marks period of lowest trade depression in English iron prices.

price are traceable to the changes in the mechanism and the economy of production, and the saving of materials is not a small part of the achievements which dominate the price.

The output per furnace in 1788 is stated by Sir I. Lowthian Bell as $15\frac{1}{2}$ tons; in 1796 as 20 tons; in 1800 as 21 tons; and in 1827 it had progressed to 35 tons per week only. At the present time the product in England's largest furnace does not exceed 600 tons, while in America furnaces are built which produce 1400 tons a week. This is as much and more per week than the whole output per year of the old furnaces sixty and a hundred years ago. The capacity beyond a certain extent is no advantage, however, as our American ironmasters are beginning to find out, and is a matter of conviction among ironmasters in England. The advantages, from the general progress made, find their expression in the improvements by which labor and fuel are saved, and not in the size of the furnace. The quantities used are not different per ton of pig-iron, whether the capacity of furnaces of equally improved condition is 500 or 1500 tons. The saving in material and in labor is the sole cause of the great price reduction.

What the Improvements have Led to.

In 1835 the first cold-blast furnace, according to the same authority, with a capacity of 70 tons a week, consumed 6 tons of coal per ton of pig-iron. The introduction of a hot blast at 650° Fahrenheit produced iron with $4\frac{1}{4}$ tons of coal. In 1855 the use of the escaping gases for steam and hot air, with a blast of 800°, had reduced the amount of fuel to 3 tons of coal. In 1865 the furnaces had been so improved that, with a blast of 1000° and a weekly capacity of 450 to 550 tons, no more than 2 tons of coal were required. At the time of my investigations in 1888 the coal consumption was 1¾ tons.

The cost of labor depends in pig-iron on the tonnage of the materials handled. Not alone that the improvements save fuel, but the extraction of the metal from the ores is now so complete that no more than what is indicated by the percentage of iron in the ore is required, whereby also great savings are realized.

All this explains why the labor cost in the furnace work of a ton of pig-iron is now less than one half what it was one hundred years ago, and even sixty years ago. It explains why the workman earns 100 per cent. more in wages, and why we can buy three tons of iron for the same amount of money that was necessary for buying one ton then.

In this saving of materials, quantitatively, we must also include the price reductions in the materials, coal, coke, and ore, brought about by the improved processes in mining, coking, etc.

Speaking of the cost of coal and iron in Alabama, *The Engineering and Mining Journal*, of January 27, 1894, has a statement of the causes that made possible the price reduction which has astonished the world. It says:

"In the matter of costs the comparison between those of the present and the past is interesting. Referring more particularly to the Birmingham district, when the red ore mines were first opened below Birmingham the soft outcrop ore, requiring almost no stripping, was loaded into cars for 30 to 35 cents per ton, but in early underground development it cost almost double this price. Now, though it is taken from considerable depths underground, and air drills and dynamite are required for the work, it is delivered on cars for 50 cents per ton, this price allowing a good profit to the contractor. With 17½ cents freight to the furnace and using 2.2 tons per ton pig-iron, the cost of ore per ton of pig is $1.485.

"In coal mining, notwithstanding the fact that a much greater distance is covered in the workings, there has been a marked decrease in cost of production. When, a few years ago, coal was loaded at the mine for 70 cents a ton, it was thought to be exceedingly low, being a reduction of nearly 10 cents a ton under the cost not long before. But at present this work is being done for 60 cents a ton, and in some few cases for less, and the coal is produced in cleaner and better condition than formerly. This reduction in cost is largely due to substituting common labor for miners in loading the coal in the mine; now the miner only cuts the coal. The freight charge from mine to ovens is $12\frac{1}{2}$ cents per ton, and the practice of the district requires 1.6 tons coal to one ton coke; consequently coal and freight per ton coke amount to $1.16. Adding to this 35 cents, the contract price for coking (the contractor keeping up the plant and furnishing everything but the coal), the total cost of coke is $1.51. At some plants 45 cents is paid for coking, adding 10 cents to the cost given. Good furnace practice uses about $1\frac{1}{4}$ tons of coke per ton iron, making $1.89 the cost of coke per ton of iron. Limestone costs on an average 65 cents delivered, and three fourths of a ton is required, or 50 cents, per ton pig.

"Taking these figures, the material used in one ton of pig-iron is as follows:

$1\frac{1}{4}$ tons coke @ $1.51		$1.89
$2\frac{1}{4}$ " ore @ .50		1.48
$\frac{3}{4}$ ton limestone @ .65		.50
Labor		1.25
Repairs		.50
Supplies		.50
Selling expenses		.25
Total		$6.37

"At one plant labor costs $1 per ton of iron, repairs 50 cents, and selling expenses 25 cents, a total of $1.75, but this is undoubtedly below the average. It is a comparatively short time since the lowest labor in the district, excepting possibly two plants, was over $1.50, and in certain known cases $1.80. A fair average now is $1.25, though a number of plants show the labor item at $1.10 to $1.20 through considerable periods. In the matter of repairs, supplies, and selling expenses, while in the instance given they amount to but 75 cents, this is at least 50 cents under the average, as repairs and supplies alone, taking a period covering one campaign, or even a year, will amount to 50 cents each, and selling expenses 25 cents more. On this latter basis $2.50 for all items other than material gives a total cost of $6.37 per ton, while in the exceptional instance given it is but $5.62. Of course these figures do not include interest or capital accounts.

"It is hardly necessary to comment upon these figures, other than that they are actual working costs."

It is but a few years ago that $9.50 was considered a very low cost of Alabama iron of the most economically worked and best built furnaces, while many of the ironmakers proclaimed this a ruinous price

The improvements in mining operations, and this applies to gold and silver production * as well, if they do

---

* The effect of the rapidly introduced improvements on gold production is illustrated in the following statement from the *New York Journal of Commerce*, referring to the new process employed in the treatment of gold ores :

"It is of interest to note a recent improvement in the chemical treatment of gold ores, by which the production of gold has already been considerably increased, and which, eventually, must largely augment the yearly output. This treatment is what is known as the cyanide process. The short inaugural period of its existence debars the possibility of complete statistics ; but an example may be cited which will show the proportion of gold extracted which heretofore has remained unrecovered. From reports of mining companies in the Rand district it is seen that during the past four years the gold output has shown a very marked and steady increase. In 1890 the total product for the year was 494,870 ounces, while in 1894 it reached over 2,000,000 ounces. It is calculated that the product of the present year will approximate 3,000,000 ounces. The reports give the number of ounces obtained by the milling and cyanide processes. It is not uncommon to find that from a third to a half of the gold produced has been chemically extracted. One mine out of a total of 4138 ounces reports 1852 ounces obtained by the cyanide process. Another, for the month, 1925 tons ore, yielding 675 ounces gold ; cyanide works, 1260 tons ore, yielding 788 ounces. Many other companies show similar results. The gold extracted by chemical treatment is nearly all clear gain, since the greater part is obtained from tailings, and represents gold actually recovered, and which would have been entirely lost in the milling process.

" In a few years we may find that the quantity of gold extracted by the cyanide process or other chemical treatments has risen to large proportions. The process, as can be inferred from the above, is adapted to poor ores. The very wide distribution of such ores, together with its application to the tailings of stamping mills and mattes all over the world, heretofore not available for remunerative treatment, will open a field of production which must very materially increase the supply of gold."

A correspondent from Johannesburg to *The Economist* (London) gives the

not outstrip, at least equal, those in all other branches of metallurgy. We have stated the gradual reduction in the cost of producing copper in a mine operated by the same company for a period of forty years to one fourth the former expense.

The causes producing this result are stated by the *Iron Age* very conclusively, and, as they cover the whole field, I will give the paragraph in its original shape:

"The lowering in cost is, of course, due to a multiplicity of improvements in every department. We need only allude to the introduction of high explosives, the use of machine drilling, the employment of modern stamps for crushing the rock, the better methods of handling, the more economical engines for hoisting and pumping, the lowering of the cost of transporting the rock, the cheapening of the supplies, the reduction in smelting expenses and transportation to market, the lessening of cost of selling, and the distribution over a larger product of the general expenses and of outlays for administration.

"As bearing on the introduction of power drills, we have come across the following data which deal with the cost of underground work at the Osceola Mine. The cost of underground work was as follows:

	1879.	1880.	1881.
Sinking shafts, per foot	$25.38	$18.67	$15.22
Sinking winzes, per foot	11.14	12.36	11.39
Drifts, per foot	10.42	10.11	8.66
Stoping, per fathom	15.33	9.72	10.78

expert information of the practical workings, that the various processes have reached so high a state of perfection, that, whereas at the beginning of the industry only 50 per cent. of the gold in the quartz was extracted, fully 80 per cent. is secured now, and that the proportion is likely to be raised after some years to ninety in a hundred. Working expenses have shrunk to such an extent that whereas six years ago several ounces to the ton were necessary to make a mine pay, a profit is now in many cases obtainable with only five pennyweights. "Better organization, as well as cheaper labor or fuel," the writer adds, "and improved processes, may even bring still poorer ores within the scope of the industry."

What bearing these new processes will have on gold production is easily imaginable. It shows plainly enough in the annual rate of production.

"In 1879 all the work was done by hand. In 1880 and since then it was done by power drills.

"While it might not be possible to trace accurately the influence upon reduction of cost of all of the important technical improvements introduced, yet there can be no doubt from a study of the vast amount of data available that the betterments alluded to are solely responsible for the very marked decline in the cost of production and in the selling prices of copper."

The effect on prices of products of a more complicated nature than the extraction of iron and other metals is necessarily equally great. It progresses in the proportion in which invention has been able to substitute machinery and the operation of newly discovered agencies for the slow processes, still in use in the more backward portions of the progressive countries even, and little different from those we find among the aborigines of this and other continents.

I have mentioned the reduction of labor-cost in steel-rail-making in America. Here we beat the world in the rapid succession of improvements. The consequence is that our latest improved plants produce rails cheaper in labor-cost than is done anywhere in the world. The continuous mill rolls the rail from the ingot as it comes from the converter, cuts it in suitable lengths, and loads it on trucks, even, all by automatic appliances. The number of men required for a train has, by the introduction of these appliances, been reduced from seventeen to five and the roller in charge of the train.

I am told that the latest mill put up by the Carnegies has improved on that rate of perfection, even. But the cost of the plant is enormous. It is said that the cost of fitting up a modern rail mill is up to $1,500,000, outside of the cost of the building.

Unless a high rate of wages were pre-existing the inducement for applying all these improvements would be wanting. In some remote countries, where wages are lowest, the old furnaces which England employed a hundred years ago would probably be considered an improvement.

I have not the space at my command to follow this improvement in methods by which the cost of labor is reduced, the chief creator of values and prices, into other branches. Every day brings new inventions and new discoveries by which the improvements of a few years ago appear antiquated.*

The saving of materials is a cause of price decline in many of the most important manufacturing branches, hardly less important than that which we have observed in the labor cost.

The recovery of waste products yields far in excess of a paying profit in quite a number of industries. The cheapness of paper-making is due to the recovery of chemicals in pulp-making, which formerly went to waste.

---

* That this economizing of materials and of labor—with increasing wages—is entirely attributable to the application of science to the productive processes of industry, and is the only cause of the fall of prices, is easily demonstrable from steel rails.

In 1865 Bessemer steel rails sold in England at £17 10s. ($85). Hematite pig-iron, used for Bessemer rails, was a little under £4, making the difference between the crude metal and the finished rail as £4 3s. for the iron, and about £13 7s. for the steel.*

At the present time Bessemer rails sell at £3 12s. 6d., about $18,—and Bessemer pig-iron at £2 3s. the ton, so that there is between the cost of the crude metal and the selling price of the rails a difference of barely £1 6s.

The rate of wages has risen in England within the last thirty years by fully twenty-five per cent. The difference of £12 (90.25 per cent.) is the part of saving due to the causes here treated as the real price-reducing factors, science and improvement, so far as this sum does not cover diminished capital earnings and royalties paid to the inventor.

* See statement of Sir I. Lowthian Bell in Part I. *Report of Royal Commission on Depression of Trade*, 1886.

The price of paper is now not more than half what it was twelve or fifteen years ago.

The by-products from gas-making, formerly allowed to go to waste, pay the full regular rate of dividend, and beside made possible the great reduction in the price of gas which we observe in England, and which we long for in America.

Agriculture and Other Industries.

New industries have been created from the utilization of these by-products. The constant cheapening in the chemical, and chiefly in the color-making industries, is based on the use made of these waste materials from gas-making, and from the greater economy practised in their reduction. To Germany her universities and technical high-schools have become sources of wealth, though this is not yet recognized as such in the economic text-books.

This cheapening process by means of the intellectual forces directed on the economy of production has come entirely from the gold-paying countries, and certain price revolutions emanating therefrom are simply enormous. Beet sugar, clearly the creation of chemical science, has been reduced to one half its former cost, because scientists have so perfected the process of extracting all saccharine matter from the beet that they obtain about 14 per cent. where 8 per cent. marked the proportion about twenty years ago.

The cheapest producers make the price which the dearer producers have to meet as soon as supply covers the full demand, and this can only be done by following the lead and adopting improved methods of cultivation. The sugar planters have had to adapt themselves to the new spirit, and are profiting by the change.

The slack from the low-grade iron ores of the Cleveland district has been accumulating for the last forty or fifty years around the Middlesborough and neighboring furnaces. They were an encumbrance on much valuable land.

In 1888 a manufacturer at Stockton-on-Tees showed me ships loading under a contract with German firms of 80,000 tons at a rate of 4s. a ton for use as fertilizers. It was the beginning of a large trade. Since then, of course, the use of these slacks, rich in phosphorus, has become much more general. Agricultural chemistry gives a value to the refuse of the furnace as well as it does to the bone heaps and the offal of the slaughtering and packing houses, supplies the carrying trade and transportation lines with tonnage of immense extent, and restores to the soil the fecundity of which exhausting crops have robbed it.

That the application of science to manufacturing industries, metallurgy and mining included, is the great price-disturbing element will hardly be denied by any one who has the smallest notion of the facts which surround the economy of production. But the decline in agricultural prices has been treated as something caused less by the changes referred to, and more by the fall in silver and an implied insufficiency of circulation.

There is more theorizing on agriculture and less practical inquiry into the results following the changes of methods than in any other human employment. To what extent improvement has followed the introduction of the best methods in the past can be seen from a comparison of the state of agricultural yield, gross and net, in Russia on the one hand (marking to-day the level of England of the fourteenth century) and of the England of to-day. (Russia's average per acre in wheat is about seven bushels, that of England thirty bushels.)

But the extent to which these differences in yield, *i. e.*, larger net profit, even under a rule of low prices, can be obtained, I noticed last year in a visit to the South. In a soil which, without fertilizing, does not produce anything, and whose sand is not distinguishable from that of the desert, truck farmers produce the most astonishing crops. I visited several of them near Savannah, Ga. One of them, who is known as one of the leading men in the industry, Major Ryal, was good enough to give me a statement of his business and accounts. He farms about 125 acres, a large part broken in by himself. The farm yields now, in years when he can favorably market his crops, as much as $25,000 in salable value, and he clears all the way from eight to ten thousand dollars. He raises generally three crops a year. First, cabbages and early potatoes, beets, and other kitchen garden-stuff. The two former are the big money crops. Early potatoes, if they do not suffer from frost and can be put on the market in favorable time, bring $4 to $5 a barrel. An acre yields him from fifty to a hundred barrels. Twenty acres in potatoes, under favorable conditions, can bring therefore as high as $10,000. In the time of my visit, to Savannah he had cleared from ten acres 1700 crates of cabbages, which netted him $5300 after deducting 43 cents per crate for freight to New York. As a second crop he raises corn, and as a third crop hay.

Of corn he gets forty bushels per acre, and of hay two to three tons. If we consider the smallness of the average yield of the farming of Georgia, which is not more than ten to eleven bushels to the acre in corn, and one and a half tons per acre of hay in Southeastern Georgia, we can better estimate the difference which divides one mode of farming from another; we can easily understand how great the influence of the application of scientific methods in farming on price decline. If farming is conducted as an industry like manufacturing, the extent of supply cannot be foreseen.

My informant uses $50 worth of fertilizers per acre; $30 of this was artificial guano, and $20 farm manure, partly produced on the farm, and partly brought from Savannah. Of course, every other part of cultivation was in harmony with this high manuring, which, however, prevails in truck farming in general, though in the South generally to a less degree than in the Northern States.

In cotton growing the same facts are noticeable. At the low price at which cotton is selling now a profit is realized where better methods of cultivation are applied. The average for Georgia is about 160 pounds to the acre in a fairly good cotton year. This is equal to three acres to a bale. This average includes the fertilized and non-fertilized land. The non-fertilized produces but one bale to five or six acres, and to this mode of farming many a poor farmer is restricted.

With an outlay of $3 (giving two hundredweight of guano) one half bale of lint cotton is produced, making a difference of 150 pounds (counting the bale at 500 pounds), or, at six cents a pound, $9 extra yield in the improved farming. Except for the picking, which is paid for by the cotton seed, the labor is not greater under one system than under the other. On the contrary, it is less because the same results are reached from confining the farming operations to a smaller extent of territory.

Where richer fertilizing is employed, as is done by some progressive farmers, most satisfactory net results are reached. The application of ten hundred-weight of fertilizers at a cost of $16 gave a yield of 750 pounds of cotton. The tendency now is more and more toward smaller farms and better cultivation. The farmer doing his own work, ploughing, etc., which is now pretty general, would realize $8.50 under the lower, and $25 under the higher fertilizing of land per acre. Allowance is here made in this statement only for hoeing and ginning, and, as explained, the picking. Leaving out the account of the highly fertilized cotton land, as of a more experimental nature, we can see in the two examples the wide difference in results of farming under poor and under proper treatment of the soil.

The greatly increased product of the last few years is generally conceded by good authority to be "due more to improved methods of cultivation and to the shifting of the cotton belt to sections better adapted to securing larger results per acre, than to larger acreage."

But, with due allowance of the increase in the newer sections, the increased yield per acre shows as well in returns for Georgia as it does in Texas and other cotton States. The "improved methods of cultivation," therefore, can be taken as pretty generally distributed.

Whatever the ultimate effect on the inner economies of the farmer and of farming, the fact is beyond dispute that the decline in the price within the last few years is due to these causes, resulting in an over-supply, and not to an attributed cause, like the fall in the price of silver. Before the over-supply of 1890–91 and 1891–92 came on the market, the price was in 1890 about the same as in 1860. The average for the ten years ending with 1860 was barely one cent higher than the average for 1881 to 1890.

It has not yet come to pass that the Bombay shipper takes

less in pay than the equivalent in rupees of the gold price in Liverpool when a rise in price takes place there on any shortage in the supply.

But with crops such as the one of 1894-95 added on to the surplus from the two previous extraordinary crop years a low price is a matter of course. It ought not to be found more surprising than the low prices obtained for cotton in 1848 and 1849, which were considerably under the common average of preceding and succeeding years for no other reason than the one which depresses the price at this time.

Within six months of this year, 1895, the price of cotton, however, has risen from $5\frac{1}{2}$ cents to over 9 cents, as a consequence of the crop turning out to be below the average yield. The consumption is at present something in the neighborhood of 7,500,000 bales. The crop is estimated at about a million below this figure. The surplus in the market at the beginning of the new crop year is estimated at not less than 3,500,000 bales accruing from the excess crops referred to above. The highest shortage estimate would still leave a surplus on hand of 2,500,000 bales to carry over to the beginning of a new crop year for which the ground has not been broken yet. And yet such influence over price has been exerted by an apprehension on so unreal a basis.

CHAPTER XII.

Reductions in other Elements which Determine Prices—Agricultural Products and Systems of Land Tenure and Cultivation—Working under Freehold and one's own Farm—Producing a Money Crop—The Influence of Extended Transportation Facilities on Crop-raising—The Resulting Gain in Increasing Fields of Supply—New Continents Made Accessible—Decline in Freight Charges—Now only Nominal in Comparison with Rates Fifty and Twenty-five Years ago—Prices Reduced to Consumer without correspondingly Affecting Producer.

"THE tendency of prices is toward the cost of production" is a truism in economics. But it leaves the question open: What is the cost of production? The question can easily be answered in products of general industry, but is not so quickly disposed of in agriculture. Here a great many points play very important parts, which enforce production to proceed whether the cost of production is covered or not.

The cost of production in agricultural products besides, is something quite different in one country from what it is in another. The methods of cultivation, systems of land tenure, whether land is cultivated by tenant farmers with hired help or by farmers owning the land and working it themselves with such help as the members of the family can give, etc., greatly affect the cost of production and change the relative cost, between one set of producers and another, very materially.

Aside of this, economic forces are at play, as we shall see, which in new countries, at least, take little heed of many elements in cost which producers in England carry as most important parts of their calculations.

This is most clearly illustrated in wheat-raising. The method of figuring of cost of English wheat applied to American wheat-raising falls short of its aim on account of the neglect of a very important consideration, the position of the American farmer as a compulsory raiser of wheat.

As far back as a dozen years ago English farmers and landlords, beginning to feel the pinch of declining wheat prices under pressure of American competition, sent experts over to investigate the cost of production. I remember reading the statement of cost of raising wheat in Michigan, from which the comforting information was given to the English farmer that it would soon become impossible for American famers to profitably compete with English-grown wheat on the basis of then existing prices.

The export price average was then in the neighborhood of $1.15 per bushel. They calculated on the exhaustion of the soil and on the necessity of putting increasing quantities of labor and capital on the soil, and on the consequent rise of price to the English level.

But the growing of wheat at declining prices has gone on ever since. Not alone the new States, but States like Ohio and Michigan, keep on raising wheat.

Leaving out the low price, the result of the financial distress in America, and great crops in Argentina and elsewhere in 1894, the average export price has come down to a mean of about 70 cents. Under this price the *London Daily News*, in a recent issue, consoles its readers that "the competition cannot go on permanently," "that there must be loss is certain."

No doubt from the point of view gained from the English mode of farming the predictions might have become true.

.Correct account-keeping in English farming proves the inevitable doom of the American farmer. Counting rent, or, if not rent, interest on capital invested or borrowed, along with labor, as so much charged against the crop, it is not unlikely that under prevailing prices, averaging hardly more than seven dollars salable value, the farmer would not make his cost. But there is the difference of farming your own land " by your own hands, living a hard life on pork and beans, exposed to all the hardships and working most laboriously," as the *Daily News* very properly states the case of the American Farmer, and farming on the English mode of raising crops. Here lies all the difference.

Theoretically right as the computation of cost of raising wheat may be, counting rent, interest on capital invested, the cost of hired labor, compute the labor of the farmer, and charge the wear and tear of farm implements, etc., certain it is that in practice the American wheat-raiser works under the compulsion of different motives. He cannot very easily stay his hands if he cannot cover his cost according to the English mode of calculation. The American farmer is not placed differently from all the peasant farmers of continental Europe. He does not farm for a profit, but for a living. If he can eke this out and has enough of a salable crop to cover his money wants, he has reason to congratulate himself. That he is not so very far removed from this goal, despite the remarkable decline of corn and wheat prices, since the hopeful augury was given expression in England, is proven by the Census reports on mortgages. Mortgages on farms have certainly not increased on old settled lands. Considering that a very large part of all mortgages are taken on land as capital to enable new settlers to have an easier start, and deducting this from the sum-total, then a great portion of the farm mortgages of ten years ago would appear to have been paid off. But even were the outlook less propitious, the wheat-raiser would have to continue to raise wheat, the corn-raiser corn, and sell these crops *in natura* or in the form of fattened cattle and hogs, the same as the cotton-raiser will have to raise cotton, all for one and the same reason. They work under a stern compulsion easily apprehended.

The settler on western lands has no other crop which he can turn into money except wheat. He may raise other produce, but in strictly agricultural settlements this would find but a limited market among his neighbors, most of whom are situated as he is.

If he can supply himself and family with the necessaries from the farm, in vegetables, butter, milk, and meat, he is well off indeed. Many of these even he has to purchase. Now, how is he to raise money for supplying himself with many of the most important necessaries of life except by raising a crop easily turned into cash?

But he has no heavy outlay, such as the English farmer. The chief farm work is done by himself, aided, perhaps, by members of his family, and, possibly, if necessary, what hired help he may require in harvest time.

The large farm, producing wheat under capitalistic management, employs by the aid of labor-saving machinery so little help that, comparative with the output, the labor counts an insignificant part. There the cultivation has reached the point of an industrial enterprise. Still it is the experience that these mammoth farms on the long run go into smaller holdings with the growth of population.

But whatever the position, at the present and for a long time to come, probably, the wheat-raiser has no alternative but to raise wheat, because wheat is the only money crop he can put his energies to. It is the same with the grower of corn, the grower of cotton, etc., each in its zone. Hired help is expensive, difficult to get, when needed, at harvesting, even at high rates, and so it is economy of labor after all which prescribes the system of agriculture which the American farmer has to follow.

The Modern Methods of Transportation.

Without railroads the farmer could not have settled any appreciable distance away from navigable rivers. The railroads have added all the intermediate lands to the food supplies of the world. The improvements in transportation, the multiplication of lines, keep the farmer in easy communication with his markets.

The consuming power is increasing, it is true; but more so is the producing power. What applies to America, applies to Australia, applies to Argentina and Chili; it applies to India, it applies to Russia, Roumania, and Austro-Hungary. They all produce a surplus over the needs of their own country.*

They are all now in line of communication, or are bringing more and more land within new avenues of communication to reach the markets the American farmer has to rely upon for the sale of that part of his surplus not

---

* The difficulty of obtaining land sends the emigrant to the new countries. Freed from the trammels which tradition and ancient law have wound around land and its cultivator in the old country, he becomes in his new and free surroundings the leveler of prices and destroyer of values, now the amazement of England and the countries of Europe.

consumable at home, and which determines the price. They are all after the same markets. The markets are limited to a few countries. The supply is growing. Here, as well as in the other countries mentioned, the same necessities impel the raising of a crop which can be turned easiest into money.

If we examine into the extension of wheat-growing in the last twenty-five years, and the increase of the marketable surpluses, it is easy to understand why wheat prices have declined, irrespective of the fall in the price of silver or any other monetary consideration.

Three years ago, with immense crops in America, the price was the highest for years because a failure of crops in other countries had created a sufficient demand for the American extra supply. Silver, however, had again begun its career downward, in which it was temporarily interrupted by the enactment of the Sherman Silver Bill. Silver-paying countries shared no less in the advance caused by that shortage in the wheat crops of the world than gold-paying countries. Whatever the relative price of wheat in silver or in gold currencies, the actual price fluctuations the world over are the same, and due alone to the causes stated above put into active operation by the railroad and the steamboat.

The steamboat a generation ago was a very poor contrivance as a carrier of bulky freight. The consumption of coal per horse power was so great and the speed so slow compared to the present conditions, that the space now available for this bulky freight was entirely absorbed by the fuel the steamers were obliged to carry.

The greatest rate of progress in these achievements has been reached within the last fifteen or twenty years, and it is not surprising that the pressure should be felt by the

English farmer, with half a dozen wheat-raising countries unloading their surplus before his very gates.*

In cotton the price had maintained itself very steadily up to 1891, although India and Egypt have extended their cultivation. Gold-paying America determined the price so long as the supply ran even with the demand. A large surplus existing cannot fail to depress prices.

In putting cotton and wheat in comparison we can see at a glance that the recent price declines in these are due entirely to the operation of the economic law known as Gregory King's law, that a surplus in the market depresses the price of a commodity in the proportion of that surplus to the usual consuming demand.

But it is a mistake to suppose that the American farmer has been equally affected as the English wheat-producer. A comparison of prices and of transportation rates of former times with those of recent dates will show this clearly. Prices at terminal points formerly were widely divergent.

The English average price of wheat for 1860 was 54 shillings per quarter, which is equal to $1.63 the bushel. The average price for spring wheat in Chicago was 97½ cents, and winter wheat $1.10. For the same time the price in New York for the former averaged $1.22½ and for the latter $1.38 the bushel. But 1860 was a year of high wheat prices, and we cannot argue very well from that year.

Let us take 1850, with wheat at $1.25 a bushel as the average price in England. Spring wheat in Chicago aver-

---

* It is strange to speak about a limit with a Siberian railroad building and millions of settlers on the alert for the new openings. But Russia itself with railroads and general improving of conditions at home could supply alone and with ease the shortage in wheat of all the rest of Europe.

aged 65 cents; winter wheat 95 cents—an average price of 80 cents. The New York average price was $1.10 and $1.25 respectively, or an average of $1.17½.

The influence of the American price on English wheat prices was then not yet appreciable. The farther back we go, the greater independence of the western and the eastern, the American and the English prices, until in distant times, the same as in backward countries of to-day, each country and section has its prices high or low simultaneously and entirely independent of other sections or countries. The average for 1846 in England $1.65, was 60 cents in Chicago and $1.10 in New York.

With the inferior means of communication the pressure of distant areas of production could exercise little, if any, influence on prices. Each centre of population had to look upon a near source of supply from where the cost of transportation did not absorb the greater part of the price.*

The Senate Finance Committee, known as the Aldrich Committee, has collected some valuable statistics of prices covering a period of fifty years.

---

* I find for one and the same year prices to vary in the most violent fashion in the different parts of France; and the same occurrence, of course, is found in every country and in every period, conditioned as were the European Middle Ages. Thus, for instance, the price per Hectoliter stands:

In 1428: Troyes, fcs., 3.62; Orleans, fcs., 10.92; Alby, fcs., 58.35.
In 1429: Strasburg, fcs., 6.40; Orleans, fcs., 19.37; Alby, fcs., 9.72; Caen, fcs., 2.51.
In 1431: Paris, fcs., 7.29; Alby, fcs., 9.72; Orleans, fcs., 5.92; Saint Leonard, fcs., 1.32; Strasburg, fcs., 5.24; Limoges, fcs., 14.60.
In 1432: Alby, fcs., 10.48; Limoges, fcs., 19.10; Saint Leonard, fcs., 6.67.
In 1433: Alby, fcs., 8.76; Saint Leonard, fcs., 16.

Not alone that grains vary between famine prices in one and superfluity prices in another section, but the abundance of one year makes room to famine prices in the succeeding year in one and the same locality, as is seen from the above statement of six years' grain prices taken without any special design by Mr. d'Avenel, except to show the basis upon which the "price averages" rest.

The price quotations for Chicago wheat in the early years are in many instances so low (such prices as 20, 35, and 38 cents the bushel) that the question may be raised whether some of the figures represent more than temporary quotations, when we consider that little would have been realized by the farmer, after paying charges and expense of carrying to Chicago.

But no doubt the figures taken from official sources correctly state in general the prices existing. The average for spring wheat from 1840 to 1845 is about 45 cents; for winter wheat 60 cents. The fluctuations are extreme; prices in 1843 vary from 20 cents to 75 cents in spring wheat, and from 45 to 85 cents in winter wheat. New York prices vary between $87\frac{1}{2}$ and 93 cents in spring and 90 cents to $1.20 in winter wheat. The prices fluctuate far less violently in New York than in Chicago, because of the constant consuming demand at the former place, a distributing centre for a large population, while at the latter place population was sparse yet and the heavy cost of freight prevented reaching out for distant markets.

The export demand exercised but little influence on prices. The exports in wheat averaged for the five years ending with 1845 but 600,000 bushels, and in flour but 1,200,000 barrels.

But what concerns us here mostly is the difference in price of western wheat and eastern wheat. Whether we compare the prices by months, or average the different months, we get to pretty nearly the same results, a difference of about 40 cents in the price of wheat between Chicago and New York. At the present time the difference is barely 5 cents between Chicago and New York prices.

The western farmer's condition has certainly been improved by the ability of reaching the world's markets at a rate of expenses which, compared with the cost of carriage at the earlier stages of railroad-building, must be considered as but a nominal charge.

The through freight charges on grain by the leading roads from Chicago to New York averaged about $1.20 per 100 pounds for November, 1865; they had fallen in 1870 for the same month to 60 cents, and averaged at that rate till about 1873. Thence in 1874 to 1880 the rates fell to 40 and 35 cents, and from there came down to rates varying between 20 and 25 cents in 1890.

What is worthy of note is that rates of freight when once lowered have never come back to old positions. Free competition among the lines insures the same results as an enactment would, if we were to follow the Belgian precept in this direction. November rates are highest, on account of closing navigation and discontinued competition by lake and canal routes.

Through freight by lake and rail 18 cents per bushel in October, 1877, came down to $7\frac{1}{4}$ cents in 1890. Lake and canal route charges in September and October, 1878, averaged $13\frac{1}{2}$ cents, in 1890 only 6 cents, per bushel.

Ocean rates have fallen more noticeably yet. The rates in the years farthest back show greatest variations. The freight room was not in as great supply as at present, and high rates followed greater demand for tonnage.

But taking the six months from July to January, when the bulk of the harvest is being shipped, we average for 1870, per bushel, $15\frac{1}{2}$ cents; for 1873, even, $25\frac{3}{4}$ cents; for 1876, 16 cents; for 1880 we have 14 cents; for 1884 we have 10 cents; for 1888 we have 8 cents; for 1890 we have about 4 to 5 cents, which is the average for 1892, and may be considered the general average rate now.

The rates for 1891, a year of great crops here and a corresponding demand in Europe, made freights rule very high for the time being. But the average was not above 8 cents a bushel. If we go back no farther than 1873 we can state that a difference in freight charges from Chicago to New York of 20 cents per bushel over the present rates have accrued to the eastern consumer, and to the western farmer alike. A further benefit to the western farmer and the European consumer is in the fall of ocean freight of fully 10 cents in this period of about 20 years.

We, in America, certainly have to take this margin into consideration (about 30 cents per bushel)—the saving of freight to the consumer of the farmer's surplus, when we speak of the fall in the price of his wheat.

In other freights, of course, similar reductions can be shown. In cotton the rates by steamer from New Orleans to New York in 1873 averaged 60 cents per 100 pounds; in 1880, 45 cents; in 1892, 32 cents. The all-rail rates from Atlanta, Ga., in 1886, were 85 cents; in 1893 they are 67 cents. Ocean freights have followed a similar course as in wheat.

If I were to bring the general freight decline into an average figure, I should say that the charges are, all around, not much above one third of what they were about twenty-five years ago.

In bulky freight this element has always been a chief factor in price-making. The lower the value in proportion to weight, the greater the share of freight in the price. Hence we see what a great part this feature plays in just those prices which have all along been used as the play-ball in the silver argument.

Transportation in the Past.

Perhaps no other branch of economic activity shows so plainly the vast advance of our modern civilization over preceding ones as the modern system of transportation. The periods of progress of all nations show the attention of rulers and governing bodies to the improvement of the means of communication. If not for civilizing and commercial ends, strategic interest sets to work to build roads and improve waterways. The perfection of Roman road-building is attested by the centuries which have brought them down to our own days as unrivalled marvels of construction. Thorold Rogers speaks of the low rates of carriage up to the sixteenth century in England and the much higher rates of later times. He ascribes this to the perfect roads in the earlier centuries, while later on in the economic stagnation of England in the sixteenth and seventeenth centuries they were left to decay. I can attribute this to no other cause than to the endurance of the roads built during the Roman invasion.* It is more than doubtful that the English of the thirteenth and fourteenth centuries could have been very expert in road-building. But it is very probable that they made more of the existing high roads by keeping them in repair, than in the succeeding centuries characterized by strife and oppression of the working-classes and the agricultural populations.

Although Charlemagne had already taken into consideration the building of a canal for uniting the navigable parts of the Danube and the Rhine, and Lombardy and Tuscany were traversed with canals as early as the twelfth

---

* Bergier, *Histoire des Grands Chemins de l'Empire Romain* (1622), is authority for the statement that England had 2579 Roman miles of roads, *i. e.*, 2380 English miles.

century, England did not see any canals until late in the eighteenth century, when the Bridgewater Canal was built.

The writers of the latter part of that century are full of complaints about the bad land communications. Marshall says that in Devonshire in 1770 all transportation was done on the pack-horse; that the Weald of Sussex was almost entirely without roads in 1791, and that the neighborhood of Birmingham saw no improvement of its roads from the time of the old Mercian Kingdom to 1770.

In the seventeenth century the charge for timber, bricks, hay, corn, as quoted from the Oxford records by Thorold Rogers, runs from 8½d. to 1s. per ton per mile. This is about fifty times the present rail rate. The carriage of a ton of grain 200 miles to any place of scarcity was a charge of from $1 to $1.20 for freight on every bushel of wheat so carried.

To speak of carriage over greater distances in a low-wage period, I will cite a load of goods weighing 10¼ cwts., brought from London to Smithhills near Bolton in Lancashire in 1588. The distance is 197 miles. The charge is 5s. 6d. ($1.33) on the cwt., which is £5 10s. ($26.73) on the ton. It would not cost the tenth part to-day to bring a ton of wheat from Chicago to New York, a distance five times as great. A load of hydraulic lime is carried in 1693 from Bishopsgate, London, to Cambridge, a distance of 50 miles. The weight is 26¾ cwts., and the cost of carriage is 64s. 8d. ($15.74), just about 1$s$. per ton a mile. This is four times the value at London at that time.

Carriage by water was lower, of course, but still very high in the light of the present day.

In 1608, 28½ loads of timber are shipped a distance of 22½ miles at a cost of 6s. 2d. ($1.49) per load or ton. The rate per mile per ton is therefore 6¼ cents.

A load of stone carried to Oxford in 1661 costs nearly eight cents per ton a mile to carry. In all coarse goods the cost was easily doubled and trebled by freight charges if carried any considerable distance. In manufactures, which were not carried to any very large extent, except at the time of the fairs, the proportion of freight charge to the value of the goods was smaller, but still it made a not unimportant addition in the price. It is easy to comprehend that not all is said, when merely the price at the place of production is mentioned in past price-periods.

But all this is in the memory of living men, is the case in backward countries to-day, and was universal not more than fifty or sixty years ago.

CHAPTER XIII.

Other Causes which Made Prices High in the Past—Changed Conditions in the Course of their Removal.

VERY various are the causes which contributed to make prices high in the past. Next to the inefficiency of labor, the stagnant condition of agriculture and the wretched means of communication, we have to consider the great risks and dangers, the multitude of exactions, duties, and other charges on traffic, the interference of the state, the privileges of the guilds, the monopolies giving whole lines of commerce into a few individual or corporate hands, as barnacles on trade and instruments for raising prices.

The line of burdens is by no means exhausted by the enumeration. But I name only the chief ones acting on prices and carried over from primitive conditions of society into our days.

The survey would not be complete, the magnitude of the load and the consequent effect of its removal would not be appreciated, did I not make, at least, passing reference to them.

The Risks of Commerce.

The high cost of foreign, southern, and eastern produce has been referred to above. It is well to observe that with the high cost of transportation by the pack-horse or the camel over thousands of miles of desert and wretched roads, the account was by no means complete.

The predatory bands had to be paid, either in buying from them protection against other robber bands or in losing the property and, possibly, life in defence of the property. Up to the time of the discovery of the sea route to India, the products of the East were obtainable in this way alone. Cairo and Alexandria were the transmitters. Proceeding from Venice or Genoa, the merchants suffered exactions no less burdensome, though the robbers were devout Christians and did penance before the shrine of the Holy Virgin.

When the bulk of the carrying trade took to the new ocean route the risks were not diminished. Piracy was considered an honorable occupation. Elizabeth's partnership with the pirates is a well authenticated fact. The destruction of the enemy's fleet was a road to honor and to wealth. And the enemy was everybody who carried anything worth risking life to take.

Armed convoys were therefore a necessary accompaniment of the trader's fleet. In the fifteenth century, Venice had a regular system of convoys. The fleets to Alexandria were accompanied by four, to Syria by four, and to the near shores of Africa by two armed galleons. Convoying was kept up by Spain well into the nineteenth century for its silver ships plying between Spain and America, and money shipments were, as a rule, made on men-of-war within comparatively modern times.

Macaulay, in speaking of the English navy and the men who manned it in the reign of Charles II., says:

"The chief bait which allured these men into the service was the profit of convoying bullion and other valuable commodities from port to port; for both the Atlantic and the Mediterranean were so infested by pirates from Barbary, that merchants were not willing to trust precious cargoes to any custody but that of a man-of-war. A captain, in this way, sometimes cleared several thousands of pounds by a short voyage; and for this lucrative business he too often neglected the interests of his country and the honor of its flag, made mean submissions to foreign powers, disobeyed the most direct injunctions of his superiors, lay in port when he was ordered to chase a Sallee rover or ran with dollars to Leghorn when his instructions directed him to repair to Lisbon: and all this he did with impunity." *

This gives an idea of trading conditions in time of peace. They continued well into the last century. The risks in war time, of course, were eminently greater. And war on the oceans during the seventeenth and a greater part of the eighteenth century was in permanency.

Where such charges had to be borne in regular trading, and tremendous losses had to be encountered on extra occasions, it is natural that compensation was sought in high profits. While now ten per cent. would pay the great trading houses a very handsome return, and five per cent., a mere commission, is a satisfactory return on the turn-over after paying expenses, a hundred per cent. was a regular profit charge in earlier trading, with, frequently, much higher charges. To this day " A Dutchman's one per cent.," in popular parlance, means one hundred per cent. As the Dutch had the carrying trade of the East for a long time, it is easy enough to see how they measured their profits, and what the people thought about it.†

---

* Macaulay, *History of England*, ch. iii.

† A hundred per cent. was recognized in the capitularies of Charlemagne as the legitimate rate of merchants' profits. In the middle ages, as in all times of undeveloped trade, the rate of profit is high. Smallness of the transactions and the limited purchasing capacity of the people make this a matter of course.

The merchants at the fair at Kabul consider a profit of three to four hundred per cent. not excessive, according to Ritter (*Erdkunde*, vii., 244).

An example of the profit of caravan trading is expressed by an instance of ten million piasters brought back from the Soudan in return for one million of merchandise taken there by a caravan from Morocco.

For the greater part of the seventeenth century the carrying trade lay in their hands. In 1669 Colbert estimates the vessels of all merchant marines as 20,000, of which he allows 15,000 to 16,000 to the Dutch, and only 600 to France.* The blame for raising prices by the exercise of monopoly lies, therefore, at their doors.

The Carrying Trade.

In dealing with this chapter of the price history of the time most important for our discussion, it is, therefore, necessary to speak of the Dutch more than of other nations. This does not by any means imply that these other nations were more modest in their demands or more moderate in the treatment of the weak peoples whom they made tributary to their commerce or victims of their avarice.† The Dutch, being the most refined and most civilized trading nation of Europe of the time, were probably not more exacting or cruel than those from whom they had taken the trident or those who were to succeed them in the following century. Still their grasping and grinding tendency is a matter of history, and can by no means find extenuation.

To give an example of the spirit which animated the great trading companies, I cite the fact that in order to

---

*An idea of the preponderance of the Dutch carrying trade and the insignificance of all other is conveyed by the statement of Hume, according to which the Dutch at about the end of the reign of James I. traded to England with 600 ships, England to Holland with 60 only.

† In example, the treatment of the Irish by the British in the seventeenth and eighteenth centuries, the butcheries, the confiscation of their lands under the appropriate cry "to Hell or to Connaught," the destruction of the Irish industries by acts of Parliament, and many other shining proofs of the spirit which filled that period.

advance the price of spices, the Dutch in 1652 destroyed the shrubs and trees on the spice islands. They paid the native rulers and their dependants for destroying trees which might become accessible to others, and thus interfere with their monopoly.*

---

* " I assign the fact " (of the rising price of spices in the middle of the seventeenth century) " to the monopoly which the Dutch had obtained on the spice islands to the energetic means which they took to secure or extend the monopoly, and especially to the practice they adopted of bringing or forcing the native princes to destroy all the trees to which possible interlopers might have access. We are expressly told that the English had numerous factories in the spice islands, that they abandoned some of them and were squeezed out of others by the Dutch. Now, it will not be surprising that the East India merchants were able to instigate that bitter hostility to Holland which can be found in all seventeenth-century English literature and, indeed onwards, and to foment those prejudices to which Selden, Swift, Arbuthnot, and Defoe gave expression. I feel sure that the extreme unfairness with which the English Government treated Holland was the outcome of that unhappy commercial policy under which Dutch trade was more unwise and grasping than even the English and Spanish colonial systems were." (Thorold Rogers, *Hist. of Agr. and Prices*, vol. v., p. 454.)

Holland was one of the great-powers of the seventeenth century. She had the means still in 1704 to keep an army of 160,000 men (Van Noorden, *History of the Eighteenth Century*). But Holland shared the fate of all trading republics. Victors against tremendous odds so long as the spirit of freedom and independence is active and arms rich and poor to sacrifice life and property in the defence of the fatherland. They go to pieces when wealth creates an inseparable gulf between rich and poor, when wars of rapacity and conquest are undertaken, and the defence of the country, even, is left to mercenaries and hired soldiers. Wealth keeps growing, profits are big, Amsterdam is the banker of the world, until London is ready to take hold of the strong box of Europe. But the Tromps, the De Ruyters, disappear. No more deeds of valor like that of the self-organized fleet of fishermen, who take it into their heads to sail into a Spanish harbor and destroy the Spanish fleet collecting there against their country. Henceforth the elements are expected to do the fighting, and the jealousies of the powers do the rest in preserving the independence of Holland.

The foreign commerce of the maritime nations in the seventeenth century soon became absorbed by stock companies. Privileges and trading monopolies were granted with a lavish hand by the kings to favorites, or bought from the crown, or obtained through bribery and corruption. But although the gross profits were enormous, as the original cost was little more than the cost of cultivation, gathering, and getting ready from the place of embarkation of the produce of countries in a low state of economic development, and the prices were so much higher than they are to-day, as shown in some of the previous chapters, yet the net results were by no means as satisfactory to the stockholders as would appear from a mere consideration of these facts. A French writer in 1769 gives a list of fifty-five monopoly companies for foreign commerce which had failed. The Dutch East India Company paid 987 per cent. in dividends from 1605 to 1648. But from 1613 to 1693 its total net profits did not exceed 48.3 millions of florins, equalling about 10 per cent. of its capital, per annum. From 1693 the losses exceeded the gains. Up to 1779 the former reached 85 millions of florins, and when it went to pieces in 1794, the company was found with liabilities of 127,553,280 florins, and assets of only 15,287,832 florins. The English East India Company paid during most of the time of its existence an annual dividend of 10 per cent., from 1791 regularly 10½ per cent. But in 1835 its liabilities amounted to £31,326,000, and its assets to £19,649,399.

What contributed so much to these unsatisfactory results lay chiefly in the nature of these monopolies, which fostered narrow and grasping characters, and an eagerness for gain that overshadowed all other considerations. Their cruel treatment of the natives, where they exercised political power, is well known, and caused the mother country frequently to interfere and abridge their rights long before they were abolished.

The officers of the companies used their places as means for enriching themselves. Since the middle of the seventeenth century the Dutch had no other end in view in entering the service of the company, and the practice of making frequent changes, adopted in the beginning of the eighteenth century, did not diminish the abuse. Besides, they traded on their own account, to the neglect of the interests of the company. The salaries were poor, and all prohibitive injunctions did not avail against this abuse of a trust.

The frequent loss of vessels was ascribed to a large extent to overloading on private account. The running into different ports to dispose of the goods of this underhand traffic not alone required nearly half as many more ships than necessary for the trade of the company, but also extended the return time to unusual and wholly unnecessary length. The vessels of the English East India Company required eighteen instead of eleven months from China to Europe, because the officers and crew traded in all the ports along the route. The freight per ton amounted to six times the amount it would have cost if carried by private shippers. As all foreign commerce, and chiefly the eastern and southern trade, down to a comparatively recent period, lay in the hands of these monopolies, the above recital of conditions under which it was conducted, easily explains a very important element in the history of *high prices in the past*.

Monopolies and Guilds.

The raw materials of industry brought from distant countries were made so excessively dear, partly by the natural conditions of trade and transportation, and partly by the exercise of grinding monopoly, that it remains a surprise that so great a traffic in them could be maintained prior to the introduction of a new industrial system, and the abolition of burdens which mistaken social and governmental views had imposed upon industry and commerce, or decaying mediæval conditions had left them saddled with.

But these taxes on the material were left in the shade by the trammels on industrial production still in operation in parts of Germany up to the middle of this century, according to my own recollection, and in Bavaria to a later day even.

First of all, the privileges of the trade-guilds were of such a nature that they gradually developed from the most beneficial civilizing and liberalizing institutions of the Middle Ages into burdensome and reactionary organizations, retarding progress and preventing the introduction of improvements.

F. von Schroeder, *Schatz-und Rentkammer*, 1686,* calls them " die vermaledeiten und als die aergste Pest von ganz Deutschland verfluchten Zuenfte," † and names them as the cause why manufacturing industries could not come up. The Diet frequently threatened to suppress them. But outside of Prussia things remained as they had been for a good long time far into the present century. An exception of this was in the trans-Rhenan provinces. There the powers left the Code-Napoléon in operation as a memento of the sway of modern enlightenment against ante-revolutionary conditions restored to the

---

* Roscher, Wm., *Nat. Oek. d. Handels und Gewerbfleisses*, § 134.

† "The damnable trade-guilds cursed by all Germany as its worst plague."

rest of Germany by the rulers in grateful recognition of the services of the people in the war for freedom.

In Saxony, prior to the introduction of liberty of trade, no fewer than seven trade-guilds disputed before the courts in the exercise of the right of making skates. In 1849 the town-guilds petitioned for a prohibition of the manufacture of window-frames in the country, because the towns were unable to compete on account of the division of the work between the glaziers, the locksmiths, the carpenters, and the painters—who were separated by impassable barriers, while in the country none of these trammels existed.

If by a change of fashion a trade lost its markets, those practising it were prevented by the guild regulations from entering even one most nearly related to it.

In the last century the shoemakers of Bremen carried the prohibition of bringing shoes from outside to Bremen. This applied even to the fairs. Foreign and German states took retaliatory measures. But the guilds declared that they would rather forego all foreign custom than have their home-monopoly infringed upon to the slightest degree.

But France, before Turgot's time, seems to have been the ideal of trade restriction and monopoly. The division into branches could scarcely be carried farther. The reason is that the state made the granting of concessions and privileges a source of revenue.

Colbert had certainly far-reaching views for his time. His endeavor to improve the finances and to raise revenue was, of course, paramount. He knew, however, that this could not be done except by raising the industrial status of the kingdom, which was very low when he took charge of affairs. How he succeeded is a matter of history. If he introduced new burdens, he certainly abolished a great many others, or tried to reduce them to a less oppressive point.

Had not an ambitious, vain, and profligate king squandered the resources of the kingdom in attempts upon neighboring countries, there is little doubt that many of Colbert's measures would have been reduced to much milder form. The necessities increasing after his death made the seeds planted by Colbert blossom luxuriously. When the war with Holland broke out, Colbert himself made the taxing of corporations a source of income. He collected a tax from all trade-guilds for the confirmation of their privileges, and ordered that all trades should organize themselves into guilds. In consequence, the Paris guilds, numbering 60 in 1674, had increased to the number of 124 by 1691. On the principle " that the king alone had the right of creating masters of a craft," that is to say, that every one owed to the king alone the right of exercising his trade,* an edict was promulgated in

---

* It is necessary in order to understand the spirit of the seventeenth and of, at least, the first half of the eighteenth century to remember that the king claimed everything as his own. Absolutism claimed the right of ownership over life and property of the individual. The individual itself had no conception yet of the idea of personal freedom and equality under the law. This is a matter of later growth. To feudalism the idea was foreign. The independence, rights, and freedom of the town, the community, the province, if you choose, were jealously guarded and defended. Every one of the estates, states, and communities exercised its own jurisdiction and defended with zeal, perhaps, the rights of its subjects or members against the encroachment of the king or the of rising dynastic houses. But every person's minutest doings were subject to carefully prepared rules and regulations. The guild was at all times a ready regulator of every detail in the life of a member of a craft. The individual was well trained in the rule of submission to the dictation of a superior body, though himself a voting member of it with full rights and privileges. With the decay of mediævalism in the

1691 by which every one coming to be a master had to pay a tax to the state, varying from ten to forty livres according to the importance of his trade. The guild-master's office was made hereditary and purchasable. And this was considered an improvement over previous conditions.

The abuses of the guilds had become a crying evil. The extreme prolixity, the high dues, the expense of the

---

seventeenth century and the breaking up of the feudal territorial forms of government, the centralization under the crown and the introduction of absolutism became a matter of course. No one at the time found the statement of Louvois preposterous in his political testament addressed to the king: "All your subjects, whoever they may be, owe to you their persons, their goods, their blood, without the right of claiming anything. Sacrificing all to you, they give you nothing, as it all belongs to you." In his instructions to the Dauphin, Louis XIV. says: "The kings are absolute lords and have, naturally, the full and free disposition of all possessions." (" Les rois sont seigneurs absolus et ont naturellement la disposition pleine et libre de tous les biens, qui sont possédés.")

The crown's prerogatives, extending over almost everything, were soon an important instrument of taxation. Monopolies and privileges of commerce were farmed out with rights to the possessors over the individual barely conceivable in our days. In England even, private persons in control of a monopoly could penetrate into the interior of houses. Those in possession of the saltpetre monopoly collected regular tribute from those who would be free from vexatious visitations, etc.

. The character of the system is well illustrated by the fact stated in Lingard's *History of England* that the new monopolies, which Charles I. created and gave to *regulated companies*, paid a net revenue to the state of £1500, but to the companies £200,000.

A system of taxation, in the modern sense, was absent. For a long time yet the officers of the state were made to pay themselves by way of levies on the unfortunate inhabitants. The large incomes of many of the high charges without having fixed salaries shows a system of administration as now only found in Turkey and, possibly, Russia in modern Europe. The effect upon prices of all this, no matter how legitimate in descent such a system of government, is easily understood.

masterpiece, and the feasting, as part of it and, in fact, of every event of importance in the guild, and the intriguing connected with electing the guild master, would seem to have made the new arrangement a change to the better. But the thing was merely a financial scheme. An edict issued by the Council of State, in 1693, gave the guilds the right to purchase back their old privileges. Louis XIV.'s financial measures were continued on this line. All offices were purchasable. Those relating to trade and industry were multiplied *ad infinitum* to be sold for cash.

As an example :

"In October, 1704, the king created 'inspecteurs généraux, commissaires-visiteurs et contrôleurs des manufactures des draps et toile et gardes-concièrges.' In December, of the same year, these offices were abolished again on the payment by the guilds of 1,200,000 livres." *

Industrial Regulation by the State.

The multiplication of offices was carried on so wildly that it was found on various occasions, that the same offices had been created twice over. These offices were all direct taxes upon the guilds. They were responsible for their payment. Neglect was followed by abolition of their privileges. The admission of masters by the state, on payment of the official tax, soon brought contumacious guilds to terms. The result of all this was, that the guilds overburdened with taxes, which all fell heavily on production, were forced to make admission more and more expensive and difficult to obtain. Besides the taxes directly borne by the members, the guilds were all heavily in debt ; some of the Paris guilds, by the middle of the eighteenth

---

* Henry W. Farnam, *Die innere franzoesische Gewerbepolitik von Colbert bis Turgot.*"

century as high as 400,000 to 500,000 livres.* The debts of all the guilds of France were estimated, in 1758, at 30,000,000 livres.

The many technical improvements introduced in the course of the eighteenth century gave rise to interminable contentions about the infringement of one trade upon the privileges of another. The courts were filled with applications for redress. The annual expense of the guilds of Paris on this head were estimated by Savary as amounting to from 800,000 to 1,000,000 livres. In one year not less than 30,000 cases were found pending; some of course of ancient date. The tailors and clothes-menders had been in legal dispute since the year 1530, about the right of the latter to make new clothes. To show the kind of vexatious restrictions which hampered production, I mention the case of the cloth weavers of St. Lô, who brought suit against those of Fouquières in 1721. The complaint was that the latter made their cloth one *aune* wide and that the law of 1669 gave them the right to only five eighths.

The regulations seriously interfered with the expansion of trade. Foreign demand could not well be satisfied by a trade which was hampered at every turn by ancient prescriptions as to width, texture, number of threads in the chain, finishing, dyeing and so on. Up to the middle of the century the severity of the law and the arbitrariness of its execution grew in intensity. As far back as the fourteenth and fifteenth centuries, I find that Ulm, one of the centres for the manufacture of woollen cloth and fustian, had official cloth inspection. The piece, not up to the regulation, was cut into three lengths.† Strassburg

---

* Savary, *Dictionnaire de Commerce*, 1761.

† See Eugen Nuebling, *Ulm's Baumwoll-industrie im Mittelalter*.

and other centres had similar regulations.* This was not to hamper trade but to promote it. Ulm did an enormous exporting trade to the north, south, and east. It was very proud of its trade-mark. The cloth of Ulm was of such repute that the stamp of the town added fully twenty-five per cent. to the value of cloth not so stamped. Many suits were brought to the Imperial Court for protection against pirating rivals. The cutting of the cloth was to prevent its exportation and thus prevent any lowering of the high standard abroad. With slight loss to himself, the weaver could retail it at home. Here the town and the guild co-operated for the preservation of the best interests of the trades upon which the greatness and prosperity of the free-towns were built.

Not so in the time of absolutistic government. Here the interference of the state was simply nothing but "l' état c'est moi," paternalism run mad, because not tempered by regard for the good of the people it may have been originally intended to benefit.

In the year 1717, a law was promulgated by which a reduction in the number of warps in the chain was made the subject of a fine varying according to the degree of the omission. Beyond a certain degree of inferiority the cloth is confiscated and cut to pieces. In 1729, however, the law is made public that all cloth not coming up to the full width is to be confiscated and cut. Even cloth made too long is subjected to a fine. In the year 1719 it is ordained that all looms not up to the regulations are to be changed or rebuilt according to the official standard. The law of 1729 says simply, that the implements not coming up to the mark shall be destroyed.†

---

* G. Schmoller, *Die Strassburger Tucher-und Weberzunft.*

† " Les dits rots et lames seront rompus et brisés en présence de l' inspecteur des manufactures."

These stringent laws, burdensome and preventive of a beneficial growth of industry and trade, proved abortive in the very particulars which they were intended to protect. The complaints of fraud in manufactures multiply, and decline of trade is made a general preamble in ordinances calling upon the officers to enforce the regulations.

From about the year 1750 a relaxation sets in. The Economists begin to make their influence felt. The opposition against what we to-day call "Colbertism" manifests itself. One by one the barriers are lowered, until Turgot, in his reform acts, speaks the great redeeming word for which the ages had been waiting and warring. With the fall of Turgot, it was undertaken to put many of the old obstructions up again, not to make progress too fast. But on the whole trade remained free fom the old interferences, and in the act of 1791 the Constituent Assembly put a resting epitaph on the remains. Nevertheless it has ever since been the anxious endeavor of a confused statesmanship to resuscitate it, and set it up again in the place of the young freedom under whose sway the world is blossoming into a state of unexampled and otherwise impossible prosperity.

The trade of the past was trammelled and hindered in every conceivable way. To enumerate the risks and burdens a commodity had to carry from the distant place of production would exhaust the whole vocabulary of commerce. To sketch them even briefly would fill a respectable volume. I have contented myself with giving an outline of the most comprehensive ones, such as were calculated to enhance prices most effectively. It remains, however, to call attention to the most grievous instrument for increasing the prices of commodities:

Duties and Taxes.

I have pointed out in another part of this chapter the burdens laid upon commodities by the exercise of the taxing power possessed by the lords of the highway on land and on sea. The modern state has relieved the knight of the duty of protecting the caravan of trade from his covetous brother. It assumes this duty as a right, and puts a tax upon commodities when they enter the boundaries of the state. In countries where the boundaries of several states could easily be traced from a church steeple in a straight line, as in Germany, during the years of the old Confederation,* for instance, this was not a light burden—nor were other dues to state, township, and commune. Tolls, dues, and taxes for bridges, roads, rivers, and canals were collected at every crossing. The navigation of the Main, Rhine, Danube, the Elbe, and Scheldt has been made free from duties only within comparatively recent times.† The tax-gatherer had his hand open all the time. The tollgate was always in your way.

---

* Up to 1866 from the steeple of the cathedral at Frankfurt one could look into the territories of Nassau, Electoral Hesse, the Grand Duchy of Hesse, the principality of Homburg, and Frankfurt itself, all exercising the right of sovereignty and of independent taxation in customs matters, up to the time of the creation of the German Zollverein.

† In the building of the Cathedral of Xanten the stone had to be brought from the "Siebengebirge." It was carried by ship on the Rhine from Andernach to Xanten, a distance of less than a hundred English miles. Duties were collected on transit, during the passage at Bonn, Bredestrom, Duesseldorf, Rheinberg, Kaiserwerth, and Buederich. Though in the two first places relief from paying duties had been obtained through the Count of Geldern, the duties summed up 19 gold florins (about $41.00) on a cargo valued at 95 florins, or about 20 per cent.

Though this refers to the fifteenth century, it describes, with equal force, conditions existing in comparatively modern times.

It was certainly a very great advantage to trade, and an important step in advance, that Colbert reduced the interference of the customs officers to the wider circle of the national boundary. Up to then, 1664, the provinces had levied taxes on imports and on exports. In the preamble to his edict, in pointing to this meritorious act of the king, he condemns in very energetic language the nefarious character of this system of taxation, and the chaos which was its natural consequence.

The most serious effect of customs taxation on prices was produced by the system of fostering home industries by protective tariffs. It existed previous to that time. Many kings and states put considerable duties on manufactured products from abroad, and prohibited the exportation of raw materials. But in general it may be said that duties were more in the nature of revenue duties, and were collected on imports and exports alike. The parliamentary grants to Elizabeth and James I. were 5 per cent. on imports and on exports.*

With Colbert the system expanded from decade to decade, and it soon became the prevailing principle for all Europe. Colbert himself, here as well as in his views concerning the management of guilds and trades, had very moderate ideas. He held that protective tariffs were

---

* "The exports of England from Christmas, 1612, to Christmas, 1613, are computed at £2,487,435, the imports at £2,141,151, so that the balance in favor of England was £346,284. But in 1622 the exports were £2,320,436, the imports £2,619,315, which makes a balance of £298,879 against England."—"As the annual imports and exports together rose to near five millions, and the customs never yielded so much as £200,000 a year, of which tonnage made a part, it appears that the new rates affixed by James did not, on the whole, amount to one shilling in the pound, and, consequently, were still inferior to the intention of the original grant of Parliament."—David Hume, *History of England*, vol. iv.

a bad means to a good end, which ought to be got rid of as soon as it had fulfilled its mission. To the syndics of Lyons, who came to thank him for the aid given to their industries, he replied, bluntly, that they would do well if they considered his favors only as crutches by whose aid to learn quickly how to walk by themselves, and that he intended later on to abolish the duties again.*

The exigencies of the state did not permit him to carry out this intention. But had he lived to the present day, he would have found that manufacturers never learn to walk alone so long as the state is willing to furnish crutches.

The Effect of Protectionism on Prices.

The effect of the system, however, is very pernicious, because not alone the prices of imported articles are enhanced, but also the prices of all corresponding articles produced at home. These in the long run exceed the imported quantities to an extraordinary extent; and while the state benefits only by the duties levied on a paltry quantity of imported goods, the private tax-gatherer collects revenue from the consumer on all the home productions coming under the same heading, at least until the home supply equals the demand.

To cover the whole question by an illustration from practical life, I will mention the recent change in price produced by the abolition of the duty upon raw wool, the rate on the manufactured cloth being left as high as before, *i. e.*, the old ad valorem rate of 50 per cent. Only the specific duty, which in previous tariffs compensated for the duty upon the raw wool, was abolished.

---

* Roscher, *Nat. Oekonomik des Handels und Gewerbfleisses*, quoting Clément, *Système protecteur.*

I shall give the prices of American cloth called sackings, a sort of so-called ladies' cloth, used for ladies' dresses. In these the American manufacturers held the field uninterruptedly for a number of years. Even under the high wool duties and the correspondingly high prices of American wools, foreign goods could not be imported by a wide margin to sell against American cloths.

Yet the abolition of the duty on raw wool sent wool prices down to such an extent that, even before the tariff took effect, the cloth prices could be reduced as much as the difference between the figures of the second column and those of the first, which represents the prices when wool was still under the full influence of the wool tariff. The third column presents the prices ruling in the spring of this year, after the new tariff had been in force for a time on woollen manufactures likewise. The free wool tariff, be it remembered, became effective at once, August 28, 1894; the tariff on manufactures of wool not until January 1, 1895.

Here are the effects:

PRICES OF ALL-WOOL SACKINGS.

	1892, October. Cents per Yard.	1894, October. Cents per Yard.	1895, April. Cents per Yard.
Mailand, 35 inches	32½	23	19
Mailand, 50 inches	45	35	29
Pensanze, 50 inches	57½	42½	36
Franklin, 50 inches	62½	50	39
Franklin, 54 inches	70	55	44
Fancy dress goods, 36 inches	42½	32½	27
Broadcloth, 50 inches	75	62½	52½
Average for seven numbers	55	43	35¼
Decline of October, 1894, price from 1892 price		22%	
Decline of April, 1895, price from 1892 price			36½%

This class shows smaller differences than other woollens. It had been selling at considerable price reductions below other manufactures of wool under the old tariff, for reasons given and explained in full in my book, *The Economy of High Wages.*

This example may therefore be considered as an exponent of the price situation created by tariff-protection, but modified by pressure of home-competition upon prices, and of the net effect on prices of so onerous a burden upon industry, as a duty upon raw materials.

The United States import, in moderately active years, large quantities of woollen goods. They will amount under the present tariff to fully $55,000,000. The American goods with which these have to compete will amount to something like $250,000,000. As these foreign goods can be brought here and pay a duty of something like 50 per cent., it is evident that the American goods are not sold at very much lower prices than the foreign duty-paid goods. The whole amount, of foreign and of domestic origin, is therefore equally affected by the change in the tariff-law.

I will here add prices of woollen goods and ladies' dress goods coming in actual competition with foreign, and show the price changes in these. They will give a fair idea of the change in prices falling on woollen and worsted fabrics both of domestic and foreign origin.

The foreign prices quoted here are the actually paid prices at the shipping point for goods of an identical character. To make even selling value with American goods quoted in columns 1 and 2 something like 10 to $12\frac{1}{2}$ per cent. will have to be added to cover carrying expense and commission as these are included in the domestic prices but not in the foreign prices:

PRICES OF WORSTED CLOTH AND OF LADIES' DRESS GOODS OF DOMESTIC PRODUCTION BUT SUBJECT TO AN ACTIVE FOREIGN COMPETITION.

	Domestic prices from the mill.		Foreign shipping price of competing goods.
	1892.	1894–95.	
Worsted cloth, 54 inches wide.			
Quality XXX Clay, 16 ozs.	1.75	1.12½	60
" " 16 "	1.65	1.00	55
" " 14 "	1.40	90	49
" " 12 "	1.30	82½	44
Ladies' Dress Goods.			
Cashmere J., 38 in.	37½	27½	16½
" 45 "	50	32½	19

With this allowance made the reader can make his own deductions as to the effect of tariff taxation on the prices of imported articles as well as on those of domestic manufactures.

The consumers in the United States are saved no less an amount than $170,000,000 * in their outlay for woollen

---

* I arrive at this estimate in the following way:

Product of American mills in 1890.		$338,000,000
Allow for amount not selling up to duty-paid foreign prices, computed to represent.		$50,000,000
		$288,000,000
Add 15 per cent. to cover increase in population.		$42,000,000
		$330,000,000
Add importations of wool and worsted manufactures, 1889–90, $54,000,000		
Duty at rate under McKinley Act	$53,000,000	$107,000,000
Net value of foreign and domestic goods.		$437,000,000

goods a year by this very moderate measure of tariff-reform.

I have taken only a few prominent examples, but they will suffice to convince the reader of the powerful disturbance of prices by the exercise of the taxing power, wisely or unwisely wielded by the state.

Prices for the last hundred years, especially, have been subject to this influence, and it is at all times wise to take this point into consideration along with all the others here treated, when we make comparisons.

General Observations.

The numberless causes which operate on prices cannot all be dealt with. I have to content myself with treating only the leading ones. I have singled out such as are general and have had a very pronounced influence in the past in keeping prices high, and as by their abolition or by radical changes in them, prices have become lower and lower until they have reached the phenomenally low range which causes so much agitation at the present time, the fact completes the demonstration that prices are the results of inherent causes and not of merely accidental ones,

Brought forward..	$437,000,000
Add discount, commission, freight and distributing expense, and wholesale and retail profit = 60 per cent...	$263,000,000
Amount of consumers' value of woollen goods, at full cost under late tariff act,	$700,000,000

Against this the cost under the new tariff, as proved by the price examples given above, and under the influence of free wool, stands as follows:

Net value of foreign and domestic goods.................................	$437,000,000
Less difference caused by tariff reduction, equal to 49 per cent. of the old duty or 24¼ per cent. of the duty-paid value............................	$106,000,000
Leaving net value of domestic goods from mill, and of imported goods, duty paid, of..	$331,000,000
Add to cover items as above, at the same rate, 60 per cent...............	$199,000,000
Amount of consumers' value of woollen goods under new tariff...........	$530,000,000
Consumers' value under old tariff..	$700,000,000
Balance saved to consumer through tariff-reduction.....................	$170,000,000

as the greater or smaller supply of the money stocks would be. It is true, prices have become extraordinarily low. But as cheapness is the result of plenty and of law and order, it is difficult to see how the phenomenon can be changed except by turning the hands on the dial backward, drowning inventors and destroying the improved tools, as was the practice in the past.*

It has not been found necessary to draw speculative causes into the discourse other than by the general reference to them in the preceding chapters. In speaking of the causes which make prices, I had reference to permanent price-making agencies. Causes which come and go with the seasons or follow in the wake of political or even economic disturbances have certainly a very deep influence, and sufficient consideration has been given to these extraordinary causes in the part devoted to the history of prices. Their presence explains violent fluctuations which we notice very frequently, but we cannot give them a place here, when causes are considered which mark the prices of great periods, when the prices of the past and the present are contrasted under the operation of economic, social, and industrial, conditions which have produced them.

The views of those who demand an artificial standard to be substituted for the commercial standard, *i.e.*, the gold-standard of civilized trading nations, are the outcome of the idea that an increased quantity of circulation is required for the maintenance of a certain level of prices.

---

* As late as the end of the sixteenth century the town-council of Danzig had the inventor of a mechanical ribbon-loom drowned and his machine destroyed. This is perhaps the latest case of a government applying in this drastic manner the principle of protection. But the "conseil des prudhommes" in Lyons ordered Jacquard's loom destroyed and the inventor himself narrowly escaped assassination three times.

The beneficial influence of the money *quantities* must necessarily be supposed to be of a general and lasting effect. The controversial points seem therefore to be fully covered by the permanent causes which I have named as the true causes of prices.

It is not specifically stated what range of prices the agitators for an artificial standard and of increased money supplies would wish to see prevail. The price level, undoubtedly, is to be high enough to create general contentment among all who have commodities to sell. That even this cannot be realised, unless the currency be depreciated in value at the same time, whereby price-increase would be nominal only, has been demonstrated by the price-history of England, France, and Germany, for a period of six hundred years.

That wage earners and those living on salaries and fixed incomes are most acute sufferers by all such stratagems, has been shown with a fulness of detail which cannot possibly leave any doubt on the subject. That the working classes, and these are the only ones which need concern the public conscience, can only look to a reign of low prices as a guarantee for high earnings and general well-being, is an equally well established fact. Indeed a decline in this condition, as has been shown in preceding chapters and is still more graphically proved in the tables of the appendixes, dates directly from the time when high prices began to change the general level of the three preceding centuries, at about the middle of the sixteenth century, with the evil of high prices culminating in the seventeenth century. This is the time when the currencies were most persistently and violently deteriorated.

It is only within the lifetime of this present generation that prices of grain and the rate of wages compare as favorably as they did in the three centuries preceding 1550 in the three countries of Europe dealt with in these pages.

It is the opinion of Thorold Rogers that the debasement of the coins by Henry VIII. and the guardians of his son caused the decline in the condition of the working classes, which all the statutes of labor from Edward III. onwards were not able to effect. All the price facts adduced here prove completely the correctness of this view.

APPENDIX A.

A Summary of the Price History of England, France, and Germany, giving in Parallel Columns Grain-Prices and Wages, with their Purchasing Power in Bushels of Grain, from A.D. 1351 to 1882.

For the purpose of illustrating in a graphic manner the price history treated in the preceding pages, I annex tables of comparative prices of wheat and of barley of the three countries in parallel columns, reducing them at the same time to

I.—PRICES OF WHEAT AND BARLEY RULING IN ENGLAND, FRANCE, AND GERMANY IN THE PERIODS NAMED BELOW, IN THE MEASURES AND PRESENT MONEYS OF THE RESPECTIVE COUNTRIES, AND IN EQUIVALENTS OF THE UNITED STATES.

Periods.	England.				France.				Germany.			
	Wheat. Quarter.	Barley. Quarter.	Wheat. Bushel.	Barley. Bushel.	Wheat. Hectolitre.	Barley. Hectolitre.	Wheat. Bushel.	Barley. Bushel.	Wheat. Malter.	Barley. Malter.	Wheat. Bushel.	Barley. Bushel.
	s. d.	s. d.	$ cts.	$ cts.	Francs	Francs	$ cts.	$ cts.	Mrks.	Mrks.	$ cts.	$ cts.
1351–1450	18.0	11.6	0.58	0.35	6.89	2.81	0.48	0.20	9.20	5.75	0.47	0.29
1451–1550	18.4	11.9	0.59	0.36	4.56	2.48	0.31	0.17	11.00	6.35	0.56	0.32
1551–1580	15.0	9.11	0.44	0.30	12.00	6.00	0.78	0.39	21.25	14.05	1.05	0.70
1591–1612	35.0	19.5	1.06	0.59	17.00	6.60	1.11	0.43	32.75	18.20	1.64	0.92
1613–1652	42.8	23.4	1.28	0.71	18.70	8.20	1.21	0.54	35.00	21.25	1.86	1.08
1653–1702	40.5	21.5	1.21	0.62	14.75	6.12	0.96	0.41	30.00	19.70	1.50	1.00
1715–1765	35.0		1.06		10.80	5.25	0.70	0.38	22.50	15.75	1.12	0.79
1766–1800	54.0		1.64		15.00	8.20	0.97	0.51	18.20	9.82	0.91	0.49
1801–1830	86.0		2.61		19.80		1.28		*17.00	10.40	0.85	0.52
1882.....	44.0	32.0	1.32	0.97	21.00		1.43		*30.00	18.00	1.48	0.88

* German prices from 1800 on are based on the thaler standard.

American money and measure. I also give the current rates of wages of occupations on which continuous information can be gathered. I bring the comparison up to the time at which the English Corn Laws ceased to exert an influence on prices. The price quotations from 1882, with the ruling wage rate appended, give us an opportunity for measuring the price and wage history of the past by present rates and prices, with which every one is conversant.

In regard to the selection of occupations, it will be understood that the choice is ready at hand. The building trades are fully developed at a time when other crafts are still conducted in a manner in which they are incapable of treatment in a historical examination of wages.

In the next table I give the rates of wages paid during the same average periods in England, France, and Germany. When the two are combined, the prices of grain and the rates of wages, their real import becomes apparent.

II.—RATE OF DAY-WAGES OF CARPENTER AND MASON RULING IN ENGLAND, FRANCE, AND GERMANY IN THE PERIODS NAMED, IN THE MONEY OF THE COUNTRIES AND OF THE UNITED STATES.

Periods.	ENGLAND.				FRANCE.				GERMANY.			
	Carpenter.	Mason.	Carpenter.	Mason.	Carpenter.	Mason.	Carpenter.	Mason.	Carpenter.	Mason.	Carpenter.	Mason.
	d.	d.	Cents	Cents	Francs	Francs	Cents	Cents	Mrks.	Mrks.	Cents	Cents
1351–1450.	17¼	16¾	35	34	1.04	1.07	20	21	1.75	1.85	41	44
1451–1550.	20⅝	18	41	36	0.97	0.87	19	18	1.40	1.60	32	39
1551–1580.	12	10½	24	21	1.01	0.96	20	19	2.	2.	47	48
1591–1612.	13½	14	27	28	1.19	1.20	23	23	2.60	2.65	62	63
1613–1652.	16½	19	33	38	1.25	0.90	24	18	2.80	2.85	68	69
1653–1702.	24⅞	27	50	54	1.10	1.10	21	21	2.40	2.52	58	60
1715–1765.	30	31	60	62	0.96	0.98	19	19	1.70	1.90	40	45
1766–1800.	30	33	66	66	1.20	1.15	21	22	1.35	1.70	30	40
1801–1830.	63	63	126	126								
1882 .	66	66	132	132					2.50	3.00	60	71

The equivalent in wheat of a day's wages of a carpenter and a mason is shown in Table III., and the equivalent of barley in Table IV., for each of the three countries, in parallel columns.

The showing proves the positions which I have taken in the preceding chapters. A few words of explanation will not be out of place to make the meaning clear. It will be noticed that the range of prices and the rates of wages of the three countries vary materially held against one another. As regards wages, the lowest rates are those for France. For the whole time dating from the middle of the sixteenth century, the purchasing power is barely one-half of what it was in the century following the conclusion of the English wars. The

III.—PURCHASING POWER OF A DAY'S WAGES EXPRESSED IN BUSHELS OF WHEAT FROM 1351 TO 1882.

Periods.	ENGLAND.			FRANCE.			GERMANY.		
	Price of Wheat per Bushel.	Wages of Carpenter and Mason.	Equivalent in Wheat.	Price of Wheat per Bushel.	Wages of Carpenter and Mason.	Equivalent in Wheat.	Price of Wheat per Bushel.	Average of Wages of Carpenter and Mason.	Equivalent in Wheat.
	$ Cts.	$ Cts.	Bushels	$ Cts.	$ Cts.	Bushels	$ Cts.	$ Cts.	Bushels
1351–1450	0.58	0.35	0.66	0.48	0.20	0.42	0.47	0.42	0.90
1451–1550	0.59	0.39	0.66	0.31	0.19	0.61	0.56	0.35	0.62
1551–1580	0.44	0.23	0.52	0.78	0.19	0.25	1.04	0.48	0.46
1591–1612	1.06	0.28	0.27	1.11	0.23	0.21	1.64	0.62	0.38
1613–1652	1.28	0.35	0.28	1.21	0.21	0.20	1.85	0.69	0.36
1653–1702	1.21	0.52	0.43	0.96	0.21	0.22	1.50	0.58	0.39
1715–1765	1.06	0.61	0.57	0.70	0.19	0.27	1.12	0.43	0.40
1766–1800	1.64	0.63	0.38	0.97	0.21	0.22	0.91	0.31	0.34
1800–1830	2.61	1.26	0.48	1.28	0.48	0.33	0.85		
1882	1.32	1.35	1.05	1.43	0.78*	0.55	1.48†	0.65	0.44

* I have taken the average of wages for the principal towns of the Departments as being on a fairer basis for comparison, with German wages quoted, at least. The average for Paris is about 7.50 fcs.; for the Departments about 4 fcs. a day.

† The original prices from 1800 on are given in the thaler standard.

average wage rate changes but little from 1351 down to the end of the eighteenth century, rising very slightly only in the dear years. The difference in wheat prices from the lowest range, in the period 1451 to 1550, to the highest, in 1613 to 1652, is, however, as 1 to nearly 4. In consequence, a day's wages in 1451 to 1550 bought 0.61 bushel of wheat or 1.12 bushels of barley; in 1613 to 1652 the day wage procured only 0.20 bushel of wheat or 0.39 bushel of barley for a mason or a carpenter.

It might appear singular that wages in France respond so little to the rise in grain prices. We note in the tables for Germany that wages are more responsive to the rise, though

IV.—PURCHASING POWER OF A DAY'S WAGES EXPRESSED IN BUSHELS OF BARLEY FROM 1351 TO 1882.

Periods.	England.			France.			Germany.		
	Price of Barley per Bushel.	Average of Wages of Carpenter and Mason.	Equivalent in Barley.	Price of Barley per Bushel.	Average of Wages of Carpenter and Mason.	Equivalent in Barley.	Price of Barley per Bushel.	Average of Wages of Carpenter and Mason.	Equivalent in Barley.
	$ Cts.	$ Cts.	Bushels	$ Cts.	$ Cts.	Bushels	$ Cts.	$ Cts.	Bushels
1351–1450.	0.35	0.35	1.	0.20	0.20	1.	0.29	0.42	1.45
1451–1550.	0.36	0.39	1.08	0.17	0.19	1.12	0.32	0.35	1.10
1551–1580.	0.30	0.23	0.77	0.39	0.19	0.50	0.70	0.48	0.70
1591–1612.	0.59	0.28	0.47	0.43	0.23	0.53	0.92	0.62	0.67
1613–1652.	0.71	0.35	0.50	0.52	0.21	0.40	1.08	0.69	0.65
1653–1702.	0.62	0.52	0.84	0.41	0.21	0.51	1.00	0.58	0.58
1715–1765.	......	......	......	0.38	0.19	0.50	0.79	0.43	0.55
1766–1800.	......	......	......	0.51	0.21	0.41	0.49	0.31	0.63
1800–1830.	......	......	......	......	......	......	0.52*	......	......
1882.	......	......	......	......	......	......	0.88*	0.65	0.74

* Prices from 1800 on, in the original quotations, are based on the thaler standard.

they express but to a very small extent the altered price conditions.

Xanten, from which place the prices are quoted, as already pointed out, is in immediate touch with regions where all the industrial, commercial, and civilizing agencies were most actively engaged to procure a higher state of well being during times in which France was subjected to the bad conditions described, and in a state of backwardness in industrial development barely credible from the point of progress it holds to-day.

The prices and wage rates at Xanten must, therefore, be taken with the allowance that they are specific, and those for France, as general average prices.

The retrogression for the Germany of the lower Rhine region from the second half of the sixteenth century is, however, not the less pointed.

The conditions from the middle of the thirteenth to the end of the fifteenth century were the most favorable in Germany's position, as pointed out heretofore. It finds expression in the above price comparisons.

At a time when England is only agricultural in its economic development, the middle of the fourteenth century, magistrates of German towns begin to issue ordinances limiting the expenditures in dress, to reduce the cost of what they deemed luxurious living.

The town council of Strassburg in 1370 orders that no woman is to spend more than 30 goldflorins for a single dress. The goldflorin containing then 3.55 grams of gold (66 to the mark fine of Cologne), was worth $2.35 in present value. The value of a dress at $70 was, therefore, frequently exceeded by the burgher's wife, else an ordinance naming 30 goldflorins as the maximum would not have been found necessary. Schmoller says : " The beautiful costumes of the thirteenth century give way to all possible excrescences of fashion. The well-to-do classes indulged in the most fanciful and luxurious changes of color and style, until the Reformation diffused, also in this direction, a more severe and measured taste." *

The effect on the trades of the towns could, however, not have been otherwise but beneficial. The trade of the weavers, and of all those connected with the industry, was necessarily enhanced by it, and the progress made through the influence of an extensive home demand for finer fabrics than the cloth supplied by the wife or the female slave in the eleventh and twelfth centuries could not fail to arouse a demand from abroad. Schmoller but expresses the causes leading to the activity in trade and the advantageous position of the working classes when he says that "this increased demand formed the common basis for the development of the German textile industry, which had begun in the thirteenth, and made its progress in the fourteenth and fifteenth, centuries. The home-loom in country and town could no longer furnish the desired materials in quantity, and far less in color and in quality." That all other trades were equally stimulated and advantageously affected is self-evident.

In a general way, much as the grain prices vary between one country and another, the purchasing power of a day's wage is the same in the time where equally favorable political conditions exist. This is the century closing with 1550. Generally speaking, it is a century of peace, devoted to the cultivation of the higher aims of life, the period of the Renaissance.

During that hundred years a day's wages buys more wheat and barley in France than at any time before or after, considered in same general average periods.

From thence on, the furies let loose by fanaticism hold their destroying carnival. The decline of the fervor finds other hallucinations, as the favorable balance of trade theory, ready incentives for governments to fall upon neighboring states and lay them waste, so that they themselves may prosper the more.

---

* Gustav Schmoller, *Die Strassburger Tucher- und Weber-Zunft*, page 57.

The effect is made evident in the above comparisons, where the periods are classed more in relation to the historical events than with regard to regular chronological dividing lines.

The period 1451 to 1550 shows an equally high rate of prosperity of the working classes in the three countries, measured by the purchasing power of their wages. In all of them the decline in the seventeenth century is marked, but to a less degree in the German quotations than in those of England and France. The reason is, as stated, in the more fortunate position of the lower Rhine country in all these periods. This condition was, however, not enjoyed by the rest of Germany. The decline of Xanten gives an idea what it must have been elsewhere. That it was of the serious nature described in the preceding part is made manifest enough by numerous recitals from the records. The laments over high prices, famines, and complaints of the workingmen that they cannot exist at the old rates are of constant recurrence in the second half of the sixteenth century. The conditions become more and more aggravated with its closing decades.

As an instance of the frequent cases of dearth and famines cited, a case is given of a woman who begs intently for a scheffel of rye, for which she offers all her ready money, 2 thalers and 13 albi (52 albi to the thaler). The scheffel is the fourth part of a malter; the malter at $4\frac{4}{5}$ bushels gives the scheffel at about $1\frac{1}{5}$ bushels. The thaler was then at the ratio of 8 to the mark fine, hence of a value of \$1.20. The scheffel price was, therefore, $2\frac{1}{4} \times 1.20 = \$2.70$, which is equal to \$2.25 the bushel.

The sad part of the story is, however, that the woman could not get the rye she so anxiously asked for.

The relations of the moneys, as said before, are not as accurately stated as would have been the case had the author from whose tables I took my data striven only to give the prices in the money equivalents of the present time, instead of

APPENDIX A.

giving a bewildering account of all sorts of moneys, few of which have a bearing on the prices and on the subject.

The only safe guide is the statement giving the relations of the mark of the chapter in which the prices and wages are quoted to the Reichsmark of to-day. Up to 1550 the alterations are not very violent. From that time to the early part of this century the decline is from a value of about 5.50 rmks. to the low value of $\frac{1}{2}$ rmk.

The decline from $5\frac{1}{2}$ to $4\frac{1}{2}$, from $4\frac{1}{2}$ to 3, from there to $2\frac{1}{2}$, 2, $1\frac{1}{2}$, $\frac{2}{3}$, to finally $\frac{1}{2}$, is stated at certain years. But we are left in doubt when the change has taken place as bearing on prices. It is well known that the changes were gradual, and by no means came with sufficient regularity to enable one to decide when they had become definitely settled. I have thought it safer, therefore, to accept the extreme and permanent changes noted in the price columns as indicating the time when the lowering of the standard had become a settled fact. With this guidance, I took an average between the two extremes as expressing nearest the actual value of the moneys of the period which were left somewhat in doubt from about 1580. The difference, however, is not great. Besides, the benefit of the doubt is given to the lower range of price equivalent, dating from the time of the continuous debasing of the coins, than would follow from a strict adherence to set dates for this computation.

From the middle of the eighteenth century to the year 1830 prices of corn were lower in Germany than either in France or England. This was especially the case in the first half of this century. Wages, however, had kept more than even pace with this decline. I have no data of wages for Xanten. The statement given elsewhere of the wages paid by Alfred Krupp at Essen in the year 1827 shows a rate of not over one-half that paid in 1451 to 1550 at Xanten, which place is not many miles distant from Essen. But low as the corn prices were in the early part of the nineteenth century in Xanten,

APPENDIX A. 319

they were still 50 per cent. above the average of the Quinto Cento period. While a day-wage of a carpenter or mason bought 0.62 bushel of wheat then, in the nineteenth century it bought but 0.21 bushel, or about as much as in France in the worst of times of war and frequency of famine.*

This, however, is by no means the lowest rate of earnings in those deplorable years. In Saxony and other parts of Germany a day's wages, even in cheap years, of the latter part of the eighteenth and the first part of this century is quoted as equal to 0.05 hectolitre or 0.14 bushel of rye. But rye holds a nearer relation to barley in price than to wheat.

It must not be forgotten that wheat played a smaller part in the domestic economy of the working classes of the past of

---

* On page 239 I speak of the rate of wages per day paid to iron-workers at the works of Krupp, at Essen, in the year 1827, as 16½ cents for casters and smiths, according to Mr. Alfred Krupp's own statement. The average price of wheat was 83 cents, of rye 53, and of barley 44 cents. If a workman had laid out his wages in grain he would have obtained either 0.20 bushel of wheat, 0.31 bushel of rye, or 0.37 bushel of barley.

In 1887 I visited Essen, and obtained, among other very valuable information, a statement from the managing director of the works as to the wages of the men.

The average of all employed is 3 marks (72 cents), and exclusive of boys, invalids, and pensioners under the old age insurance act, the average is 3.40 marks.

This average divides as follows :

Common laborers and firemen, 2.40 marks (58 cents); while about 40 per cent. of the men earn 4 marks (95 cents). These represent the smiths, the class spoken of in the statement for 1827. I must say, however, that the lad who showed me through the works told me that his father, being paralytic and drawing 40 marks monthly pay from the pension fund, when able to work at his trade of a puddler, earned 35 marks as two weeks' pay. This does not show more than an average of 3 marks, or 72 cents, a day. This is not introduced here as opposed to the statement of the firm, but to show that even among so important a class as puddlers in the iron industry there were men who did not earn more than 3 marks. I am certainly justified to draw an average between the two statements for establishing the rate of pay in 1887 of the occupations referred to by Mr. Krupp in his address to his

England and France at least, than at the present time. Barley, was of great importance in the workingman's beer in England and Germany, and so was rye as a bread corn. Rye taken at about one-fifth above barley prices will give a fair expression of the general run of prices of this cereal for comparison.

With this allowance made, a comparison with the figures of Table IV. gives an adequate idea of the misery to which the German working-classes had become reduced by the early part of this century, when 0.14 bushel of rye, equal, in barley price of the same time to about 0.19 bushel, expressed the earnings of an able-bodied workingman in the industrial centres even.

---

workingmen. A rate of 3½ marks (84 cents) would therefore mark the present (1887) wage rate, against 16½ cents of 1827, in the same works, for the same occupations.

Expressed in bushels of grain these wages bought, according to the following prices ruling in the neighborhood—wheat $1.17, rye $0.78, barley $0.70 the bushel—0.72 bushel of wheat, 1.08 bushels of rye, or 1.20 bushels of barley.

The relations of wages of 1887 to 1827 stand as something over 5 to 1 expressed in money, and as something over 3½ to 1 expressed in grain.

This shows the progress made in the condition of the working classes solely by the improvements in the economy of production of which the last fifty years have been so prolific. The greater productiveness of labor resulting therefrom enabled the paying of these higher wage rates. The cost of production has become reduced at the same time to an almost fabulous degree in the very industry where this wage development has taken place. With this phase of the argument the reader has been made familiar in the pages treating this subject.

I will add that if we take sections, as in the mountain districts of Germany, where the old methods are still in practice, the earnings to-day are not higher than they were at Essen some seventy years ago. For this statement I have also recent positive proof in hand.

Turn it as we may, we always come back to the same proposition: The only divisible quantity is the product of labor.

The greater the productiveness of labor the higher the rate of wages and the profit share of all engaged in·the creation and distribution of products.

APPENDIX A.

The effect of the Corn-Laws in English prices is made plain by the comparisons here afforded with contemporaneous German prices.

By the act of 1804 the duties on foreign wheat were, when under 63s. the quarter, £1 4s. 3d.; at or above 63s., but under 66s., £0 2s.6d.; at or above 66s., £0 0s. 6d.

By the act of 1815 the importation of corn was prohibited when under 80s. the quarter or 10s. the bushel. Care was therefore taken that it should not go below 8s. the bushel; and as this was not deemed sufficiently remunerative a price, the later twist was applied to bring it up to 10s. ($1.94 and $2.43 the bushel).

The last price quotation in the tables shows reversed positions. The price of grain in England is the free-trade price, and is about as much below the Continental prices as the rate of duty amounts to which the paternal governments of the Continent were pleased to put upon the bread of the people in their solicitude for the welfare of the landed proprietors.

The great price differences existing between one country and another can permit of no other interpretation than that they were the result of inherent causes which bore a direct influence on them.* Their nature has been sufficiently explained to need special reference here.

That the increased money supply had nothing to do with

---

* This is illustrated with particular clearness by the prices of grain of the second half of the sixteenth century. The prices for the century 1450 to 1550 are on the general level of the preceding century. English and German prices vary but a few points from one another. French prices, generally lower in the early period, but on a comparatively higher basis during the period known as the time of the Hundred Years' War, have gone back again to the low rates ruling before the English invasion under Edward III. But in the second half of the sixteenth century French and German prices rise to abnormal heights, while English prices are lower up to 1580 than in 1450 to 1550. England enjoyed a period of peace and settled conditions under Elizabeth, while Germany and France were torn by civil and religious wars, with dearth and famine in their train.

the price changes could not be demonstrated more plainly than from the comparison of German grain prices of the latter part of the eighteenth and the first part of the nineteenth century with the prices of the sixteenth and seventeenth centuries. They have gone back to positions not very far removed from the prices previous to the time from where the great rise began in the second half of the sixteenth century.

I have examined corroborative tables of grain prices in Mr. Bein's publication, referred to heretofore.* I find here for Saxony very high prices in the seventeenth century, low prices in the middle of the eighteenth century, and for a number of years, from 1763 to 1772, prices three to four times as high. From then on to about 1830, with the exception of a number of dear years between the year 1800 and 1816, the general price average is about $2\frac{1}{4}$ thalers for barley, 3 thalers for rye, and 4 thalers for wheat the Dresden scheffel. This scheffel, equal to 104 liters, measures something like 3 bushels English. Reckoning the thaler at 75 cents, as it was of a somewhat higher value in the last century ($13\frac{1}{3}$ thalers to the mark) than in its later conversion in the 14-thaler ratio per mark fine, we get $1.69, $2.25, and $3.00 as the price for the scheffel of barley, rye, and wheat; or, reduced to bushels, 56 cents for barley, 75 cents for rye, and $1.00 for wheat.

Grain prices for Plauen and the Voigtland are generally higher than in other parts of Saxony or Germany, as stated by Mr. Bein, on account of the less favorable conditions of soil and climate in relation to agriculture, and the relatively greater density of population.

This corroborates, therefore, the statements in the preceding tables, and proves again, if any further proof were needed, that the high prices of grain, beginning in the second half of the sixteenth century, were entirely due to other causes than the increasing money supply. But whatever part of these

---

* L. Bein, *Die Industrie des saechsischen Voigtlandes.*

causes is traceable to the debasing of the coins, which raised prices nominally, or to the influences depressing agriculture, so powerful during the latter half of the sixteenth and the entire length of the seventeenth century, the fact stands out in bold relief, from the price history of the three countries, that the effect on the fate of the working-classes was disastrous.

APPENDIX B.

INFLUENCES BEARING ON PRODUCTION.

INTRODUCTORY LETTER TO THE AUTHOR'S REPORT ON TECHNICAL EDUCATION.

January 11, 1888.

Hon. T. F. BAYARD,
　Secretary of State, Washington, D. C.

SIR :

Pursuant to my instructions I proceeded to examine by personal observation into the condition and prospects of Technical Education in the principal industrial countries of Europe. It was evident, and my instructions point this out, that an inquiry of this nature could not confine itself to the pedagogical side of it, but would have to extend over all the phenomena of industrial life. A study of the economy of production in the different countries which are to-day competing for the prize in the world's markets seems to be the broader ground upon which an inquiry, as demanded, was to be founded. Technical Education not alone as given by the school, but by school and life, tradition, theory, and action. The school and the workshop, the college and the factory, the art school, the museum and industrial art works, as well as the practices of the people, would, under this view, become necessary subjects of inquiry. That this would have to be the line upon which to proceed became evident after even a superficial examination of, and acquaintance with, the methods of the people. The closer we get to them the more we realize how great the influence which habits, association, and inherited views exercise upon the formation of national character.

The methods employed in production are largely governed by these causal influences. They impress their stamp upon the output even, on the work measured quantitatively and qualitatively. Of this phase, the elementary one, a visiting of schools hardly gives an adequate idea. It becomes clear to us, when we observe the people engaged in their daily occupations, that the busy marts of life, the shop and the factory have to supply the requisite measure for an understanding of the relative positions nations occupy in the industrial progression of their time. The aim and end of all industrial activity are the supplying of food, clothing, shelter, and necessaries of life to the worker and his dependents. What we call luxuries are only the necessaries of a more advanced state of civilization. A people's state of civilization can therefore be measured best by what its working classes consider necessaries of life, or their standard of living—the working classes preeminently. It must be taken for granted that the well-to-do classes enjoy in all times and zones relatively the sum and substance of comforts known to their age. Varying as this standard of living is, varying as the wants of nation and nation, time and time, zone and zone are, so we find, with the greater or smaller force of this incentive, activity increase and prevail with greater or smaller force. Under this varying standard we find the widest divergence both in the demands of the laborer and in the product of his activity by which he supplies these wants. What by one would be considered comfort and plenty, another nation's standard would stamp as poverty and want.

If we have, therefore, no common standard of living, of the wants, we have a still more varying standard of production, of the means employed for supplying the wants. The results of a day's labor in one and the same industry per hand employed in different countries are of a most diverging nature. In one and the same line differences are so pronounced that it becomes at once apparent that the old standard of measurement, from which economic deductions have usually been made, the day wages, is entirely illusory. The means employed, the tools, machines, and methods are seldom the same. Even when apparently the same agents and methods are employed, on examination we find that they differ in their nature, or employment, or in both, so materially that no reliable comparison and deductions could be made from the mere fact of the employment of these agencies in production.

It may be taken for granted that in cotton manufacture the same kind of machinery is employed in America, England, Switzerland, Germany, and France. The same power is likewise employed for speeding the machinery. Steam-power in England, Germany, and France, and water-power supplemented by steam-power in America and Switzerland. The day earnings of the operatives (weavers) vary so much between one country and another, that weavers in Switzerland earn but $2\frac{1}{4}$ to $2\frac{1}{2}$ francs (44 to 49 cents), in Germany on an average 2 marks (48 cents), in French mills $2\frac{3}{4}$ to 3 francs (53 to 58 cents), with a working day from five o'clock in the morning to half-past seven in the evening, and $2\frac{1}{2}$ hours of rest in the day; in England about 65 cents, with nine working hours, and in America from 80 cents to \$1.12$\frac{1}{2}$ a day of ten working hours. (Average 85 cents, taken from the work account of a mill.) If all things were equal, if with the same machines and working agencies the results of a day's work per hand employed were the same, of course the countries where the higher earnings prevail would be in a hopeless condition in competing with the others. The above-mentioned factors, however, exercise so powerful an influence, that the reverse is the truth. In fact, the cheapness of the labor product stands in an inverse ratio to the weekly earnings of the operative. The cost of weaving—in wages—of one kilogram of print cloth, $15\frac{1}{4}$ yards, 64 x 64 standard, in Switzerland, is 50 centimes, $9\frac{3}{8}$ cents, or .606 cent a yard. For Germany I have not been able to obtain data for this count and width. Printers in Mulhouse and

Elberfeld tell me, when they use it for export, they get it mostly from England,—a drawback of the duty paid to the government is given upon re-exporting the prints. This sufficiently proves that the cloth cannot be made at less cost in Germany. In England 22d, or 44 cents, is paid per cut of 80 yards, equal to .55 cent per yard.* In America 20 cents is paid per cut of 50 yards (from another source I have 18.15 cents per cut of 45 yards), or .40 cent a yard as the weaver's wages. Putting daily earnings side by side with the labor cost of weaving we have

	Daily wages.	Wages per 100 yards.
In Switzerland, and we may include Germany..	$0.44 to $0.49	$0.606
In England...................................	0.65	0.55*
In America...................................	0.85	0.40

From this we have a right to conclude that the average rate of wages customary in the country, the supplying of the wants and necessaries of life, must have a direct bearing upon the productive power of the people—the operatives. I confine myself here strictly to this induction—and specific case. And here this is demonstrable to an absolute certainty. The number of looms operated by one weaver is:

In Switzerland two to three for the more expert weavers.
In Germany and France two and very seldom three.
In England three, and for expert weavers four.
And in America six to eight looms.

The work account of a mill in Lowell, for which I am indebted to the kindness of the lamented Mr. Dupee, the late treasurer of the Hamilton Mills, gives me

232 girls operating 6 looms.
 43   "   "   7 "
 20   "   "   8 "   and only
 11   "   "   5 "   each.

* See ante, pp. 242 and 243 for statement giving results of later inquiry.

This shows that the high standard of working power in America is very widely distributed. The speed of the looms has been held to be so much greater in England than in America, that thereby the advantages gained by the running of a greater number of looms by one hand becomes neutralized in a measure. Even this I do not find to be the case. In America 180 picks a minute is the average, and some run as high as 210 picks a minute. In England 200 is considered very high speed, run by the best and most improved looms. Whatever objection might be raised on this point would be met by the weekly output as given by the earnings, which are piece-price earnings and not day-wages. In England, taking $3.90 as the average of weekly earnings, at the rate of 55 cents per 100 yards the weekly output would be 709 yards of print cloth. In Switzerland, taking $2.80 as the average earnings of weavers, at the rate of 60 cents per hundred yards the weekly output would be 466 yards; while in America, taking 6 looms indicating a low average, or $4.86 (as taken from the pay-rolls of my informant) at the rate of 40 cents per 100 yards the weekly output would be 1,200 yards of print cloth per weaver. (The average number of looms worked in this mill by one weaver is $6\frac{1}{4}$, with the earning proportionately raised to $5.08, brings the output to 1,270 yards.) In the spinning of the yarn for this cloth I find about equal cost of labor per pound in English and American mills and a higher cost in Switzerland. The time earnings stand relatively in the same positions with the respective countries as in the weaving, necessarily indicating higher individual exertion, skill, energy, or whatever term we may apply to cover this economic manifestation.

I speak here of a branch where the same plant and technic is assumed to be used by competing nations—enjoying relatively the greatest amount of social, intellectual, and political advantages of the age—and still how different are the results of exertion aided by the same motors and appliances.

If equally accurate data were at hand for the lowest stratum of wage earners—the operatives in the cotton mills of India—a still stronger verification of this parallel could undoubtedly be brought out. The fact of the great spread of cotton manufacture in the last decade is attributed to the low wages and to the depreciation of silver. With the latter imputed cause I have not to deal here, though I may say incidentally that the price of cotton in Liverpool or Manchester would never be affected thereby in any but a nominal way. Ten dollars worth of India cotton would bring, let us say, $7.00 gold, plus freight and charges, in Liverpool, and re-exported to Bombay in the nature of yarn or cloth be again $10.00 in silver plus labor—and freight and charges. The differences in exchange could only bear upon the added items. Freight charges even would be subject to the same nominal influences as the price of cotton. It is a fact, however, that India works successfully only the coarser yarns, Nos. 10 to 20, where the least labor is expended in the pound of cotton, while the finer numbers are imported from England in a larger degree even than the spread of Bombay cotton manufacture. Now the spinning wages in one hundred pounds of cotton yarn in Fall River are:

For No. 14............$0.33 For No. 20 ....$0.45
For " 16............. .35 (And in Lancashire for No. 20. .50)
For " 18............. .40 For No. 40................. .98

India has the seeming advantage of freight. The average rate of freight the year around on a ton of cotton from Bombay to Liverpool is 22s. 6d. or $5.46. Freight from Liverpool to Bombay of a ton of yarn is 12s. 6d. or $3.06, total $8.52, or about the spinning wages in Lancashire and Massachusetts for the coarse numbers made in Bombay. This apparent protection, however, is partly offset in the higher cost of coal, higher cost of mill property and machinery, superintendence, etc.

APPENDIX B.

Practically it may be said, therefore, that the basis of cost, the material, upon which labor operates in India, offers only these advantages to the home spinner. The difficulties of the Bombay manufacturer increase with the increase in the ratio of labor to the pound of cotton. There the greater productivity, relative cheapness of high-cost labor, shows itself in its greater potency. In lieu of a more specific and more closely defined measure, we may take the relative output.

A mill in Bombay, of which I have an account, of 35,000 spindles, turns out 8,000 pounds of No. 20 yarn a day. Against this we may set the output of a mill in Lawrence, which produces two pounds a week per spindle of No. 18 to 20 yarn. For 35,000 spindles this would represent an output of 70,000 pounds in Massachusetts a week, against one of 48,000 pounds in Bombay. The mill in Massachusetts, however, makes miscellaneous goods, and does not, as the superintendent informs me, represent as high a working capacity as a mill would which runs without changing, and on a large scale, the same numbers. Such a mill would, therefore, under more favorable arrangement, represent a much higher working capacity. We can, therefore, deduce from this that, irrespective of the number of hands employed, for an equal quantity of work produced, the same plant and improved machinery turn out in a given time a very much greater number of yards of yarn in Massachusetts than in the cotton mills of Bombay.

If this be so when we deal with what is apparently like and like, how much more are we justified in expecting quite important modifications of ruling impressions when we examine into industries which are conducted among different nations by entirely different methods. Here we find one nation clinging tenaciously to small domestic industries; the people work in family groups, or masters with helpers; some still employ hand-tools of ancient construction, others use modern inventions and labor-saving machinery made serviceable for domestic industry. Along with this the factory runs. But even here the use made of machinery is quite different in one country from what it is in another.

Here the insufficiency of the commonly adopted standard of measuring relative efficiency, *i. e.*, productivity of labor, or cheapness, by the rate of wages, becomes more distressing yet. In a sense more closely allied in methods of proceeding to the just-mentioned industry than what I shall point out below is calico printing. In Elberfeld and Mulhouse the work is conducted practically on the same principle as in Lowell, Fall River, Providence, etc., by printing machines with engraved copper rollers driven by steam. Yet I was told by owners of extensive print works at both places in Germany, that it is useless for them to attempt competition with America in neutral markets; that they had lost the Mexican market, and would run the same risk elsewhere where American cloth, width and quality, have established markets. They cannot compete in price. From the rate of wages standard this would seem incredible. In Lowell print-works which I visited, a printer gets $4.50 a day. In Mulhouse not above one-third; in Elberfeld not much over one-fourth would be the day wages of a printer. Truly a formidable difference. When, however, we know that one printer at $4.50 and a helper at $1.50 suffice to tend one printing machine; and that one printing machine, printing up to three or four colors, turns out daily 400 pieces of print of 50 yards, or 20,000 yards; and in prints used for furniture, etc., with eight to twelve colors printed simultaneously, 250 pieces or 12,500 yards, then we see how immaterial the question is whether the wages for tending the printing machine are $6, $3, or $4, .03, .015, or .02 cents per yard. The labor cost becomes here a vanishing quantity on the one side, while on the other side causes may come in which make it an important factor, even if nominally of a very low rate. The German printers say they cannot work on the American basis of running for days and weeks one pattern on one machine. They have to run much slower, use more time and care. They have to collect their trade from almost every country in the world. It comes in dribblets. They have to accommodate themselves to everybody's whims, make patterns, styles, and colors for every zone and taste. The large trade is in the hands of England, and they can only obtain and retain trade by ready acquiescence to all the exactions of fashion in the finer prints or national predilections in the cheaper goods. This not alone increases the cost of production, but, perhaps to a greater extent yet, the cost of distribution, and may be called a new element of disturbance in making comparisons in like industries among different nations. Methods in distribution as well as methods in production. They are dissimilar in every country, and both have their influence on prices and cost of production.

Along with this advanced system of printing, bearing such different results so far as price-making is concerned, runs block printing yet to a considerable extent. Apparently hopelessly expensive if brought in competition with roller printing—still under certain conditions it may be much cheaper—or no other process applicable. Roller printing would be ruinously expensive in a small output or applied to a small industry of a changeable nature.

We have found all of these divergences in reviewing manufacturing conducted by similar methods. How much greater must we expect these divergences to be when we compare production conducted here by an industrious toiler with his hand tools; there with improved hand machinery; and in another place by minute subdivisions of the best organized labor, aided by machinery of the subtlest construction or by automatons, which with iron teeth and fingers cut steel and copper, turn screws, nails, pins, make the heads, sharpen the points, and drop the finished work into a ready receptacle, or cut iron and twist and knit it into chains, etc. The labor employed here consists simply in putting a coil of wire or a rod of steel or copper into the machine, which then does all the work with greater regularity and precision than the most skilled workman could do by hand. In more complicated work than the making of these units great skill is required of the workers under both systems. Still it is skill of quite a different nature—the one in doing one and the same kind of work repeatedly day in and day out, like the automaton which makes the parts; the other in making a complete piece of assembled parts inclusive of the parts. Great as the skill and technical knowledge must be of making a complete piece of so fine and subtle a mechanism as a watch or a clock by hand with hand tools, the skill required in the manipulation of the other system is of an equally high though of a different character. In the assembling room of an American clock factory I found one girl putting together the parts of 240 movements as one day's work. This requires great dexterity and exactness. The work in all the manipulations is paid for by the piece. High earnings can only be obtained by great quickness, deftness, and uninterrupted attention and application, qualities which again can be supplied by none but the best conditioned labor, enjoying the highest standard of living. Nowhere is so high a degree of intelligence and brightness in manner, looks, and appearance observable among work people as where these conditions prevail; where the highest known earnings in like industries lead to the lowest cost of labor. A clock is sold at 90 cents, an alarm-clock is sold at retail at $1.25, a Waterbury watch at $2.50. It is the surprise of Europe. The factory sells it at $1.50 to the retailer. On a recent visit to the factory I was shown all the numerous operations of the manufacturing process. The material is all worked from the plainest condition. It enters the factory as rolled steel and brass, and sheet-iron, and leaves it as a well-regulated watch in a pasteboard box lined with colored satin. The making of the spring, of the wheels, screws, pins, pinions, the perforating of the plates, etc.; the assembling, the finishing, the regulating, all are done with as much care and precision as if for a piece of five times the value. Yet all these collected processes do not cost in labor more than 50 cents a watch. The company has a pay-roll of $4,500 a week, and turns out 1,500 watches a day, or 9,000 a week, which makes the labor exactly as stated. The machinery is as interesting a study as the labor employed in the making and finishing of this product of skill and enterprise. The number of people employed in the factory is 420, fully one-half of whom are women. The average earnings are $10.71, which is about four times as high as in the Black Forest or in Switzerland. Here the lower cost is not due to cheap wages, but to excellent machinery and skill, and great quickness of labor employed at a very low cost by the piece. The great variety and complexity of machinery and consequent great expense of plant can be borne profitably because of the very large output. The labor, the machinery turning uninterruptedly the same work, is here employed and utilized to the full. Improvements in machinery follow on one another's heels when they are so profitable that, for instance, two machines and two men make 1,200 to 1,500 springs a day, while a short time ago, on now obsolete machinery, it took twelve men to turn out 1,000 springs. Neither in the Black Forest nor in Geneva have I seen machinery, meant for the same purpose, utilized in any way approaching that in which it is utilized in America. Nor does hand labor move with the swiftness of hand labor in American factories. Here it is also a matter of minor significance that a girl gets $9 to $10 a week, when she is thereby enabled to fasten the wheel in 1,600 watch-cases, handling four pieces in each case (the wheel, two washers, and the pinion wire), as a day's work. Only with such labor, appliances and systematizing is it possible to make a watch containing 58 pieces, which collectively have passed through 370 single operations, at so abnormally low a price.

The relative indifference of high day wages when brought side by side with such astonishing results is more apparent yet when we deal with industries where automatic machinery is employed almost exclusively, screw-making, nail-making, pin-making, etc. In the latter industry the coil of brass wire is put in its proper place, the end fastened, and the almost human piece of mechanism, with its iron fingers, does the rest of the work. One machine makes 180 pins a minute, cutting the wire, flattening the heads, sharpening the points, and dropping the pin in its proper place. 108,000 pins a day is the output of one machine. A factory visited by me employed 70 machines. These had a combined output per day of 7,500,000 pins, or 300 pins to a paper—25,000 papers of pins, allowing for stoppages and necessary time for repairs—say 20,000 papers. These machines are tended by three men. A machinist with a boy helper attends to the repairing. It will not materially influence the price of pins whether the combined earnings of these five men be $7.50 or $10 per diem. The difference would amount to one-eighth of a cent on a paper of pins. The likelihood is that when cheaper help is employed a greater number of hands would be employed for the same work and the same output.

This applies to all industries, but principally to those which can be conducted by highly developed and organized labor. The boot and shoe industry is a brilliant example. I found on samples, the products of Lynn factories, which I had brought with me for comparison, that no foreign manufacturers were able to compete with American factories in the cheapness of the labor price. Here at Lynn a pair of ladies' gaiters is made as low as 35 cents for the labor, including the making of 24 buttonholes and sewing on of buttons, and in country shops as low as 25 cents for the same kind with about 10 buttonholes in each. I made comparisons in different places. In Vienna, in Berlin, in Frankfort, and in Offenbach I found the labor cost to be double, while the earnings were less than half what they are here. In Erfurt, where wages are lower yet than in any of the mentioned places, the cost is lower; but the goods are inferior, and still fully 60 per cent. higher in the labor cost than in my sample of country-shop gaiters of American manufacture. The factories work with American machines, but the output falls way behind ours. Along with this a great deal of handwork made in the homes of shoemakers—domestic industry—is run in, both for export and home trade. I do not enter into an explanation of these phenomena here, neither their bearings or their causes. I shall in a later report, with fuller data, attempt to point out the causes which produce these varying effects. I only desire now, in a cursory review of the methods under which the world's industries are conducted, to enforce the necessity of conducting investigations specifically, and not from a "general average" standpoint, which necessarily leads to erroneous deductions.

To show the extent to which industrial production persists in the line marked out, I point to Germany, certainly now one of the most progressive states. Still, according to the Industrial Census of 1882, more than one-half of all its population engaged in manufactures, where small groups of workers can at all be employed, were employed in groups of less than five to each establishment. In

	A Total of	Worked in groups of less than 5 persons	Worked in groups of more than 5 persons
In metals．	459,713	298,125	161,588
In machinery, instruments, etc.	356,089	127,565	228,524
In chemicals.	71,777	16,867	54,910
In textiles.	910,089	440,573	469,516
In paper and leather industries.	221,688	107,293	114,395
In wood industries	469,695	367,688	102,007
In nutriments, food and drink.	743,881	468,652	275,229
Total.	3,232,932	1,826,763	1,406,169

Organizations large enough for profitable employment of power machinery would have to be aggregates of many more than five persons. The number of people employed in domestic industries, those working in their own homes, for account of business-houses, merchants, exporters, or manufacturers, is very large. A total of 754,550 persons are so engaged. The kingdom of Saxony alone employs 138,000 persons, and Rhenish Prussia and Westphalia 102,000, in domestic industries. 230,000 are engaged in textiles, mostly in weaving. Hosiery still occupies over 40,000 people in house-industry. The principal lines in textiles occupy in home-industries the following position ; I set side by side the total of all engaged in the representative branches :

Percentage of all Employed.	Per cent.	Engaged in House-Industries.	Total in Industry.
Silk weaving and velvet (Rhenish Prussia, 49,022)..........	70	53,286	76,264
Woollen weaving	22	23,799	108,007
Linen "	40	41,045	103,808
Cotton "	42	52,295	125,591
Mixed goods weaving..........	30	22,212	73,750
Knit goods, hosiery (kingdom of Saxony alone, 30,513)..........	55	40,528	73,828
Total..........	42	233,165	561,248

In woollens 22 per cent., in mixed goods 30 per cent., in cotton 42 per cent., in silk 70 per cent., and in knit goods 55 per cent. of all weavers are still plying their looms or work their frames in their own homes in the fashion of the fathers.

In boots and shoes, of 398,757 shoemakers, only 25,768 work in groups of more than five persons. But even these are not of a higher ratio than 14, being distributed over 1,839 establishments.

In metals, a line where so much of our automatic machinery is so tellingly employed, the employment groups are of an equally low ratio.

APPENDIX B.

	Total No. of employed.	In groups of less than 5.	In groups of more than 5.	No. of establishments.	No. of persons in larger groups employed in each establishment.
Coppersmith ware..................	9,198	6,940	2,258	147	15
Lead and tinware	4,610	2,158	2,452	113	22
Composite metals	30,003	7,410	22,693	760	29
Tinsmith ware....................	46,158	34,884	11,274	457	25
Nails, screws, etc.................	23,609	11,784	11,825	267	44
Safes and heavy ironware, blacksmithing, etc........................	63,467	51,127	12,340	976	12
Cutlery, etc......................	55,889	34,312	21,577	825	26
Watch and clock making............	26,208	21,100	5,108	156	33
Mathematical instruments, &c.......	15,073	7,591	7,482	384	20

If the classification into groups were carried farther than "groups above 5," and groups of 5 to 10 and of 10 to 20 were given, we should see plainly what the above figures indicate—the small number of people employed in establishments conducted on a basis large enough to make production on the plan on which it is conducted mainly in America at all possible.

If these illustrations and figures prove anything, they prove beyond doubt the necessity of basing comparisons on homogeneous positive facts.

It is a common belief that, with the rapid exchange of ideas, the closer relations of nations, characteristic of our age, the methods and systems under which work is conducted by an industrially more advanced nation will soon be taken up by all competitors. Measurably this may be true ; so far as outside appearances go, even to an appreciable extent. On close examination we find, however, that the thick crust of imperturbability, of national predilections is not easily penetrated by new ways, methods, and ideas. Many counteracting influences have to be overcome before one nation's system of work will perform the same result after adoption by another. The spring to man's activity, to the exercise of all his functions, lies deeper than that mere arbitrary will or individual action exercised from without could effect rapid and violent changes. While these differing features in the productive methods of nations are visible at a first glance, it is evident that production must also be largely influenced by them; preëminently, production taken quantitatively. But much as the results of labor measured by numbers, length, or whatever term may be called in for covering dimensions, may be influenced by the methods and factors mentioned, the side which cannot be measured by the common standard, the side appealing more directly to the eye—taste—is still more greatly influenced by these national, popular, latent instincts. It would be useless to expect of one nation the same coloring, expression, ornament, or artistic production as from another. In one the sense of color predominates, in another the sense of form. Here, more than in any other side of production, the national habits, the means and methods exert a great influence. Here, in quite a number of instances, the same results could not be obtained by any other method than the prevailing one. We cannot expect production mainly conducted by machinery, or with an eye to turning out big quantities, to cover the same ground or bring out like results as where painstaking regularity, inherited skill, and an intuitively trained eye direct the hand of the worker tied to his domestic industry and produce an individualization of products not obtainable otherwise. In one country the traditions, habits, and aims of government unite to make the people persevere in the old methods. The small industry of the craftsman, the hand-loom weaver, the decorator, the metalworker in his own smithy, the domestic industry is fostered and considered the ultimate goal to which we have to return again. In another country, where traditions and habits do not so strongly point in that direction, industry is left more to itself to shape its own course. Everywhere, however, we detect the most varied manifestation of national activity. The methods by which production is carried on are as varied as the products themselves. Different as these are in all respects, it is as unreasonable to expect of one nation the same work and results as of another, as it would be useless to engraft upon one nation an exact copy of the methods of another because the latter have been found to bring out good results there.

What can be said of the methods of industrial life and work can also be said of the school, and here especially, the schools for Technical Education. To understand properly their aims and directions and the degree of their utility, it is above all necessary to study the various phases of industrial development among the different nations. The lessons of life are as essential in Technical Education as of the school; the school is to give idea, direction, and elevation to industry, to raise the standard of the work by raising the standard of the worker. The school at best is a means to an end, be that means ever so powerful. It would be difficult to understand the bearing of this means, without thoroughly inquiring into the social and economic fabric of the nation whose system of Technical Education we study. The shop, therefore, gives perhaps a clearer insight into the makeup of this fabric than the school. The school very often is a creation from without, or an engrafted branch, not always sure to bear the fruit expected. The shop has grown and developed upon nature's own soil. We know little of a nation if we do not see it at work. We know little of the utility of systems of Technical Education unless we know also this phase of it upon which it is to operate.

With so extended a subject to investigate and to report upon, I assumed that the Department did not expect me to complete the inquiry in the brief period assigned, afterward extended, but to gain a general knowledge of the industrial conditions and of the state of Technical Education in the most advanced countries, and to leave to a later period the instituting of more minute inquiries. I found it useful, before proceeding to a report upon any branch of my inquiry, to have procured as much general knowledge of the subject by travel and direct investigation as was possible in the limited time,—limited, necessarily, by the school year terminating in July for general and technical education, and for many industrial and trade schools as early as the Easter vacation. A primary review of the whole field was necessary, merely to enable me to decide to which nation's system to devote the first part of my general report.

I visited France, the western part of Switzerland, Germany, a part of Austria, Belgium, Holland, and, on my return from a second visit to France, parts of England and Ireland. I became impressed with the fact that the elements of Technical Education upon the broadest basis imaginable—the public schools—were more thoroughly distributed in France than in any other country in Europe which I had visited. I deemed it of value to devote my first report to Technical Education in France. The public schools of France are of recent creation. The statesmen organizing the system could study the systems of all the advanced nations, and select the best and most fruitful methods. Even from the results of private and isolated attempts it became evident to them what an efficient guide and lever of a child's understanding it would be to have its sense of form, of color, of outline and proportion, trained at an early age to cultivtae a knowledge and love of work under the guidance of practised teachers able to direct it playfully in the elements of handicraft and of art. It was found that a nation endowed with a larger degree than any other with a sense of color, with intuitive skill in assembling and arranging parts into a harmonious pleasing whole, was losing ground. Nations which a generation ago were not considered formidable competitors were making heavy inroads even in what France used to consider her own special domain. It was held that this was due to the influence of education, to the more thorough training of mind and eye, to the art schools and industrial schools which had taken so rapid a development in neighboring countries.

But whatever may have impelled them to action, the statesmen of France planted upon a wider basis than the neighbors from whom they could borrow and profit. They made the public school system the instrument for laying the groundwork of technical knowledge in the make-up of the future workmen. One may assume that institutions for artistic, technical, and scientific instruction are either as a rule quickly introduced wherever the need of them is manifested, or, as lending lustre to the fame of rulers and statesmen, have always received, and always may be expected to receive, due attention from the powers that be. The masses, the nation, the millions of workers are not reached thereby. They are not reached by technical high-schools, academies, or schools of industrial art. A nation of indifferently trained workmen may co-exist with a very efficient and even brilliant corps of directors and leaders educated in these institutions. To bridge this gulf was the avowed aim in France. How far the French system will succeed in this the near future will demonstrate. One visiting schools and workshops, observing the young and the adult, could, however, not fail to carry away with him the impression that a great revolution was preparing in the mental make-up of the nation, proving the wisdom of this new departure in education.

From this brief explanation it will appear logical that I commence my report with a description of the French system, and then describe the systems of other nations, where other conditions and institutions prevail and cover ground perhaps left untrodden in this first report. The systems of Technical Education differ nearly as widely as the methods and systems of work. Each has its lessons, and in each will be found worthy subjects and examples for study and imitation, modified, perhaps, according to the differing conditions which they are to serve, and which call them to their aid.

It would be premature were I, at this stage of my inquiries, to speak of these. My inquiries have not been terminated. They were sufficiently comprehensive, however, to enable me to view the part submitted from the standpoint gained by a general acquaintance with the wider subject. This enabled me to decide upon the method of proceeding, and upon the scope and sequence of the reports necessary to cover the investigation assigned to me.

The present report will be followed by reports on Technical Education in Germany, Switzerland, Austria, Belgium, Holland, and Great Britain. Another report planned, for which I am collecting the data, and a necessary parallel of this, is a report on "The methods employed in production in different countries." The methods employed in production by different nations, and the results in competing industries, are very important subjects of study. It will be readily understood that the inquiry must be extended over the same field in the United States. A general review will then enable us to perceive whatever may be of advantage for us to adopt. We shall easily discover by comparison our points of weakness and of strength.

For this reason I have refrained from making any suggestions. It is essential in the first instance to collect the facts not alone of Technical Education, but of the whole broad subject, the facts underlying the economy of industrial life.

Our literature is as full of the philosophy of industrial life as it is wanting in facts regarding it—facts as they present themselves under the influence of modern development. We have, therefore, to gather the data, collect the facts of production with careful minuteness. The economy of production with careful minuteness. The economy of production will have to be treated in the same analytical manner of investigation by which all the natural sciences have made such wonderful progress within the last fifty years. National biology is as truly a positive science as individual biology. Abandoning the hazy abstractions of the speculative past, science has, by the aid of the microscope, the balance, and the retort, brought to light some of nature's most deeply hidden secrets. Under the results of this great scientific upheaval, life has become a changed condition. Industrial life, conditions and means governing production, transportation, distribution, all have experienced changes as pronounced as are the differences between the life and aspiration of the American mechanic and the life and aspiration of the Hindoo workman. The application of electricity and steam power to production and transportation has revolutionized industrial and economic conditions and the lives and prospects of the working classes to a greater degree than any other event in the history of man. Still it is not too much to say that the economic generalizations of the day are largely founded on the facts of a past era.

Incontrovertible evidence of the facts of industry, of production, its means and methods, cost and conditions among different nations, and the results to the working classes derived therefrom, if it corroborates what has been stated above, will contribute most powerfully toward a happy solution of what is the great question of the day all over the civilized world.

From this view facts are the only essentials. The collection of facts must for some time occupy the attention of public authorities. I have the honor to be, sir, etc.

INDEX.

A

Absolutism succeeding feudalism, 294
Agricultural laborers, Wages of, 196
Agricultural land, Price of, 178
Agricultural states and trade, 57
Agriculture and science, 253–270
Agriculture, State of, 136, 154, 181, 192
Alluvial gold deposits, 47
American farming, 273
Animals, Price of, 108, 122
Assignats, French, Decline in value, 6
Augsburg, Leading position of, 73–85
Aureus, The, 38, 92
Australian silver product, 52

B

Bacon, Price of, 22
Banks, 85
Barley, Price of, 119, 135, 153, 157, 182, 194, 205, 206, 320, 321, 322
Beans, Price of, 119, 135
Beef, Price of, 22, 106, 138, 162, 210
Bein, Louis, *Die Industrie des saechsischen Voigtlandes*, 227, 229, 322
Beissel, Stephan, *Geldwerth und Arbeitslohn im Mittelalter*, 80, 96, 203, 204, 206, 210
Bell, Sir I. Lowthian, 258, 264
Bergier, *Histoire des Grands Chemins de l'Empire Romain*, 282
Bimetallism, 26

Blacksmiths, Wages of, 216
Boars, Price of, 122, 138
Boeckh, *The Economy of the Athenians*, 108
Bohemia, Low wages and high cost, 233
Bolles, Albert S., *Financial History of the United States*, 4
Bonnemère, *Histoire des Paysans*, 187
Bread, Price of, 107, 157, 183, 195
Brentano, Lujo, *Relation of Wages to the Product of Labor*, 227
Bricklayers, Wages of, 125, 142, 158
Bricks, Price of, 124, 141, 209
Bulk and freight, 281
Butter, Price of, 22, 103, 123, 138, 160, 164

C

Candles, Price of, 124, 141
Capitularies, Carlovingian, 37
Carlovingian coins, 90, 91, 92, 99, 175
Carpenters, Wages of, 125, 142, 158, 196, 206, 216, 236, 312–314
Carrying trade, The, in past, 288
Cattle, Increase of, 107
Changing relation of silver to gold, 42–44, 203
Cheese, Price of, 22, 103, 123, 138, 164
Chevalier, Michel, 21
Chickens, Price of, 210
Cicero, Transfer of credit by, 58
Cinnamon, Price of, 130, 146, 170

Cloth, English, Low character of, in Middle Ages, 110
Cloth industry, The, in France, 297
Cloth, Price of, 105, 128, 144, 169, 200, 211
Cloves, Price of, 130, 146
Coal, Price of, 11, 22, 117
Cochineal, Price of, 172
Coffee, Price of, 10, 172
Coinage of England, 100, 116, 134
Coinage of France, 98, 99, 175, 176
Coinage of Xanten, 97
Coins of Frankish Monarchy, 37, 90, 92
Colbert, 192, 202, 288, 294, 301, 302
Colbert's views on protection, 302
Collars, Cost of making, 244
Cologne, Money of, 95, 97
Cologne, Trade of, 212
Colwell, Stephen, *Ways and Means of Payment*, 64, 65
Commodities, Changing character of, 107, 110
Commodities, Fall and rise of, 9
Comparisons, Rules for, 89
Computation of fines, 37
Confederate issues, 4
Continental money, 4
Convoys, Armed, 56, 68
Copper mining, Declining cost and rising wages illustrated, 249, 250
Copper, Price of, 10, 168
Corroborating proofs, 212
Cost of carriage, 280, 285
Cost of production in agriculture, 271, 273
Cotton and wheat, present position analogous, 277
Cotton cloth, Price of, 10, 17, 23
Cotton, Improved methods of raising, 269, 270
Cotton, Price of, 10, 13, 23, 172
Cotton prices and supply, 18, 270
Cotton spinning, Cost compared of, 230
Cotton yarn, Price of, 10, 17, 223
Cows, Price of, 122
Credit money, 56-68
Credulity of writers, 78
Crops, The raising of certain, compulsory, 273, 275

D

Dareste de la Chavanne, *Histoire des Classes Agricoles en France*, 185
Davanzati, *Lezione sulle Monete*, 19
D'Avenel, G., *Histoire de la Propriété*, etc., 174, 185, 194, 202, 204, 278
Dearth, Prevalence of years of, 198
Debasement of coinage, 100, 143, 176
Decline in price of silver, 31, 51
Del Mar, *History of Money*, 42
Demonetization, Effect of, on prices, 21
Demonetization of silver, 8
Demonetization of silver, Cause of, 32
Denier, The, 38, 91, 204
Depreciated currency and competition, 230, 239, 240
Depreciated money, 3
Drafts and bills of exchange, 56, 72, 90
Dress fabrics, Effect of removing duties on raw material on price of, 305-308
Dutch, Grasping character of the, 288, 289
Dutch, The, as traders, 288
Dutch, The, East India Company, 289-290
Duties and taxes, burdens on production, 300-306

E

Early institution of drafts, 56
Eastern competition, Fear of, ungrounded, 230-232
Economist, The, 8, 9, 162, 164
Eden, Sir Frederic, 25, 110, 153, 219, 220
Eggs, Price of, 22, 123, 138, 160, 210
Elizabeth, Coinage reform of, 101, 115
Ellison, *The Cotton Trade*, 224
English East India Company, 290
English farming, 273
Erroneous wage views, 217

INDEX.

Exaggerated accounts of silver production in sixteenth century, 78
Exports of wheat and flour, 279

F

Fall River and Bolton rates, Comparison of, 221
Fall River and Burnley, Labor cost, 243
Famine, Frequency of, 187
Farnam, Henry W., *Die innere franzoesische Gewerbepolitik*, 296
Fertilizers, Effect of, on cotton raising, 267–270
Financial history of England, 131, 149, 151
Flax, Price of, 10
Fleetwood, Price quotations by, 116
Flemings, Influence of, on England, 110, 121, 136, 145
Florence and the florin, 40
Florin, Character of the, 40
Fluctuations in wheat prices in past periods, 278
Forced issues, Nature and fate of, 6
Forty-to-one bill, The, 5
Free coinage of silver, 26
Free land and farming, 272
Free trade and prices, 163
Fuggers, The wealth of the, 75
Furnace practice, 258, 259

G

Geese, Price of, 122, 138
Geiler von Keysersberg, 72
Geld, Meaning of, 7
Geometrical theory of prices, 24
German and English labor cost, 226–228
German and English wages, 228
Germany, Decline of, in sixteenth century, 211, 215
Germany, Price records of, 203, 211
Germany's trading pre-eminence in fifteenth and sixteenth centuries, 72–85
Ginger, Price of, 130, 146
Gold coins of Saracens, 38, 40, 95
Gold deposits, 47
Gold mining, Reduction of cost, 261

Gold mining, Progress in, 261
Gold production, 27–30, 46, 151
Gold standard, Rule of, 39
Goldsmiths' notes, 150
Gold the standard of progressing nations, 256
Grain, Increasing supply of, 188
Guanajuato, Mines of, 28, 49, 75
Guilds and monopolies, 292–296
Guinea, The, 66
Guyot, Yves, *La Science Économique*, 215, 216

H

Hemp, Price of, 10
Henry VIII., Debasement under, 100, 115, 117
High prices in Middle Ages, 74, 102
Hoards in plate, 78
Horses, Price of, 103, 104, 122, 138
Humboldt, Alex. von, *Essai Politique sur la Nouvelle Espagne*, 27, 50, 76, 77
Hume, David, 20, 81, 121, 132, 137, 145, 288, 301
Hundred Years' War, Influence of, 180

I

Imports and exports, 135, 183
Inama-Sternegg, *Deutsche Wirthschaftsgeschichte*, 37, 43, 91, 95, 100
Index numbers considered, 13
Index numbers, Unreliability of, 238
India, Competition of, 230
India cotton and silver relation, 17
Indigo, Price of, 10, 172
Individual rights, 295
Industry of England, State of, 127
Intellect, The rise of the, and wages, 225
Ireland and England, Contrasting wages of, 234
Iron, Bar, Price of, 13, 23, 124, 126, 141, 168
Iron, Fluctuations in, 23, 257
Iron law of wages, Fallacy of, 217
Iron, Pig, Price of, 10, 13, 23, 124, 126, 141, 168, 200, 256, 257

J

Janssen, Joh., *Geschichte des deutschen Volkes*, 35, 73, 78
Jews, The, and credit money, 56–58
Jews, The, and trade, 72, 90
Jews, The, as preservers of methods of civilization, 56–58, 72, 90

K

Kipper and Wipper, The, in Germany, 131
Krupp, wage rates contrasted, 239, 318, 319

L

Labor cost and wages, 216–219, 224, 225, 227, 233, 241, 243
Labor cost, German and English, 226–228
Laborer, Wages of, 142, 216
Labor product and wages, 219, 225, 241
Land in common, 35, 36
Lard, Price of, 22, 123
Laveleye, Émile de, *De la Propriété, et de ses formes primitives*, 35
Lead, Price of, 10, 141, 168, 200, 209
Leather, Price of, 10, 23
Levasseur, Émile, 174, 177
Levi, Leone, *Wages and Earnings*, 106, 162–164
Lime, Price of, 124, 141, 209
Linen, Price of, 128, 144, 169, 211
Livre tournois, The, 98, 99, 175
Locke, John, 19, 189
Low cost of labor and high wages, 216–253
Low earnings and high cost labor, 216–253
Low wages in competition, 239, 241, 243

M

Macaulay, *History of England*, 143, 149, 150, 287
Maccann, *Argentine Republic*, 107
Maine, Sir Henry, 35

Malt, Price of, 119, 135
Markets, Opening of, affecting prices, 160, 275
Mark of Cologne, The, 95, 97
Mark of Xanten, The, 96, 97, 204, 318
Masons, Wages of, 125, 142, 158, 196, 216, 236, 313, 314
Meadow land, Price of, 178
Meals, Price of, 182, 183, 195
Meat, Price of, 10
Metallurgy, Progress in, 247, 262
Middle Ages, High prices in, 74, 102
Mining, Progress in, 248, 261, 262
Mining, Risks not preventive of, 47, 54
Mints, Closing to silver of, 8
Molinari, G. de, *Cours d'Économie Politique*, 98, 99
Money, Cattle as, 35–37
Money economy, 84, 88
Money, Meaning of, 7
Money of account, 63–68
Money payments, Infrequency of, 61
Money supply and prices, 7, 8, 19, 25, 151, 184, 201
Monks, Medieval, transfers through, 56
Monopolies and privileges, 72
Montanari, *Della Moneta*, 19
Montesquieu, Theory on Money 19,
Moreau de Jonnès, *État Économique*, etc., 184, 186, 189, 201
Mulhall, Michael, G. index numbers,

N

Nail making, Labor cost and wages in, 252
Nails, Price of, 22, 124, 141, 209
Nuebling, Eugen, *Ulm's Baumwollindustrie*, 297
Nuremberg, Leading position of, 73, 85

O

Oats, Price of, 119, 135, 157, 153, 182, 194
Oils, Price of, 10
Oxen, Price of, 122, 138

P

Painter, Wages of, 196
Patriotism, ineffectual, When, 6
Payment by weight of silver, Rule of, 113-116, 176
Payments by accounts, 64
Peas, Price of, 119, 135
Pepper, Price of, 74, 130, 146
Phœnician traders and exchange, 58
Piccolomini, Aeneas Sylvio, 78
Piece workers, Proportion of, in factories, 246
Plague, Change of conditions following the great, 118
Plasterer, Wages of, 196
Plate as hoard and money, 78
Plumbers, Wages of 125, 142, 158
Poor, Effect of high prices on the fate of the, 155, 158
Pork, Price of, 22, 139, 210
Potosi, Mines of, 28, 49, 75
Price and supply, 18, 210
Price comparisons, 22
Price decline and money increase, 171, 201
Price variations, 10, 108
Prices and money supply, 87, 151
Prices and transportation facilities, 159, 278, 284
Prices and wages, 16, 125, 143, 157, 208
Prices expressed in wheat, 104
Prices of
  Animals, 108, 122
  Bacon, 22
  Barley, 119, 135, 153, 157, 182, 194, 205, 206, 311
  Beans, 119, 135
  Beef, 10, 22, 106, 138, 162, 210
  Boars, 122, 138
  Bread, 106, 157, 183, 195
  Bricks, 124, 141, 209
  Butter, 22, 103, 123, 138, 160, 164
  Candles, 124, 141
  Cheese, 22, 103, 123, 138, 164
  Chickens, 210
  Cinnamon, 130, 146, 170
  Cloth, 128, 169, 200, 201
  Cloves, 130, 146
  Coal, 11, 22, 117

Prices of
  Cochineal, 10, 13, 23, 172
  Coffee, 10, 172
  Copper, 10, 168
  Cotton, 10, 17
  Cotton cloth, 10, 17, 23
  Cotton yarn, 10, 17, 123
  Cows, 122
  Eggs, 22, 123, 138, 160, 210
  Flax, 10
  Geese, 122, 138
  Hemp, 10
  Indigo, 10, 172
  Iron, Bar, 13, 23, 124, 126, 141, 168
  Iron, Pig, 10, 13, 23, 124, 126, 141, 168, 200, 256, 257
  Lard, 22, 123
  Lead, 10, 141, 168, 200, 209
  Leather, 10, 23
  Lime, 124, 141, 209
  Linen, 128, 144, 169, 211
  Malt, 119, 135
  Meals, 182, 183, 195
  Meat, 10
  Oats, 119, 135, 153, 157, 182, 194
  Oils, 10
  Oxen, 122, 138
  Peas, 22, 139, 310
  Pepper, 74, 130, 146
  Pork, 22, 139, 210
  Rails, Iron, 22
  Rails, Steel, 22, 264
  Rice, 130, 170
  Rope, 124, 141
  Rye, 119, 135, 194, 317, 321, 322
  Salt, 124, 141
  Saltpetre, 172
  Sheep, 122, 138
  Silk, 10, 172
  Silver, 10
  Slate, 209
  Starch, 22, 138
  Sugar, 10, 72, 74, 130, 146, 147, 170
  Tallow, 10, 138
  Tar, 124, 141
  Tea, 10, 172
  Tiles, 124, 141, 209
  Timber, 10
  Tin, 10
  Tobacco, 10, 13, 23

350   INDEX.

Prices of
  Wax, 123, 209
  Wheat, 10, 20, 22, 116, 119, 135, 153, 157, 159, 183, 194, 205, 206, 277, 278, 311, 320-322
  Wheat flour, 22
  Wool, 10, 20, 123, 138, 165, 166, 167, 200
  Yarn, 10, 17, 223
Privileges and monopolies, 72
Product, Annual, of the United States, 21
Production of gold, 27-30, 46, 151
Production of silver, 27-30, 46, 151
Profit rate in past periods, 287
Progress in mining, 261
Protective duties and prices, 303-305
Protective tariff injurious, 301

Q

Quantity relation of silver to gold, 32
Quincy, Josiah, views on paper money, 5

R

Rails, Iron, Price of, 22
Rails, Steel, Price of, 22, 264
Ratio and production, 28, 29
Ratio of silver to gold, 43, 44, 203
Raw materials and manufactures, 157
Raw materials, Taxes on, 301
Reduction of weight in coinage, 93, 113, 205
Regulation of trade by the state, 296-299
Reichsmark, Relation of, to money of Middle Ages, 205, 206
Rem, Lucas, Diary of, 73, 75
Resumption of specie payments and prices, 22
Revenue from land, 178
Rhenish gold florin, The, 95, 97
Ricardo, Erroneous views of, 218
Rice, Price of, 130, 170
Rising prices in fifteenth century, 74, 84
Rising wages and declining prices as incidents of progress, 254, 255
Risks of commerce in the past, 285
Ritter, E., *Erdkunde*, 287

River navigation, Charges on, 300
Roads, Roman, in England, 282
Rogers, John Thorold, 43, 55, 80, 100, 111, 113-147, 153, 155, 282, 283, 289, 307.
Rope, Price of, 124, 141
Roscoe, *History of Lorenzo il Magnifico*, 85
Russia, Report on agriculture, 235
Russia, Wages in, 235
Rye, Price of, 119, 135, 194, 317 319, 321, 322

S

Saddlers, Wages of, 125
Salt, Price of, 124, 141
Saltpetre, Price of, 172
Saracens, Gold coins of the, 38, 40, 95
Saracens, Influence of, on Middle Ages, 89
Sauerbeck, index numbers, 9, 15
Saunois de Chevert, *L'Indigence*, etc., 185
Savary, *Dictionnaire de Commerce*, 297
Sawyers, Wages of, 125, 142
Say, J. B., *Traité d'Économie Politique*, 216
Schmoller, G., *Die Strassburger Tucher- und Weberzunft*, 111, 298, 316
Schneider, *Heer- und Handelswege der Roemer*, 36
Schoenhof, J., *Consular Reports*, 106, 225, 242
Schoenhof, J., *The Destructive Influence of the Tariff*, 127
Schoenhof, J., *The Economy of High Wages*, 225, 304
Schoenhof, J., *The Industrial Situation*, 21, 233
Schoenhof, J., *Report on Technical Education*, 242
Schultze-Gaevernitz, *Der Grossbetrieb*, 225, 226, 241, 242
Science applied to industry, 258
Settlements at fairs, 59
Shaw, W. A., *The History of Currency*, 43
Sheep, Increase of, 107

INDEX.   351

Sheep, Price of, 122, 138
Shirts, Cost of making, in Berlin and in New York, 245
Shoemaking by machinery, 253
Silk, Price of, 10, 172
Silver, Changing relations of, 42, 43, 44, 203
Silver, Closing of mints to, 8
Silver, Decline in price of, 31, 51
Silver, Demonetization of, 32
Silver, Free Coinage of, 26
Silver, Low cost of production, 51
Silver, Production of, 27–30, 151
Silver, Price of, 10
Silver, Quantity relation of, 32
Silver, Ratio of, to gold, 28, 29, 43, 44, 203
Singer, Dr. I., *Die Baumwoll-industrie in Boehmen*, 233
Sismondi, *Histoire des Républiques Itatiennes dans les Moyens Ages*, 85, 99
Slate, Price of, 209
Smith, Adam, Grain prices, 25, 105
Smuggling, Prevalence of, 183
Soetbeer, Dr. Adolf, 9, 48, 63, 75, 78
Solidus, The, 38, 91, 204
Southern produce, Prices of, 130, 146, 170
Spinners' wages, 219–224
Spinning cost and wages, 219–221, 224, 226
Spinning, Piece rates and wages compared in, 221
Standard of value, 35, 38
Standard, Change of, 100, 116
Starch, Price of, 22, 138
Statistical Society, Numbers of, 8, 13, 162, 164
Steel Mills in America, 263
Stonecutters, Wages of, 216
Stucco-workers, Wages of, 216
Sugar, Price of, 10, 22, 130, 146, 147, 170, 174
Summary of price history, 311–323
Supply and prices, 18, 270

T

Tacitus, *Germania*, 42
Tallow, Price of, 10, 138
Tar, Price of, 124, 141
Taxation and prices, 186, 191
Tea, Price of, 10, 172
Tennessee Coal and Iron Company's cost of making iron, 257
Textile industry, State of, 127, 137, 145, 158, 201, 298
Thatchers, Wages of, 125, 142
Theory of money quantity and prices, 19, 21, 25, 184, 201
Thirty Years' War, 71
Thirty Years' War and prices, 187
Thun, Alfons, *Landwirthschaft und Kleingewerbe in Mittel-Russland*, 235
Tiles, Price of, 124, 141, 207, 209
Tilers, Wages of, 125, 141
Timber, Price, of, 10
Tin, Price of, 10
Tobacco, Price of, 10, 13, 23
Tolls, 300
Tooke, Thos., *History of Prices*, 24, 25, 110, 153, 157, 166, 173, 257
Trade follows sound money, 65
Trading risk, 62
Truck farming, 267, 268
Turgot, Reforms of, 293

V

Vauban, *La Dime Royale*, 192, 193
Venice, Bank of, 63–65
Vineyards, Price of, 178
Vintners, Wages of, 196

W

Wage rate by the piece, 145, 217, 221, 241, 243
Wages and labor cost, 216–219, 224, 225, 229, 233, 241, 243
Wages and prices, 16, 125, 143, 157, 208
Wages expressed in flour, 223
Wages expressed in grain, 311–323
Wages of
  Agricultural laborer, 196
  Blacksmith, 216
  Bricklayer, 125, 142, 158
  Carpenter, 125, 142, 158, 196, 206, 216, 236, 312–314

Wages of
    Laborer, 142, 162
    Mason, 125, 142, 158, 196, 236, 312–314
    Painter, 196
    Plasterer, 196
    Plumber, 125, 142, 158
    Saddler, 125
    Sawyer, 125, 142
    Spinner, 219, 220–224
    Stonecutter, 216
    Stucco-worker, 216
    Thatcher, 125, 142
    Tiler, 125, 142
    Vintner, 196
Wages, Rising tendency of, 16, 220
War periods and prices, 156–159, 180–193, 207
Wasteful methods in silver mining, 50
Waste, Recovery of, 264
Watchmaking by machinery, 252
Wax, Price of, 123, 209
Webster, Daniel, views on paper money, 7
Wheat flour, Price of, 22
Wheat, Price of, 10, 20, 22, 116, 119, 135, 153, 157, 159, 183, 194, 205, 206, 277, 278, 311, 320, 322

Wheat raising as a money crop, 275
Whitwater Strand gold mines, 33, 45
Wool, Price of, 10, 20, 123, 138, 165–167, 200
Wool supply and prices, 166, 167, 201
Woollen manufacturers and protective tariffs, 302–306
Wright, Carroll D., Labor cost, Statements of, 251

X

Xanten, Record of prices, 80, 203–212, 311, 314, 317

Y

Yarn, Character of, 110
Yarn, Price of, 10, 17, 223
Young, Arthur, 24, 157, 165, 201, 218

Z

Zecchino d'or, as money of account, 63
Zimmermann, Wm., *Geschichte des grossen Bauernkriegs*, 74

www.ingramcontent.com/pod-product-compliance
Lightning Source LLC
Chambersburg PA
CBHW032043220426
43664CB00008B/844